Christ or Hitler?

Wilhelm Busch

Christ
or Hitler?

Stories from my life and times by
Pastor Wilhelm Busch
(1897–1966)

Compiled and translated
by Christian Puritz

 BOOKS

EP BOOKS
Faverdale North
Darlington
DL3 0PH, England

www.epbooks.org
sales@epbooks.org

EP BOOKS are distributed in the USA by:
JPL Fulfillment
3741 Linden Avenue Southeast,
Grand Rapids, MI 49548.

E-mail: sales@jplfulfillment.com
Tel: 877.683.6935

First published 2013

Printed by Bell and Bain Ltd, Glasgow

British Library Cataloguing in Publication Data available
ISBN: 978-085234-914-4

Photographs supplied by members of the Busch family, kindly made available by Dr Martin Rüther of the NSDokumentationszentrum der Stadt Köln.

Contents

Preface

Wilhelm Busch, a Lutheran pastor, was born in 1897; his father was also called Wilhelm, and was also a pastor, and some of his life story forms the first part of the present book. The son, who is the author and main subject of the book, served in the German army in the First World War and was converted during that time.

After studying theology he spent some years as an assistant preacher in Bielefeld, then in the Essen Altstadt congregation, and finally from 1929 as Youth Pastor in Essen, in which post he continued till his retirement in 1962. He died in 1966 while returning after preaching in communist East Germany.

Wilhelm Busch requested that no biography of him should be written, and this request has been honoured. However, he left a great deal of published autobiographical material, from which this book has been compiled.

I first came across the book *Freiheit durch das Evangelium* (*Freedom through the Gospel*), which described Busch's encounters with the Gestapo. This was a transcript from two recorded talks that

Busch gave during the1960s. I enjoyed reading it and decided to translate it with a view to having it published in English. One of the publishers I approached liked it in principle but said it needed more material.

That started me on a quest for more books by or about Pastor Busch, and I found there were plenty. Two of the main sources for this book were *Pastor Wilhelm Busch erzählt* (*Pastor Wilhelm Busch narrates*) and *Plaudereien in meinem Studierzimme*r (*Chats in my study*). The former contained relatively short incidents; the latter was about men of God whose pictures Busch had in his study, men who had impacted Busch's life in some way. The chapters in this were longer.

As mentioned above, Busch's own biography of his father, *Dr Wilhelm Busch, ein fröhlicher Christ* (*Dr Wilhelm Busch, a cheerful Christian*), has been drawn on in this work, as have various other shorter books of anecdotes, some published quite recently. There is also near the end a brief extract from Ulrich Parzany's *Im Einsatz für Jesus: Program und Praxis des Pfarrers Wilhelm Busch* (*On Mission for Jesus: the Programme and Practice of Pastor Wilhelm Busch.* Ulrich Parzany was the successor of Wilhelm Busch as youth pastor in Essen).

Wilhelm Busch junior confesses that he could see no faults in his father; but he is very candid in describing his own failings, giving glory to God for his grace. In particular he has a vivid sense of his share in the guilt and timidity of the generation that lived under the Nazi regime, as he shows at the beginning of Chapter 9 and also in connection with a visit to the Norwegian Bishop Berggrav near the end of Chapter 12.

However, I received the following from Ulrich Parzany, here translated from his German:

Preface

Dear Mr Puritz, there were, thanks be to God, many opponents of Hitler who survived the Nazi time. Wilhelm Busch was among the few pastors who refused to take the oath of loyalty to Hitler. Together with his brother Johannes he saw to it that the West German Young Men's Union (today the YMCA West Union) held to the Confessing Church. He criticised the readiness for compromise of the Evangelical (i.e. Protestant) Church. You will find more about Wilhelm Busch and the NS time in my book *Programme and Practice of Pastor Wilhelm Busch,* which I wrote in the '70s. Cordial greetings, Ulrich Parzany.

The gripping way in which Wilhelm Busch tells of the varied experiences he had before, during and after the Nazi years have made the translation and compiling of this book a real pleasure, which I hope will be shared by the reader.

I am grateful to Mark Robins for help with the typing, to Paul Kendall for his encouraging and helpful comments on a draft version, and to George Noble for a striking early version of the front cover.

I am also deeply grateful to my late father, Gerd Puritz, for his persistence in keeping my and my brother's German alive and well after we moved from Germany to England in 1948 when I was seven and Rupert was four. He kept talking to us in German and making us read German books long after we were more fluent in English. Without his endeavours I could never have undertaken the writing of this book.

Christian Puritz
July 2013

Prologue:
Christ or Antichrist

Desperately I fought to save my house. The terrible air raid of two days ago had turned the city into a sea of fire. All around me they had given up the struggle; only soot-blackened walls remained, with clouds of smoke silently rising from within.

There was not much I could save. The two upper storeys were gutted; but if I could put out the fire, then I could salvage my valuable library and a few pieces of furniture.

Eyes were inflamed with smoke and weariness, hands were burned. We used poles to pull the fire apart. Water had long been unavailable.

Then — heads were raised. What was that? Yes! The telephone still worked! It seemed ridiculous that in the burning wreckage of a house, with the blue spring sky looking in from above, the phone was ringing. I rushed towards it.

'This is the Secret State Police. Come here immediately.'

'But I can't. My house is on fire!'

Christ or Hitler?

'When the State Police call, you are to appear immediately. We expect you in half an hour.'

So there I sat in the Gestapo office facing an elegant official who gave just a fleeting glance at my burned clothes and then informed me about one of the petty restrictions with which the evangelical youth work was constantly being tormented.

'I wouldn't mind having your worries!'

I was rather shocked at the words that had escaped me. But the important man was very gracious. 'Why?' he asked simply.

'Well, here a world is coming to an end. And you have the effrontery to summon me to your office for a thing like this!'

At that he suddenly became very serious and said, 'This matter is very important to us. You see, we have been observing you carefully, and we noticed that you have not cancelled any service or youth meeting. When your halls and churches were destroyed, you went into the cellars. And when a cellar was destroyed, you arranged to meet in the next one.'

I had to smile: 'Yes, the triumphal march of the gospel goes on!'

At that he flared up: 'And our conflict of world views goes on as well! Even if the world comes to an end!!'

We looked each other in the eye and sensed, each in the other, a tremendous determination.

'In that case you are admitting,' I said slowly, 'that the theme of this dreadful time is: "Christ or Antichrist"!'

Prologue

'I agree with you. It is just a question of whether your imagined Jesus is to go on holding minds in captivity — or whether we and our world view are to rule. That is the real issue of our time. All the rest is only accompaniment.'

I could not help myself; I put out my hand to him and said, 'Although worlds separate us, you and I understand something more than all those who do not grasp what this is really about.'

And then I said to him that Jesus Christ is not imaginary, but that he lives.

As I was going home, I suddenly remembered my burning house. I had completely forgotten about it.

And that was good. After all, it was not a question of house and possessions. And my heart became joyful in spite of all the trials, because I was allowed to serve a Lord whose victory is certain since he cried on Golgotha: 'It is finished!'

1.

My father and mother

My father

Father was noticed wherever he went: a big, powerful man with a goatee beard and bushy moustache, and an expressive face that could show both exuberant joy and deep earnestness.

He made it clear that Christians are not to be whiners and complainers. After all, why should a man who has peace with God look miserable?

I remember how he once travelled with us children to the Rhine. As we left the train and marched down the magnificent road underneath the Rheinstein Castle he said, 'Children, I just need to let off some steam!' And then he began to bellow and yodel and cry out with unbridled *joie-de-vivre* and holiday mood.

Another time we were lying in the rough alpine pasture on some high mountain and enjoying the view of the quiet wooded valley below. Then he jumped up: 'Come on boys, let's run down!' And thus began a wild race down to the valley. Or the children laid themselves down in order of size on a grassy slope, and then he started to count 'One, two, three!' and there was a rolling race down the mountain, which he enjoyed all the more when the children's legs got thoroughly mixed up together. That was how exuberant he could be.

He had a great sense of humour, which also made for cheerfulness. The whole Busch family was once going on holiday in a fourth-class train compartment. The train was packed and tempers were high among the other passengers, who were sweltering in the heat. One of them was complaining loudly about the train operators, the fellow travellers, the children and anything else he could think of. Father tried to calm him down, but the man had a go at him.

'Do you mean to say you love this crush?'

'No,' he said dryly, 'I love my wife!' and he gave her a radiant look. At that the spell was broken. Everyone laughed, and they had a happy journey.

But he could also be serious. What holy earnestness showed in his face when he stood in the pulpit! And when in the tumult during a family meal, he would slowly and emphatically knock on the table with the napkin ring, everybody went quiet!

Father once heard of a parishioner who was seriously ill. Immediately he set off to visit the man. But he had hardly entered the room when the man flared up: 'You damned parson! If I could only get my hands on your throat…!'

The thundering reply came: 'And you shameless fellow! You will immediately keep your unclean mouth shut!'

The man stopped short, deeply shocked — that was not what he was expecting. But then he began to laugh, so Father could sit down next to him, and soon the two became good friends.

My father and mother

This drastic manner showed one side of his character, but he could also be very gentle and tender. Many a sad soul can speak about that, having experienced his help in times of great sorrow and trouble. His faithful sexton declared after his death: 'He never treated me as a subordinate.'

It was in fact all a matter of love. 'Strive after love' was the melody that accompanied my father's steps through life. In big things and in little things this was his motto.

The love he had for his poor people made him content with the meagre rations that were prescribed for everyone during the First World War. He trusted in God to bring him and his family through with very little. Cheerfully he sat down to the table during the difficult years and gave an example to his children: 'Not what we eat is important; but that we are together, that is a feast!' He valiantly led them in eating, even if it was turnips yet again, so that the children just had to follow suit; for any complaint about God's gifts he would not tolerate.

From love came also the unlimited hospitality that Father showed, which treated every member of the congregation as belonging to the family. He especially opened his house to young people who were far from home. It was wonderful how he never found guests to be too much trouble even when he came in tired and drained from the congregation or from church meetings. He welcomed them gladly and enjoyed the lively conversation that often followed.

Great and small in the kingdom of God, or not yet in it, all kinds of guests came and went, leaving stimulation and often blessing behind them. Many were attracted by my father's joyful, hearty love which opened hearts to him, so that he could give much more than just food and drink at his table. Thus he became, as Paul says, 'all things to all men'.

Christ or Hitler?

There was much singing and music in his house. He himself was an accomplished pianist, which once led to an amusing experience. During a ramble in Switzerland we had entered an inn. After the meal he sat down at the piano for a little while and played a merry tune. The guests listened. Then came the landlord, laid his hand on the shoulder of the supposed musician and said, 'You can stay with me for four weeks! Free lodgings, good food! You only need to play a little music each day.'

At that Father laughed: 'No, I'm afraid that's not possible.'

'And why not?'

'Because I will soon have to continue my work as a pastor.'

The landlord's eyes widened as he replied: 'No offence meant!' But Father played him another piece for free.

Once a friend said to him, 'Busch, you are a blessed man!' He replied with heartfelt joy and deep emphasis: 'Yes, indeed I am!'

How my father became the man he was

There was a children's home outside the gates of Elberfeld, where my father spent the first years of his youth. His father had been a teacher and became the director of this big institution. Anyone who grew up there saw something of the hardships of life; children came there from unhappy broken-home backgrounds and from deep poverty.

My grandfather Busch was a serious man. He didn't spoil his children, but tried to show his love to them by letting them feel in their youth something of the hard realities of life.

My father and mother

My father often said how valuable this rough schooling had been for him. The house-father's children were not given any preferential treatment over the children in the institution, and free time was spent working in the field or garden.

'Now I know quite well,' Father said later, 'that work is not anything to be ashamed of. But in those days it seemed a great imposition to me that I, the dignified grammar school student, had to go out to the field with a hoe on my shoulder. Yes, I was so foolish as to hide when I saw my classmates passing by near the field, so that they wouldn't see me.'

So my grandfather didn't treat his children softly. And yet those were lovely years of youth; for even with the strict upbringing the children sensed their father's great love. For instance, every child had his or her own seedbed in the garden. With loving interest grandfather helped each of his children to sow and tend their plants.

Sundays were great days when grandfather really devoted himself to the children. In the morning they went to the house of God. In the afternoon they all went out to the forest, where they romped and played happily. And then, best of all, they settled themselves round their father on the grass and he began to tell stories. No one could do that the way he did it. Sometimes a hero would rise up from the past and be portrayed in such a lifelike way that you forgot everything else and travelled with the hero through the wide world, joining him in his adventures.

My father was only thirteen when suddenly this period of his youth came to an end; quite unexpectedly his father died.

The impressions received at his father's deathbed never left the boy. Death is terrible and can produce particular shock and horror in the heart of a child. Something of the awfulness of dying was there in the death of my grandfather; for ten days he went through dreadful sufferings.

But over all this shone the light of eternity. One little incident from that time has been passed down to us. His wife handed the dying man a spoonful of wine and said, 'Father, here is some refreshment for you.' At that the fatally ill man sat up, looked at his wife and said with a clear voice, 'The greatest refreshment when dying is the forgiveness of sins!'

Such impressions made the boy more receptive than a child of his age would normally be. How hard it was to say farewell to his father; and now the family was being torn apart. The boy came to live with kind people, but it was no longer home.

All this was a God-given preparation for his confirmation. I guess there are not many people who have received life-changing impressions from their confirmation; but my father did. He was given the words: 'Fear not, for I am with you; do not be afraid, for I am your God! I will strengthen you, I will help you, I will uphold you with the right hand of my righteousness!' (Isaiah 41:10).

These words gave him the strong certainty on which he was to base his life. The verse is engraved on his gravestone; that was his wish when the time came for him to die. He knew that his life was surrounded by the joyful comfort of this God-given promise.

Early days of service

After his student days Father spent some time doing pastoral work in an alcoholics' institution, helping businessmen, lawyers, officers and layabouts in their fierce conflict against the horrors of bondage to alcohol.

My father and mother

An anecdote from that time impressed my father deeply. He used to tell it with great feeling:

> There was a man who was a so-called quarterly boozer. He did not have to drink constantly; there were times when it came on him, and then nothing could hold him back till he had drunk himself into a state of unconsciousness. He had fought hard against it, wrestling to get free, but the compulsion was too strong. He owned a hotel and once gave the keys of his wine cellar to a friend, when he realized that he was about to succumb. That night the craving became so strong that he broke into his own premises.

> This man entered the institution and became very ill. When he was about to die the poor addict became happy, and he spoke the words from the 126th psalm: 'When the Lord released the captives of Zion, then we were like those who dream. Then our mouth was full of laughter and our tongue full of praise.'

Later Father was assistant preacher in Wuppertal (Barmen) where he really got to know what work with a congregation was like. It was a poor district, and in so many wretched homes there was deep bitterness and hatred: against the rich, the government, the church and the pastors.

He went visiting in his district, being convinced that house visits were an important part of his work. It was tiring! Not just in body, but more so in spirit: everywhere the same hard words, the same rejection and enmity.

Once, when feeling very despondent, he met one of the Salvation Army officers who had been experiencing the same kind of reception. There in an archway they encouraged one another, prayed together and then shared in the work: one took one side of the street, the other took the other.

After my father's death a few sheets were found in his desk, in which we read a little about this time:

> I came as a young clergyman to a big industrial workers' district in the city of Barmen. There I was to do pioneering for the church under the leadership of an older pastor. I didn't feel very confident, as I knew that the whole district had come under sustained political propaganda, and I was aware of the mood of that time against the church.
>
> It was like coming into an ocean without a shore. I didn't know where to begin and where to end. I started going through the great tenement blocks from the basement to the garret. It was not easy and there was little encouragement. I kept going out of a sense of duty to the Lord, and prayed continually for open doors, but it seemed that doors and hearts were closed to me.
>
> Things went on like this for a time, till suddenly a remarkable change took place. People began to open their doors and show friendliness; they were willing to listen to me, and here and there the Word of God began to work. For a long time I couldn't explain this change, till someone from the district told an acquaintance of mine that I had done something that had won the hearts of the people. I had done this without any such motive, but God had blessed it so wonderfully and through it given me the entrance to many hearts:
>
> In a little attic room in a great block of flats lived an old war veteran. He was a strange fellow. Hardly anyone was allowed to enter his flat. He looked after the place himself,

and did his own cooking. The flat did not look very clean under a man's care. A resolute neighbour woman had once tried to come in and do some thorough cleaning, but he had decidedly sent her packing.

I visited him now and then and found him lovingly stroking his fat cat, who was obviously his close and only friend.

One day I found him completely desolate, bewildered and sad. His cat had disappeared; she had evidently gone for a prowl around, been caught and probably ended up in someone's frying pan. I felt so sorry for the man, who had lost the only thing that brought joy into his life, and I decided to get him a replacement.

I went to a merchant who had many cats in his warehouse and asked him for one. 'If you catch one you can have it,' was the answer. As a pastor you learn to do some things you haven't done before! I went outside and got hold of three boys I knew and went cat hunting. It wasn't long before we had caught the dearest little kitten. Then I went to the merchant, let him pack me a basket full of useful food, put the kitten in the middle, and went off in triumph, the boys following behind…

Sadly the account breaks off here. We must now picture the happy ending of the story ourselves, and the result has already been described.

Distractions from a Bible study

Father was once asked by some members of his congregation to begin a regular Bible study. Of course he was happy to do this.

Christ or Hitler?

However, there were many in that part of the town who wanted nothing to do with church or Christianity. When they heard about the proposal they thought: 'We'll give these Pietists and their pastor a good send-off,' and they hatched a plot.

When the study was due to be held for the first time, there was a great crowd of people outside on the street. They howled and screamed and made a great spectacle with trumpets and other similar instruments.

Worst of all, just above the meeting room someone kept banging on the floor with a sledgehammer: 'Boom, boom!'

Father, with his little group — there were just two men and a few fearful women — first sang a verse, though it didn't really sound right. Then he did the Bible study, a little shorter than he had intended. When he finished, the people were afraid to go home because the demonstration outside was still going on. So Father went to the door and called loudly into the crowd: 'Make room please! Can't you see that the people want to go home?' They were a bit taken aback, and a proper alley was formed, so that his little sheep could go through the noisy crowd and get home unharmed.

Then my father went upstairs to the human knocker. He was still hitting away with his heavy hammer, but you could tell that by this time his arms were tired. When he noticed the pastor he stopped and looked at him in amazement. 'Good evening,' said Father, 'I just wanted to let you know that we have finished now.' At that the man's eyes grew even wider.

'Listen,' asked Father, 'what does a worker earn these days for an hour's overtime?'

'Half a mark,' said the man, looking rather embarrassed.

'Good, then I want to pay you that so that you have not worked for nothing.'

With these words Father pulled out his purse and placed 50 pfennig for him on the table. 'Good evening,' he said, pressing his hand, and went.

When the Bible study happened the second time there was no more banging. Some people had indeed gathered on the street to make a disturbance, but Father just said calmly to them: 'Children, go home and make the racket there; that's much nicer.'

It worked! They gradually withdrew, and from then on they never appeared again. The small study group continued and grew into a flourishing fellowship.

Marriage

It was funny how my father, the young Dr Busch, came to Hülben where he found his wife in the old teachers' house.

A close friend said to him one day, 'Do you know, it's time I got married. I haven't found the right one yet, so I want to take a journey through the whole of Germany and see the daughters of the land. Perhaps I'll find one that suits me. Would you like to come with me?'

Father agreed, and they set off together. In the end his poor friend didn't find a girl he really loved (though later on he did find the right one). But as for Father, who had only come to be a witness to this strange search for a bride, he did find the right one, though he had not been looking for one. And he knew from the first day he saw her, 'This wife is a gift to me from God!' There has seldom been such a happy marriage, in which each saw the other as God's gift.

In the land of Württemberg in the south of Germany lie the beautiful Swabian mountains. If you ramble from the health spa of Urach to the majestic ruin Hohen-Neuffen, the way takes you through Hülben. Every visitor to the village is struck by a huge, ancient house. Why is it there?

Well, the teachers of Hülben have lived in this house for the past two hundred years. It is a unique feature that a teacher dynasty was formed here, going back to the year 1722. That was when a Kullen first became the teacher in this village, and from then on the son always followed the father.

They were rooted in the soil, these teachers. Even today they are not just teachers but also farmers. Under the big, dark red roof of the schoolhouse there is not only the schoolroom, but also the cattle stable and pigsty, the teacher's flat and the threshing floor.

The schoolhouse in Hülben was one of the centres of a spiritual movement that has a special significance for Württemberg, that of Old Pietism.

In almost every village in the mountains, and for miles around also in the lowlands, there was a so-called meeting hour. On a Saturday evening or a Sunday afternoon men and women, simple lay people, came together to look into God's Word. They didn't leave the church; they considered it important to take part in the services of the congregation. But in great freedom they formed and developed their own life of fellowship.

In the Hülben schoolhouse my father, the young pastor Busch, found his wife. It was a lovely day, his wedding day on 26 September

1894. Many dear friends came from all over the place to celebrate the happy feast with them.

The first few years of married life were spent happily and fruitfully serving in the little village of Dahlerau, which up till then had never had its own pastor.

Elberfeld

Back in the industrial city of Elberfeld-Barmen in Wuppertal the former assistant preacher had not been forgotten. And one day they fetched him back to be their pastor.

Elberfeld was a battlefield. Long, dreary, dirty streets, with terraced houses stuck together in monotonous uniformity. The people who lived here knew the darker side of life. It was so different from Dahlerau: there the hearty personal relationship between employer and employee, here mostly joint-stock companies, where the shareholder knew nothing of the worker and the worker didn't know his employer. And just as the worker didn't relate to the mechanical work he was doing for someone he didn't know, so also in most cases the personal relationship to the home had been lost.

It was shocking to see how many workers in Elberfeld in those days were so unsettled. When people wanted to do spring cleaning, usually on 1 May, they just moved into another apartment. Then all the meagre furnishings were placed in the street and were soaped down; and the evening meal was eaten in a new apartment. But the children sang:

The month of May has come,
the trees are coming out,

the bits and pieces fly
out of the window fast.
As clouds move in the sky
So do the people move
throughout all Elberfeld.

There were, indeed, many poor people who lived here. Day in, day
out, without any holidays, the soulless work in the factory ground on.
Badly paid, looked down on by those better off, housed in narrow,
musty tenement blocks, embittered by continual harassment, the
workers were also inwardly impoverished, because an extremely
inadequate party political press was their only mental nourishment.

It is hard to describe the deep needs of an industrial parish.
Facing such wretchedness the pastor loses all illusions and wishful
thinking, as he finds himself confronted with the harsh realities of
life. There he learns to value and depend on the truths of his faith.
Here are the 'labouring and heavy laden'. Such work is not easy.
Father soon noticed that. How was he to get close to such people?
The natural man resists the idea of even seeking to get close.

'…It's going to be hard for me to have to get into all that moral filth
and depravity…,' Father wrote on one occasion.

This was where he was to proclaim the glad tidings. The forces of
resistance were mighty and were freshly encountered with every
individual. The materialistic, earthbound way of thinking held the
people totally in its sway. And on top of that was the deep mistrust
of the workers towards the representative of the church, whom
they regarded as the 'agent of capitalism', the hypocrite in the pay
of economic and political groups.

And yet my father managed to penetrate these strong defences. He
had a quick-witted and fearless personality. Beyond that was the

spiritual power he fought for in prayer. There was really only one way to make progress in such work, namely to seek people with love coming from the heart. He learned the truth of 1 Corinthians 13: 'If I spoke with the tongues of men and of angels and had not love, I would be a sounding brass and a tinkling bell.'

The people came to sense the genuine love in their new pastor.

My father had a special aptitude for helping people to abandon their hostility. One day he came into a sick room. As soon as the man saw the pastor coming he turned round defiantly in his bed and faced the wall. Father said nothing, but got himself a chair and sat down next to the bed. And then it was quiet in the room while he waited. The minutes passed. From the twitching of his back it was clear that the situation had become embarrassing for the man. At last father interrupted the silence: 'So, now I have seen your back long enough. Now let's have a look at you from the front.' At that he turned round quite relieved, and the conversation could begin.

Another time he entered an apartment, only for the man to jump up, stand right in his way and bellow at him: 'Now I am throwing you out!' Father stood there broad and tall with his legs spread out, gave him a friendly smile and replied: 'Why don't you try it?' The man was nonplussed by his energetic pastor, but there was no more word of 'throwing out'.

Odd things could happen. Once when my father was going down the road a young man jumped out of a ground floor window looking utterly terrified. Behind him flew a slipper, and at the window appeared the face of the tender spouse, flushed with anger. As Father looked more closely he realized that it was a couple that he had married the day before.

On one of the early days in Elberfeld, Father went quite unhappily to his wife in the kitchen: 'I have never had a Saturday like this one. I just can't get down to my sermon. People keep coming to talk to me, wanting me to help them.' While he was still lamenting, the door bell rang again. The poor pastor's wife was a little afraid: 'What will happen now? The unlucky person who comes now and meets an unfriendly pastor won't know how often he has been disturbed today.'

But no; it went well and resulted in something lovely. After a while Father came back into the kitchen full of cheer, to share the joyful news with his wife. Who had been there? A grammar school boy had come with the request that Pastor Busch might start a small Bible study group with him and a few of his friends at school. A true pastor is glad to give up his peace and quiet if a seeking soul comes with such a request. The study group stayed small for a long time, but that did not deter my father; and by the time he left Elberfeld it had grown to a substantial living flock.

Episodes in pastoral life

There was the old lady doctor, who regarded herself as very pious till one day the Word of God so touched her heart as to bring her into agony and soul conflict. A sin committed in youth, which others might not have considered very bad, so stood before her mind's eye that she could no longer lift up her eyes to the Saviour. The word that expressed her desperation was: 'My sin is ever before me.' Father tried to set before her Jesus's grace in various ways, but nothing helped her. Her reply was: 'My soul is very frightened' (Psalm 6:3). She felt only God's wrath upon her, realizing that she deserved it.

Then one day my father came to her: 'Doctor, I have read through the Bible many times. There I found the verse "God so loved the world that he gave his only-begotten Son so that all who believe in him should not perish..." but the verse "...all except Dr X", *that* I have never read anywhere.' This helped her; she accepted forgiveness with gratitude and became a joyful Christian.

It is a great thing to be able to help in this way. My father did not always succeed; he also experienced closed doors and disappointments. Once he met on the street a young man, a former confirmation candidate, who was now a trained bricklayer. 'How are you? Why don't you visit me any more? We never see you in the service or in the Bible study either. Why don't you try coming back?'

The young man laughed. 'Yes, that's what the pastors all say. I'm doing all right without that. I want to enjoy life, while I'm young. Later maybe...'

And with that he went on. An hour later a procession of people came along the road. They were carrying a bier. On it lay the young man Busch had been speaking to previously. He was dead, following an accident at work.

Another experience also shook my father deeply. A gentleman had suddenly been taken seriously ill while on a journey and wanted to see a pastor. Father was called and hurried to the scene. There lay the man, in the prime of life, alone and dying far from home. Death was approaching, and he had no hope of eternal life. He had squandered his earthly life, and all the things he had taken pleasure in were passing before his eyes and driving him to desperation.

He was married, but was living together with another woman. This and other sins were now coming with terrible force and horror on his conscience in the hour of his death. It was dreadful, this fear of coming with an unclean soul before the judgement throne of God. He cried out and begged for help in his soul's extremity.

Father spoke to him the glad tidings: 'The blood of Jesus Christ, God's Son, cleanses us from all sin' (1 John 1:7). But he could no longer grasp it, and died in despair.

What is a mother?
(a talk I gave to young mothers)

So you are young mothers, are you? At least that's what you think. That you are young I will not deny. But — are you mothers? I'm not so sure about that…

You say, 'But we've got children!' Well, yes; but having children is just the beginning. Shall I tell you what it really means to be a mother? A real mother loves her child so much that she knows just what the child needs at any moment.

I want to give you a couple of examples. I know a young mother who always gives in to her child when it puts on a defiant face. After all, the 'little sunshine' mustn't be allowed to sulk! But when the child dropped and smashed a coffee cup — a lovely collector's item — she gave the child a severe beating… What, you think that was right? Nonsense! In the first case she could well have given her a smack. A child is not some golden toy. But the smashed cup? That was clumsiness, not wickedness.

I repeat: A real mother knows just what her child needs. I want to tell you about my own mother. When I was a schoolboy we had to do some maths homework. I was scared of it and didn't want to try it. And so in the morning I was glad when I noticed that I had a slightly sore throat. Hooray! Just what I wanted! It was nicer to lie in bed and read than to do the stupid homework.

And my mother? She said not a word against my illness. On the contrary, she took it very seriously. Quickly she came with a thick, rough, horrid woollen cloth and tied it round my neck. And then she said, 'Lie quite still! Don't think of reading! Sick people need complete rest!'

After an hour I couldn't take any more; I got up and went to school. See, that was hard but it was sound. That was just what the boy needed at the time... You laugh? Sure, but there was much wisdom in that treatment.

May I tell you another story about my mother? I was a man then, but a man is still the child of his mother. I had been arrested during the Nazi regime because I still preached despite a prohibition on public speaking. It was an everyday occurrence then for pastors to be arrested, but it was hard for us when it happened.

I was sitting very timidly in my narrow cell one day, when the iron door opened with a great din and a Gestapo official appeared. 'Here is a letter for you,' he said. I was astonished. Post was not being delivered to me in those days.

I took the letter; it was from my mother. There was no need to tear it open, as censors had already read it. My mother had had to reckon with that. But although she knew that the letter would be opened, she didn't think for a moment about the censors, only about her son.

When I read the letter I understood why it had been given to me. The official's whole expression said, 'Now you traitors have shown your true colours. Now we have got you!' For my mother had written something like this:

> My dear son! I am proud of you, that you are in prison for the sake of your service for the Lord Jesus. Please do not give in! I adjure you not to move a finger's breadth away from your testimony to the truth. I would rather see my sons dead than in the bonds of this spirit of ungodliness...

Christ or Hitler?

This letter shook me; my mother was such a kind, friendly woman, and such firmness was not at all characteristic of her. But when the truth was at stake she was utterly uncompromising. I can tell you, that was just what I had needed then: a heart that came right next to me in my humiliation and loneliness… It was a mighty, a glorious, a strong letter.

You see, that is what being a mother means: loving the child from the heart so much that you give it exactly what it needs — a rough throat cloth or some godly comfort.

Mother and the American invasion

After the Second World War they found a list in the town hall at Hűlben that contained the names of all the people who were to be arrested and executed immediately after Hitler's 'final victory.' The first on that list was my almost eighty-year-old mother.

When the war was coming to an end, the Americans fired their artillery wildly at Hűlben because some scattered individuals were still putting up a resistance. Everybody ran to the cellars. But my mother said, 'I'm too old for that sort of thing.' Then she went into the kitchen and made coffee.

When the first Americans stormed into the house with loud yells the old lady met them with a friendly greeting and a hearty invitation to the well-spread coffee table. The young lieutenant was the son of a well-known German Jewish publisher who had emigrated in time, and he understood German. But even without that help the storming invasion would have turned into a pleasant coffee time. The soldiers took in the fact that here was a person for whom there was no such thing as an enemy.

My father and mother

How could I possibly do justice in describing my mother? She was so incredibly alive, strong, happy and kind, that not only we children but also all her sons- and daughters-in-law were attached to her with boundless respect and love.

2.

My childhood

Holidays in Hülben

The schoolhouse where my mother grew up is a strange building: under one roof are two classrooms, the teacher's roomy flat, the cattle stall, the barn and a big threshing floor.

In this adventurous house I spent the holidays as a boy with my siblings, playing hide and seek in the dusky barn, going to the field on the cow cart with Uncle Albrecht, searching the attic for old paintings stored there, sitting quietly at 2.00pm on Sunday in the 'lower schoolroom' listening to a brother expounding the Bible, and drinking coffee in the huge living room on Sunday afternoons with many guests and friends; these are all unforgettable experiences.

Here I got to know my maternal grandfather. I see in my mind's eye the slender form with the friendly face and the blowing white hair. I still have a letter that he wrote to me on my fifth birthday:

Christ or Hitler?

My dear grandson!

I wish you thousand fold, yes million fold blessings for your birthday. May the dear Saviour give you a really good new year of life, so that you keep healthy and no harm befall you, and that your dear daddy and mummy and the dear little sisters don't fall ill, but can live happily together all your days.

If you come to Hülben again this spring — may the dear Saviour grant it — then with God's help we will go for lovely walks in the woods and on the rocks, and perhaps we will see beautiful birds' nests with delightful little eggs in them. And in church I will play the organ to you and your dear little sisters, quietly and loudly.

And you must help give the cows drink and feed the chickens. They like bread so much, especially white bread; but they don't often get white bread, and they will also eat barley.

On the church tower I will also show you, dear little children, the great bells.

And in the school below I will tell you about the Saviour. He is our dearest Lord! May his face shine on you and all!

Your Grandpa and Grandma who love you very much.

Why the ice cream came so late

Oh what excitement for me as a little boy when I went to a wedding for the first time in my life!

My childhood

The long journey to Stuttgart! The people in their festive clothes! The carriages in which they drove to church! The ceremony there, I have to admit, was a bit boring for me. But I could look forward to the reception.

At last we were there. In a hotel salon I sat with my sister right at the bottom end of the festive table. It was so exciting: in front of us great big napkins and wine glasses, into which apple juice was poured by an imposing waiter. He was so dignified that we hardly dared to breathe when he was serving us.

And there were cards describing the menu in full. It was all in French, and we were most surprised when ordinary potatoes and such like appeared, not looking at all French.

But at the bottom it said 'Ice cream'. That would be the highlight of the meal! How we looked forward to it!

But there was a problem: after every course some uncle in tails stood up and gave an address; sometimes a very long one. We wished the speakers would go into the never-never land!

And yet — just such a talk has stuck in my memory. Or rather, what that talk led to.

Yet again another uncle stood up ceremoniously and smiled. He was obviously going to be facetious. He began: 'There is a legend that says that in heaven there are two chairs placed ready for married couples who have never regretted marrying each other. And these chairs...' he made a long pause, during which we could hear the waiters going about their business... 'these chairs are still empty to this day!'

A few people laughed out loud.

But then it happened: my father called out across the great salon to my mother who was sitting at the other end of the table: 'Mother! We'll get those chairs!' There was such joy and heartiness in this spontaneous utterance that everybody burst out laughing and waved to my mother.

I felt such a sense of wellbeing in my heart. I didn't know exactly why. But later, when I saw children suffering because of unhappy marriages, then I knew: there is no greater happiness for a child than to grow up in a home where the mutual love of the parents provides a warm nest.

The move to Frankfurt-am-Main

It was quite remarkable how my father broke off his work, so blessed by God, in Elberfeld and started very small, almost in a corner, in Frankfurt-am-Main.

He had preached one day in Trinity Church in Elberfeld. When he came into the vestry after the sermon a gentleman was waiting for him. This was a man who afterwards played an important part in Father's life, His Excellency Dr Schmidt-Metzler, a famous throat specialist who had treated Kaiser Friedrich III, and who had significant connections with the greatest minds of his time.

When my father saw him and heard his name, he was startled; for this very same man had recently asked him to preach a trial sermon in Frankfurt, and Father had declined without further thought.

Now here in the vestry stood this important, aristocratic man and just said to father the words that had called Paul into Europe: 'Come over and help us!'

My childhood

Then my father knew: 'This is God's call!' But he still didn't quite see his way clear, so he only promised to visit Frankfurt and consider the matter.

Now Mother will continue the story:

> In front of Trinity Church I met my husband briefly. He had to go away quickly to give a special sermon. In great haste he said to me: 'There are some gentlemen from Frankfurt; they will visit you.'
>
> I replied: 'Oh, I'm not going to welcome them at all. I hope we're not going to leave here.' But on the way home I thought: 'Now I suppose the gentlemen will come and will present everything in the best possible light, how lovely it is in Frankfurt. But I will say clearly to them how dear Elberfeld is to us.' And in my mind I recalled all the beauties of our home.
>
> But when the gentlemen were led into our lovely house and I thought they were going to come out with the splendours they had to offer, their spokesman, the fine, dignified Dr Schmidt-Metzler greeted me quite humbly, begging and enlisting my support with the words: 'You know what we are up to. However we cannot offer anything quite as beautiful as you have here.'
>
> Then I was smitten. I had not expected that. When I still replied how much my husband was attached to Wuppertal, how strongly he loved his home, so that we could not think of leaving all our dear friends and relatives, then His Excellency Schmidt said in an indescribable way: 'I have prayed to God to give us the right man in Frankfurt. And Pastor Busch is the right one.' At that I was so gripped in my conscience that I said nothing more against it. I could only wipe away my tears.

Soon after that my father was sitting in the train. His heart was heavy as he thought of the wonderfully rich work in Elberfeld. He saw in spirit round him the many people for whom and with whom he had prayed. All the faithful friends who by their prayer were supporting his work passed before his mind's eye…

As he thought of all this he questioned again whether it was really God's will that he should leave this work. And then — although it was not his practice to do such a thing — he arranged a sign with God: 'If in the house of His Excellency Schmidt, to which I am coming for lunch today, things are so worldly that there is not even a grace before the meal, then I'll cancel the whole thing.'

When he arrived in Frankfurt Dr Schmidt met him in his carriage and brought him to his magnificent house, which stood by the River Main and commanded a wonderful view over the beautiful old imperial city of Frankfurt.

Here were gathered a great crowd of parish representatives who wanted to see this Pastor Busch. They went to the table. And now the head of the house did not just say a simple grace. He prayed freely from his heart, saying that they had come together for an important occasion, and asking God to guide all according to his will, that his kingdom be built up and the name of Jesus be praised.

When he said, 'Amen', Father also said, 'Amen', and straight after that 'I am coming!'

Life in Frankfurt

Now I must sing the praises of the beautiful city of Frankfurt. Standing on the old bridge you see the great river; on one side the glorious old town topped by the majestic cathedral in which the

My childhood

German emperors were crowned during the Middle Ages; and on the other bank the charming Sachsenhausen with the beautiful May Promenade and the stately looking villas.

How lovely Frankfurt is in spring! The Sachsenhaus mountain is a sea of blossoms, and the plain bounded by the blue Taunus mountains is a laughing garden of God.

What rich history this city has: in the old town hall, the Römer, several German emperors were elected. The old observation points around the town speak of the fierce battles fought by an awakened, proud citizenry. In the Hirschgraben is the birthplace of Goethe, who in his poetry sings a song of praise to this city.

Frankfurt is filled with Goethe. My way to school passed the Goethe House in the Hirschgraben and reminded me every day of this great citizen of Frankfurt. In the school curriculum Goethe was treated practically like a local saint.

But, and it's a big but, in spiritual things Frankfurt could not compare with the great cities of the Rhineland. In this city there was an astonishing indifference to God's Word. In most of Frankfurt's churches the gospel was seldom heard in those days. There were pastors who preached from the words of Goethe, giving clever and elegant lectures. These will not satisfy the needy heart of man, whether in Frankfurt or anywhere else. That way no one can find peace with God!

A focal point of spiritual life was to be the Luke Church parish in Frankfurt-Sachsenhausen, to which my father came.

There is a law in the kingdom of God that only what begins in a small and humble way like a grain of mustard seed can come to anything. And this new work did start in a very inconspicuous way. It cannot have been easy for my father to go back to such humble beginnings after the lively congregational life in Elberfeld.

The vicarage in Garden Street was a real 'house in the sun'. In the front garden the roses bloomed throughout summer and autumn. Our family experienced much love from Dr Schmidt-Metzler there. He brought my mother a bunch of chrysanthemums with an encouraging word just as she was arranging the new home with a heavy heart. He would stand beside the new pastor, ready to help with word and deed. He often brought us children home to his own wonderful garden. It could always be said of him, 'The love of Christ constrains us' (2 Cor. 5:14).

Here in the parish hall my father was to preach and diligently visit countless homes for many years to come. It was a different world from Elberfeld. Here there were well-to-do middle-class people, smug and full of endless self-confidence. There were many millionaires living in houses looking more like castles. Sometimes Father thought that it was really simpler to visit the workers' homes, where he had to hear many a hard word, rather than these posh houses where he had to get through a barrier of servants just to meet the residents, only to experience a cool politeness from them.

But soon my father learned even here to find the lost, sinful and trembling human heart behind the secure and glittering façade. And so it came about that the little parish hall filled up more and more on Sundays.

Visiting Dr Schmidt-Metzler

For us eight children it was a great occasion when we were invited to the home of His Excellency Dr Schmidt-Metzler, who had been used to bring us to Frankfurt.

'We're going to Exilence!' Yes, the title 'Excellency' was quite a problem for the little ones. They found it hard to distinguish from the biblical word 'Pestilence'. We were familiar with that. But we had not come across Excellencies in Elberfeld.

The excitement began with a great washing and tidying operation. When we were all dressed up, the rubber-tyred coach, drawn by two horses, drove up. Everyone crammed in, and off we went to the marvellous house on the River Main.

On tiptoes we children ran through the great rooms and gazed at the photographs. There was a picture of the last Kaiser with a dedication. Also the father of this Kaiser, Friedrich, was to be seen in conversation with Schmidt-Metzler. Yes, there were photos of all the great ones in Germany of that time. Especially important to us was the picture of Bismarck.

But we did not spend too long on all this. The table on the garden terrace had been laid. Wonderful chocolate was poured into our cups, and there was cake!

Then it was off to the park. There we romped and played. Quite often the head of the house would leave my father to spend time with us. I remember how he taught me to walk with stilts.

When we were older, Dr Schmidt-Metzler sometimes told us stories from his own life. I remember him telling us how he became a famous throat specialist.

As a young assistant he once sat in the anteroom of some famous doctor in England. Another doctor entered the room and soon got into conversation with him. Among other things the doctor asked him: 'What do you think of the new laryngoscope?'

'Oh,' Schmidt observed, 'that's nothing.' And then he explained to him why he didn't think much of it.

'Well,' said the older man, 'I don't think you understand how to use it properly.' Then he straight away brought out his laryngoscope, explained it to the young assistant, inserted it into his throat and let the other insert it into his own throat. And when Schmidt went he had learned something which was to have a decisive effect on his life.

Only later did he discover that his patient teacher was the inventor himself!

As one of the first German doctors who understood the instrument he soon gained a great reputation.

Now I just want to tell how, many years later, the picture of Schmidt-Metzler came into my possession. That is a nice story in itself.

Since my youth I have suffered from a strange kind of illness. Every ten years or so I get a terrible abscess in my throat. This grows and grows until I almost choke. When the trouble is at its worst the thing breaks up. Sometimes, however, it has to be cut open.

Now I had been pastor in Essen for some years, when the illness returned. One Sunday morning it had reached its height. I thought: 'Now it's all over for me. I'm going to choke!'

In her extremity my wife straight away rang up Professor Muck, a famous throat specialist who lived in our area. We had heard a lot about him; he was a man to whom people came from far and wide.

But there were also stories about how curt and abrupt he could be with patients. So when I heard that my wife had rung this man I was afraid and thought: 'Well, he's sure to be angry at being bothered early on a Sunday morning by such an unimportant pastor. My poor wife! He's going to wipe the floor with you!'

But shortly afterwards she came beaming into the room and said, as if it were the most natural thing in the world: 'The Professor will be very glad to see you. We are to get a taxi straight away and come to his residence.'

I was astonished. But I wondered even more when the great man received us kindly. He took me to his room, looked in my throat and slowly began to speak: 'This has been cut before! By His Excellency Schmidt-Metzler in Frankfurt! Round about the year 1910!'

Baffled I gurgled out — I could hardly speak at all: 'You can read all that from my throat?! That's amazing!'

Then the Professor laughed and said, 'I'll explain that to you later. First let's get you some air!' Then came the cut. I spat out blood and pus. And when — like a man who's been rescued from drowning — I lay on a sofa, Muck told me:

> Professor Schmidt-Metzler was my teacher. All my colleagues know how much I admired that man. One of them brought me the book you wrote about your father. In it I read that this man was a friend of your family. You were so close to him, that he even taught you how to walk on stilts! I really envy you such a close friendship with this man, whom I so deeply admire, and to whom I owe so much.

When some years later Professor Muck set his house in order before he died, he decided that I should inherit the picture of Schmidt-Metzler, which was so valuable to him. 'Busch is probably the only one of my acquaintances who would appreciate that picture,' he said.

47

So the valuable heirloom now hangs on the wall of my study.

'As a father pities his children'

I had a happy childhood; we had the best parents who ever lived. It still hurts me to recall a bad episode; yet that was when I really learned to love my father.

I was a boy of twelve and a pupil in a secondary school, but a very unwilling one! I think I was just lazy. Boys go through phases when the serious things of life are not to their taste.

I don't know exactly how it happened, but I got tangled up in a real web of lies. I guess it started when I had done a bad piece of work. Anxiously I saw retribution approaching. Now this bad mark would lead to other school work being checked. I would have to work terribly hard to make up for what had been missing.

I couldn't be bothered to do that. So I kept quiet about the bad mark. The next piece of work was worse. Again I said nothing at home, and when my father asked about my work I just lied to him with beating heart. He wanted to see my exercise book. I sat down at night and made up new exercise books. Then I had to get hold of some money to buy red ink so as to forge the teacher's signature. My father received an exercise book showing excellent marks.

I learned at that time that every lie spawns at least ten more. Soon my whole boyhood life was filled with covering up and cheating. The web of lies got more and more intricate. I was in the grip of a kind of panic. I would have been much better off just doing my homework. Now I was sitting up at night writing duplicate exercise books or forging excuses.

My childhood

Meanwhile Christmas was approaching. My parents were thinking hard about how they could make us happy. As for me…! When my brothers and sisters were playing merrily I was gripped by the whole misery of my ruined existence. How would I ever get out of it all?

At last the looming catastrophe broke. I can still see the scene as if it were yesterday. My sisters were playing with a ball in the corridor. And I was sitting darkly brooding on the stairs.

Then the doorbell rang — the postman delivered the letters… Not many minutes later the study door opened, my father appeared and quietly summoned me: 'Come in a minute!'

My heart was beating wildly. The table lamp was illuminating a letter that had just been opened. I immediately recognized my form teacher's handwriting.

What was in the letter?! I made vain efforts to decipher it. But then my father handed it to me. While I read it trembling he sat down in his armchair.

It was only a two-line note asking for an appointment with my father.

'Come, sit down,' said my father, 'and tell me what it's all about.'

Now I had to confess, and it all poured out of my heart: the whole tangle of cheating and deceit and lies and laziness and dirt. I myself was shocked when I saw it all spread out before me.

Oh, I could have spat on myself! There sat my dear father, who showed his love to us every day; his face seemed covered with a veil of abysmal sorrow.

Christ or Hitler?

At last I had finished. My father was totally sunken into himself. A dreadful, deep silence was between us, although both of us could hear my sisters' merry laughter outside the room.

Then my father raised himself up and said from the depth of his soul: 'You will be a nail in my coffin! Now go!'

And I went. The tears flowed down my face as I climbed the dark stairs to my little room. My sisters were shocked when they saw me.

Mechanically I undressed and went to bed. No one called me to supper. I didn't want it anyway. Later I heard my mother singing carols with my sisters. That started me crying. Dimly I grasped the fact that sin results in exclusion and loneliness.

I was in utter despair about myself. No dog would ever again take a piece of bread from me! My father would never be able to laugh cheerfully again! No one would love me any more!

Later, deep in the dead of night, I had heard all the usual sounds. My father was still at work in his study. Then I heard his door shut. Now he was going up to his bedroom on the first floor. Then my heart stopped: I heard distinctly how he continued up the stairs, up to me on the second floor! So slowly — step by step, as if he was carrying a heavy burden.

Shock thoughts raced around in my head. I couldn't remember my father ever coming into my little den. What did he want now? Was this the final reckoning? Would he turn me out of the house?

There he was at the door. I noticed how he hesitated a moment … then the door opened… he stepped into the darkened room… I held my breath. He stood quite still. Then he asked quietly, 'Are you asleep?'

I began to sob uncontrollably. I couldn't say a thing. At that he came towards my bed, laid his hand on my head with infinite tenderness and said, 'Now you're glad that everything is out in the light, my dear son!' I felt how he bent down and gave me a kiss. Then he went.

I lay there as if paralysed. And yet what I wanted to do was to jump out... I could have hugged him and said, 'My dear father!' But before I found the strength to do that I heard his door shut.

I lay alone in the darkness. Seldom have I felt such unbounded bliss. Forgiveness!! Forgiveness!! Yes, now everything, everything would become new!

The next day my father went to see the teacher. I don't know what they said to each other. With great gusto I sat down to hard work, and at Easter I brought home a good report.

My father never mentioned the matter again. It was completely put away. The guilt was forgiven: 'cast into the depths of the sea', as the Bible says (Micah 7:19).

Years later I came to know the forgiveness of sins that God gives us through the crucified Lord Jesus. Then I recalled this story from my boyhood. That is forgiveness, that our guilt is never mentioned again; it is really and truly put away.

And here — in forgiveness — lies all the power for a new life. Whoever believes and experiences it, his heart overflows with love to the Father.

Wilhelm Steinhausen and my enthusiasm for art

Next to my father's vicarage in Frankfurt was a big fenced-off building site, where we children experienced our most glorious hours. We built huts from old rags and boards and let off steam with our wild games. In the middle there was even a hill about two metres high, which we called Mount Everest. Another time it served as a spy's look-out when the German defence forces were fighting during the Herero rebellion in the colony of South West Africa.

The site was not meant to be a playground. The parish had bought it in order to build a church there one day. But at first that was not necessary. A parish hall had been built onto the back of the vicarage, and this could be made larger or smaller using partitions. To begin with only a small part was needed when a service was to be held. 'Today the church was well attended,' said the people if, instead of twenty, perhaps thirty had come.

One day in 1911, when I had just turned fourteen, all the glorious games were over. It had become clear that a mere hall was a disgrace for a rich parish of twelve thousand people, and the Luke Church began to be built. Yet we were richly compensated for the loss of our playground as there were so many interesting things to see and experience.

What a joyful day it was in October 1913 when the Luke Church was consecrated. The song of praise thundered from the assembled congregation. It was not just an audience taking part in a ceremony. It was a congregation that had come into being and one that continued to fill the great church every Sunday.

In this church building my father taught, preached and testified of Christ until they carried him out to his eternal rest.

Now this new church had to be something special. Not far from the vicarage was the big town museum on the River Main. Here the rich city of Frankfurt had set up studios for many important artists, to tie them to this city which so loved the arts.

My childhood

In one of these studios worked an old man whose life had led him more and more into the truth of the gospel. And his heart's desire was this: 'I want to proclaim the glad tidings of the Saviour of sinners once more in a great final work.'

This old man was Wilhelm Steinhausen. How happy he was when his wish was fulfilled. He was asked to decorate the interior of the Luke Church.

A hearty friendship developed between my father and the artist. Often I saw the patriarchal figure with the long white beard coming to our house to talk about something with my father or mother. He would sink down into the big red sofa in Father's study and say, 'Now tell me something!' He was hungry for mental stimulation. The conversation would often explore the deep things of the faith, or they would speak about the needs of the people and the congregation. Then suddenly he would get up and go. He had found something which could become gloriously vivid in his pictures.

I remember an amusing occurrence during one of those visits. While talking to my parents the artist had a new idea and wanted to make a quick note. Proudly he took out his fountain pen — at that time a rarity — and explained that he had recently been given this valuable instrument as a gift. He unscrewed the cap, and immediately his fingers were smeared with ink. Annoyed at this interruption of his great inspiration he just threw the pen into the waste paper basket and murmured something about this 'newfangled technical rubbish' into his amazing beard.

I was sitting in a corner and pretending to be immersed in a book. In fact I had my ears pricked to catch something of the conversation. But when the valuable item flew into the bin and Steinhausen ruefully stared at his inky fingers I couldn't keep up my detachment. I laughed out loud, the painter laughed with me

— and so I was noticed by this man whom I greatly admired, which was what I so much longed for.

For me, as a boy growing up, meeting the great painter was decisive. My connection with him did not stop after the completion of the church building, because even then he continued to paint, not on the wall now, but on huge linen sheets stretched out in his studio, which had been set up by the city near the town museum.

I often visited these painting or sculpture workshops, and felt completely at home with the younger artists. I would watch a sculptor creating from a rough stone block the picture he had already seen in it. However, I rarely ventured into Steinhausen's studio; I had such a deep awe of the man.

At that time I wanted to devote my whole life to art. I soon discovered that I did not have the gifts to be an artist myself. So I decided to study the history of art. I thought it would be glorious to be immersed in this world of creativity.

Steinhausen did not live to see the destruction by bombs of his great work in the Luke Church. In 1924 he laid down charcoal, pen and paintbrush for ever. A little while later I visited his house in the Wolfgangstrasse. His daughter Rose took me into the beloved master's studio. There on the easel was an almost completed picture, a charcoal drawing based on the text 'A bruised reed he will not break, and the smoking flax he will not quench' (Matthew 12:20, from Isaiah 42:3).

It showed a bleak room. Outside a fierce storm was darkening the sky and breaking trees. In the room was a man sunk in despair, his head buried in his hands. A lamp on the point of going out and a broken reed led the viewer to the Bible text and showed how it was with this man. The inner conflicts and storms of life were too great for him.

But behind this desperate man Jesus had come near and was bending over him, putting his hand so gently on his shoulder. It was a gripping scene, one that could only have been drawn by someone who himself had known severe conflicts.

Years later, during the Hitler regime, I was sitting in a dreary prison cell. Here I experienced one of those desperate days that only hopeless prisoners know.

Then the iron bolts were drawn back, and to my astonishment the jailer brought me a big letter. I had not had any post delivered at that time; so this was a real wonder. I opened the envelope, and out fell a small but beautifully clear reproduction of that picture of the 'smoking flax'. Rose Steinhausen, probably imagining what I was going through, had sent the picture. The fact that it actually came into my hand is one of the special kindnesses of God, who is also Lord over the hearts of hardened prison officers.

I chewed a bit of my mouldy bread and used it to fasten the little picture to the smooth cell wall. But I cannot express how much I was comforted by the old master artist, now long gone to his rest, when through this drawing he reminded me that Jesus comes to the broken in heart.

3.

First World War; my conversion

The lonely soldier

It was a beautiful evening in May 1915. But I had a heavy heart as I was standing there as a raw recruit at the door of the barracks.

Only three days before I had said goodbye at home with great, romantic enthusiasm. And in those three days all my illusions had been smashed. Until then I had viewed every soldier as a hero and a saint, but now I could see behind the façade. There was the rough sentry, who inflicted his bad temper on us with senseless bellows; the fat furniture trader who used bribery to get himself the cushiest jobs; the captain who saw in us human material but no living hearts; the comrades, who could think of nothing better to do from morning to evening but to tell dirty jokes and stories. And no one with a heart!

I was homesick. In spirit I saw my parents' home before me: how lovely it was there! Nothing but love and warmth and cleanness! I saw my father, how at my farewell he had embraced me for a moment and said to me, 'My dear son! God preserve you in body and soul!' And then: 'I won't be able to visit you in the first three weeks, because my duties will keep me here.'

Bellows of laughter sounded from the guardroom behind me. Oh how that repelled me! No doubt someone had told one of the usual 'jokes' which were more dirty than amusing.

A sorrowful dusk came over the strange town.

I was all alone! If I had not been too ashamed to do so, I would have wept at feeling so abandoned...

Just then a taxi came along. It stopped at the barrack gate and I couldn't believe my eyes: out stepped my dear father. With a jubilant yell I threw myself into his arms. He paid the driver, and off we went together. Happily I took his arm: 'Oh Papa, you did say you wouldn't be able to visit me in the first three weeks!'

'Yes, really that is so,' he replied, 'I will have to go back in an hour. Let's make the most of the hour!'

'And you came here especially for this one hour?'

He nodded. It went through my mind how tiresome travelling had become in the war: the overfilled trains and the tedious waiting around because nothing was running properly according to plan.

'Papa,' I asked, 'why did you do that?'

Then he answered — and it was as if he was opening to me his whole heart: 'I had the feeling that my boy needed me.'

Many years later I was sitting with a man who despised the gospel. He thought he had something clever to say. 'Look,' he declared mockingly, 'your Jesus says "I am with you always." It's funny how much he cares about people. I suppose he really depends on us! He is finished if no one bothers about him.'

At that moment I recalled the experience with my father, and I replied: 'Yes indeed, Jesus does care about us. But it's not because he needs us. Rather, because he knows that *we* need *him*; because he knows how utterly lonely and lost we are without him.'

At that he was silent. Had a ray of that endless love struck him?

'The world was lost'

It was Christmas time in 1915. I was at the front, a young volunteer soldier. We were stationed at the Kanonberg in a desolate, war-devastated region in the Champagne.

On the day before Christmas Eve I received a little parcel in the post. Among various welcome presents there was a yellow wax taper. 'Guys, we're going to have a Christmas tree!' was the word, when they saw the wax taper in my hand.

On the morning of Christmas Eve I set out with my comrades to look for the Christmas tree. How happy we were to find a little green shrub! Very lovingly we planted it in a tin can. With more patience than skill the wax taper was cut up and each little light was fastened with a pin to a twig.

Then came Christmas Eve. It was all quiet outside. Only here and there a stray shot barked through the night. Now the ceremony could begin.

It was a complete failure! In the afternoon a big demijohn of *Schnapps* had been delivered to us. This poison had already had a strong effect on the men, so that a bad spirit reigned. I tried to rescue what I could. The candles were lit, and I begged: 'Let's sing a carol!' One of us wanted to take a photo of us with the lighted tree. By the time he had set everything up the little candles had burnt out and the dugout was full of biting smoke from the camera flash. Everything went wrong! Why? Looking back, I think we were all homesick that evening. In short, it was miserable. And finally, full of anger and pain, I ran out of the dugout.

It was a starry night. The churned up chalky ground gleamed white in the starlight. Poor land! Here were once rich fields and gardens. Down in the hollow there had been a village. Now only a few bare fruit trees were left as witnesses of that. Even the ruins had disappeared; they had been used for road building. Two years ago joyful people had celebrated Christmas there. Where were they now, as their homes had disappeared?

I heard a sound. Someone came out of the officers' dugout, a few steps away from ours. He didn't see me, because I was standing in the shade. But I recognized him. He was a lieutenant who had always greatly impressed me. He stood there for a long time looking out into the dreary night. 'Well,' I thought, 'he's going through the same as I am. In the officers' dugout they're presumably all drunk too. And now the whole misery of the war is hitting him, so that he can hardly bear it.'

Yet — what was that he had got? From under his cape he pulled out a glistening horn and put it to his lips. And now sounded softly and strangely over the devastated valley the tones of the carol:

'Oh you joyful, Oh you blessed, grace bringing Christmas time...'

His blowing practically forced me to speak the words quietly along with him. And everything rose up in rebellion within me. 'No! No!' cried my heart. 'It is not true! There is a village that's destroyed. Every ruined house is a reminder of deep sorrow. And here are the drunk, homesick men, back home the weeping women, children calling for their fathers. Blood, death, misery … How can you play like that: "Oh you joyful…"?'

But he blew on unperturbed. And it sounded accusingly: 'The world was lost…'

'Yes,' I thought, 'now that is altogether true.' I had never perceived and seen it like that.

'Christ is born…' he blew into my thoughts. So bright, so jubilant that I had to listen: 'Christ is born! Rejoice, rejoice O Christendom!'

Then it was as if scales fell from my eyes: this is Christmas, this and nothing else: 'The world was lost; Christ is born! Rejoice, O Christendom!'

An amazing confession

What a mess that was! Just right for Verdun 1916! According to the map our trench ran through the Chaume Forest. But there was nothing to be seen of the forest apart from a few splintered tree stumps. Perhaps there had been a real wood here with trees and leaves. Maybe birds used to sing here. Now the machine gun bullets sang their menacing song. The forest had been ploughed up hundreds of times. And it stank dreadfully of corpses.

There we stood one morning, crowded close together in the trench. Over our heads the shells howled, the harbingers of death whistled and gurgled.

'Five more minutes, then — ' whispered the NCO (non-commissioned officer).

Christ or Hitler?

Yes, then! — Then we will storm out of the trench, will stumble over the barbed wire defences and throw hissing hand grenades at living human bodies. And if we're lucky, we'll have the French positions over there in ten minutes.

'Four more minutes — !'

There — a crash! Sounds of splintering, howling and clattering! Screams! Our mortars are firing, but they're firing too short. It's not surprising: we are after all only a few hundred metres away from the French.

Shot after shot hit the edge of our own trench. Now the French were also taking action. A hellish barrage began. Boundless confusion!

Over there a group collapsed without a sound. Here a man was running, bleeding and crying, through the trench. All hell was let loose! Everyone dived for cover.

I pressed myself into the hollow of a newly begun dugout. It only went a quarter of a metre into the wall of the trench; but it was at least a bit of cover.

'Three more minutes — !' What, *minutes*? They were eternities!

Then another man jumped into the place where I was taking cover. He pressed himself against the clay wall. I glanced at him quickly; I didn't know him. He was a medical NCO and had a walrus moustache. Under the helmet his face was pale as death; horror looked out of his eyes.

He spoke. He stammered. The words tumbled out.

I smiled: 'Just calm down, comrade, it will pass over!' Then he spoke more clearly. Now I could understand his words. What was it he wanted?

With great haste he told me — me, the young volunteer — that he was an adulterer. Right in the middle of the howling of the shells, the crashing of the guns, the whirring of the shrapnel, the man confessed that he had been unfaithful to his wife. And then — a new sin! When he was a young man, he had been a thief. Slowly I grasped the horrifying truth: God had seized this man by the scruff of his neck. And now all the old sins were flashing before his mind. Whether he wanted to or not, he had to confess them one after the other.

I was deeply shaken. Silently I listened to his confession. Then cries went along the trench: 'Out!'

We burst out, up the scaling ladders, right into the roaring battle, into the enemy trench.

I never saw the NCO again. He may well have fallen.

But since then I know what it will be like on the Day of Judgement. Then all that we trust in for security will be taken away. Then all our sins will confront us. There they will be openly on view, all of them, every one! And — whether we want to or not — we will have to admit them.

In those three minutes in the trench in Verdun I saw how dreadful that will be.

The Advent journey

A year after that first wartime Christmas I was an NCO in a battery. Most of the time I was lying at the front of the trench on observation duty. It stank of corpses. It rained incessantly. Every day there was the usual number of dead. We had become mindless water rats, with no thoughts but whether the pathetic rations would arrive that day (it was the time we lived on turnips); and whether we would live to see the evening.

But now Christmas was approaching. That meant that my almost forgotten home kept coming into my mind. Somewhere that still existed: warm rooms and soft beds and shining Christmas decorations and singing and real human life. And father and mother and…

'Huuii, huuuiii!' came an enemy bombardment. I pressed myself into the clay trench wall. The magical pictures were forgotten.

And then one day came the call: 'NCO Busch is to report to the orderly room.'

When the evening came I trotted apathetically to the back, grumbling about the orderly room jackasses who were harassing us through the night in all this dirt for some trifle or other.

Late at night I arrived and met the patrolman. 'Why are you so late?' he shouted at me. 'Tomorrow morning early you must report to the regiment.'

Well, in that case the best thing was just to trot on through the endless rain. What would the regimental staff want from me? Had I made a mess of something?

A dark collection of barracks loomed ahead. A lonely sentry indicated a place to lie down. I was asleep immediately in spite of having only a few boards under me. It seemed as if I had only just shut my eyes when someone was shaking me: 'Off you go to the Commander!'

I had no time to tidy up. I could only — as we used to say — wrinkle my brow so that the dirt would fall off. Then I was standing before the mighty one, who, clean and well groomed, looked smilingly at the dirty water rat in front of him. 'Now all I need is for him to bellow at me for my non-regulation appearance,' I thought to myself. But no: he smiled and said,

> Busch! You are going home to the officers' course. It begins on the 3rd of January. You are leaving immediately. Understood?

Of course I understood. I wanted to cry out and roar with joy. But today was only — what was the date? At the latest the 20th of December. We didn't have a calendar in the trench, but there was one on the wall. Yes, today was the 20th. Why should I go now? I wouldn't need thirteen days for the journey.

Then this mighty one — Oh, he seemed to me like an angel of God — continued: 'Go straight away. And before the 3rd have a Christmas holiday! Dismissed!'

I thought the sky was going to fall in on me. Christmas at home? Not in the dirty clay? Christmas tree! … Father! … Mother! … Brothers and sisters! … Bed! … O joy!…

And there I was, sitting on the train. The carriages rattled. An endless delay somewhere. It was pitch dark. We were neither sitting nor standing, we were squashed together like sardines in a can. The grumbling started. I could only laugh and sing, 'O joy … I'm going home!'

It was a dreadful journey. I was travelling for two days. My stomach was roaring with hunger. My ears hurt from all the grumbling in the dark trains that crept through the night. But my heart sang and cheered, danced and cried out for joy: 'I'm going home!'

Christ or Hitler?

My mother, who knew nothing about my leave, was just coming out of the front door when I — unbelievably dirty and unshaven — arrived. She turned pale. She had to lean against the wall. Then we fell into each other's arms.

'O you joyful, O you blessed, grace bringing Christmas time...'

Shortly afterwards I heard the joyful cries of my many siblings.

Is our Christian life not also sometimes a laborious journey home? Let us not take it so hard! We are going home — to the everlasting Father's house.

Gottlob Mundle's visit

My godfather Gottlob Mundle was well known. He was a teacher in the mission school in Wuppertal-Barmen. But he became more widely known for his skill in reaching out to children with the gospel. I once watched him tell a Bible story to a crowd of hundreds of children. That was so captivating! Quickly he gained the attention of even the most restless spirits. And they followed to the end in breathless absorption.

I must tell you now how 'Uncle Gottlob' once appeared to me as a real angel of God.

Our position at Verdun was being shelled. A piece of shrapnel tore open the palm of my left hand. The blood spurted as from a fountain.

The medical orderly bent over me. 'It's hit an artery,' he murmured. Quickly he applied a tourniquet to the arm. Semi-conscious, I found myself being carried away with other casualties on stretchers. We were left on a street devastated by gunfire, and told: 'If you're lucky an ambulance will pass by in an hour and pick you up.' Then one of them turned as he was going and said comfortingly to me: 'Comrade, if you don't have an operation within two hours that arm has had it.'

There we lay helpless on the street. And then the shooting began. A wounded man bellowed in despair: 'A car will never get here through this!' The pain made me faint.

But suddenly the noise woke me again. A car was driving up in the grey morning through all the fire and smoke. It was a wonder that the car was not hit. It stopped. We were thrown in. As in a dream I saw how the driver turned and made his way out.

I looked at my watch when I was put on the operating table in a French church and realized that there were only five minutes of the two hours left. Then some anaesthetic was laid on my face, and I sank down into unconsciousness.

I came to in an empty schoolroom and saw a face bending over me. 'But that's not possible!' I thought. 'I must be dreaming still! That's Uncle Gottlob Mundle, from home; how can that be?'

It really was he. Amazing circumstance! He was in charge of a soldiers' home in that place behind the lines. And just that morning he had come into the military hospital and seen that the surgeon had an injured lieutenant under the knife. He looked at the young fellow's face — and recognized his godson.

Oh, Uncle Gottlob Mundle! I loved you very much, but never as much as on that day when I awoke all alone in that field hospital.

Christ or Hitler?

My conversion

Now I want to tell you how my plan of devoting my life to art was broken to pieces. It was during the First World War, and I had become an enthusiastic member of the horse-drawn artillery.

The thought that the war was a dubious — even an ungodly — matter didn't even come into my mind. With heart and soul I was fully immersed into the military world and its totally ungodly atmosphere. The Christianity that I had brought from home was gone, with just tattered shreds left. And when at nineteen I became an officer in an active regiment, my pride was enormous. There were no inhibitions any more. We lived on the edge of death with the rule: 'Let us eat and drink, for tomorrow we die.'

We had a lot of losses in our regiment. I was an officer like the rest, no better and no worse. But if someone had said to me, 'You are going to preach in the church,' I would have laughed out loud ... I was far from God.

My father asked me once, 'Don't you believe in God?'

I answered: 'I'm not so stupid as to deny God. To be an atheist you need a huge amount of stupidity; I can't do that. But God has not met me, so I am not interested in him.'

It was shortly after this conversation that I was sitting with a comrade, another young lieutenant, in a roadside ditch near Verdun. We were waiting for the command to advance. We sat there telling dirty jokes — old soldiers know all about that. And then I told one, and my comrade didn't laugh.

'Kutscher,' I said — that was his name — 'why aren't you laughing?' At that he toppled over and I realized he was dead! A shrapnel splinter had gone right into his heart. I was standing with my nineteen years in front of the corpse of my comrade, and at first I was still quite unmoved: 'My dear chap, how can you be so impolite as to clear off before I have finished telling my joke?'

But then I was overcome by the thought: 'Where has he gone?'

I can still see myself standing by the ditch as it hit me like glaring light, brighter than the flash of an atom bomb, 'He is now standing before a holy God!' And the next thought was: 'If we had been sitting the other way round, then the shrapnel would have hit me, and then *I* would now be standing before God!' Not any other god, but the God who has made his will known, who has given commandments, all of which I have broken!' ... And then it was clear to me: 'If I catch a bullet, I'll stand before God, and then I'll be in hell.'

At that point the lads came with the horses saying, 'We're going forward!' I mounted the horse. There lay my dead friend. And after long years I folded my hands for the first time and just prayed: 'Dear God, don't let me fall before I know that I'm not going to hell.'

Later I went to a chaplain and said, 'Chaplain, what shall I do so that I don't go to hell?'

The poor man was dumbfounded by my question and just stammered, 'Lieutenant, don't have any scruples about that. Whoever dies for the Fatherland dies well. First we must just have the one thought: to win the victory, victory, victory!'

'You don't know the answer yourself,' I replied bitterly, and went off without saying goodbye. Is that not shocking, that thousands of young men were going into death, and no one could tell them how to be saved? And that in a Christian nation!

Christ or Hitler?

For a quarter of a year terrible restlessness tormented me. One day — we were behind the front but would be going back to it the next day — I cleared out my suitcase which had stayed with the baggage. While doing this I found a Bible which my mother had put into the case during my last spell of leave. On the first page was written, in that handwriting so dear to me: 'To my beloved son', and then the saying, 'Thy word is a lamp unto my feet and a light unto my path' (Psalm 119:105). There had to be light for me here! 'That will tell me how not to be lost!' I thought.

I leafed through it, because I was not really familiar with it. My eye was caught by a single sentence: 'Christ Jesus came into the world to save sinners' (1 Timothy 1:15).

That hit me like a bolt of lightning. 'Sinner' — that was what I was, and nobody needed to explain that to me any more. I was a sinner — that was clear — and I wanted to be saved. I didn't know exactly what that meant. I only knew that being saved meant coming out of the state I was in, and finding peace with God. 'Christ Jesus came into the world to save sinners.' If Jesus could do that, then I must find Jesus!

It took a few more weeks. I looked for someone who could show me Jesus. No one could show me Jesus. Then, when we were on the advance again, I locked myself in an old French farmhouse. It was broken down and empty, but one room was still whole. There was a key in the door.

I went in, locked the door on the inside, fell on my knees and said, 'Lord Jesus, it says in the Bible that you came from God to save sinners. I am a sinner. I cannot promise you anything for the future, because I have a bad character. But I don't want to go to hell if I get hit by a shot. And therefore, Lord Jesus, I am giving myself over to you, from head to foot. Do with me what you want!'

There was no bang, no great emotion, but when I went out I had found a Master, the Lord to whom I belonged.

This was the great turning point in my life. I experienced then how the living Lord Jesus himself seeks and calls his sheep. And I know that my parents were praying, not just for my preservation in the war, but for my eternal salvation.

From then on, it became clearer and clearer to me: you must become a pastor, and tell young people how they can be saved! This was fulfilled; I became a youth pastor, dealing with young men in the main. And if I was ever tempted to go in 'modern paths' then I couldn't help thinking, 'Perhaps there is a young man sitting here who is as worried about his eternal salvation as you were at that time. You must not disappoint him. You must show him the way to Jesus.'

So I was lost to the world of art.

4.

Student days

A romantic journey

1919! The war was over. I moved to the delightful town of Tübingen to study theology. Till the end of the course I never left Tübingen. There was no need to move, because just at that time there was a big turnover of professors, so that I did not have to change university as many students do. We stayed — and the professors changed.

Those were glorious years! The youth movement that went through the whole land of Germany like a storm drew me in its wake. What rambles we had, rich with experiences! I want to tell you about one romantic journey.

Brilliant, sunny Whitsun days by Lake Constance, near the Swiss border! The trees were blooming, the birds singing; and we students were singing as well. With a few friends I had left Tübingen for a hike. The great inflation had begun, but that was not important for us, as we had next to no money anyway.

Christ or Hitler?

In our rucksacks were a few meagre packets of soup. At midday we went to a farmhouse and asked the farmer's wife for permission to cook our soup on her stove.

Permission was gladly given, for in those days no cars had yet come to Lake Constance. Few strangers visited these lonely villages, so we 'travelling scholars' brought welcome variety to their quiet world.

While my friend was cooking in the kitchen, I sat with the farmer in the living room and told story after story. Soon there was a jug of cider on the table, and apples! And bread!

Meanwhile the farmer's wife asked our cook: 'Is that all you've got to eat? This small packet of soup? Are you so poor? Then you'd better eat with us!'

So now we could eat our fill of *spaetzle* noodles, ham and vegetables. To express our thanks we sang another song. Meanwhile the farmer's wife stuffed bread and fruit into our rucksacks. Then they waved goodbye to us for a long time, while we went on our way singing a travellers' song.

Tourism for the masses didn't exist in those days; instead there were delightful human encounters…

Evening descended. We lay at the lake's edge and kept looking across the blue surface to the snow-capped Swiss mountains. I was seeing them for the first time in my life. The war was behind us. The four of us had looked death in the eye thousands of times. We had been officers, with responsibilities far too heavy for such young fellows. Now we were making up for all the things we had missed — all that our young lives had been cheated of: youthful joys and romanticism.

Student days

White sails were coming toward the shore, one after another. 'Over there is Überlingen,' said one of us. 'There's a sailing regatta today; I saw a poster about it. There'll be lots of people there. We should go and look for somewhere to stay the night.'

I laid down the little volume of Eichendorff novels, a bit of which I had just been reading. How I enjoyed reading them in those days, the wonderful stories of the Silesian romantic, in which post horns sound through quiet summer nights, white castles beckon mysteriously and noble countesses mingle with travelling students in wondrous adventures!

Still engrossed in my dear Eichendorff I announced to my friends: 'This blue evening, coming down so gently, hardly wanting to end the brilliant day, will bring us a big surprise!'

'Surprise?!?'

'Yes! A countess will invite us to her white castle…!'

With that we shouldered our rucksacks and set out for Überlingen.

Here we found bustling activity. The regatta had drawn many visitors; the inns and their gardens were full of cheerful people.

No one bothered about us. Far and wide no noble countess appeared! A farmer, whom we asked for permission to sleep in his barn, drove us away. A policeman offered us accommodation — in a police cell. We thanked him politely and ended up in the market square. The fountain gurgled. Slowly the lights of the town went out. The tower clock struck midnight.

We were sitting on the edge of the fountain, quietly strumming on the guitar.

Christ or Hitler?

Then two ladies came across the quiet square: an older one all in black and a younger one all in white. 'The countess!' I whispered with delight.

The two went past us, but then turned back immediately. 'The gentlemen have no accommodation?' asked the lady in black.

'No,' I answered, 'we're waiting.'

'Oh! May I ask what you are waiting for?'

'Certainly.' And then I burst out: 'For a countess who will invite us to her white castle.'

The young lady in white laughed out loud. The older lady in black smiled quietly and said, 'Yes, I am a countess. But — I'm afraid I can't invite you to a white castle, much as I would like to. You are students I presume…'

I nodded, and could feel my heart in my throat.

'But…' She whispered a few words to the young lady; and then she showed that she knew German literature and had understood my Eichendorff language. She asked: 'Do you know Scheffel's "Eckehardt"?'

I nodded, delighted. How could I not know that glorious story of monks and knights! The lady in black continued: 'Perhaps you remember that it's about the unfortunate emperor Karl the Fat, who…'

'…who was dethroned because of his lethargy,' I interrupted her impolitely, 'and then lived in the tuff caves by Lake Constance.'

Student days

'Right!' said the lady. 'And just think, those caves are still there, just ten minutes from here. The farmers use them for storing hay. Wouldn't that be a romantic place for you to stay the night?'

That was great, almost like a royal castle! We thanked her profusely!

Accompanied by the ladies in black and white we set out. I can still see in my mind's eye the steep moonlit slope that we ascended. The air was full of the scent of lilac and other blossoms.

And there indeed were the caves. We said goodbye and crawled into the sweet-smelling hay. We didn't need sleeping pills…

Student life in Tübingen

I had a romantic flat up in the old Tübingen Castle, where my friends used to meet every evening for long discussions. There were many problems to talk about. The old world of the Kaiser and his empire, which had still been there during the war, had gone. A new world was rising up, and we didn't know what to make of it. On top of that came all the questions that trouble every young person.

And then Professor Karl Heim was called from Münster to Tübingen. Heim was engaged in constant dialogue with science and philosophy. He effectively opened the windows to these subjects for his students, but he also represented his Swabian Pietist inheritance with conviction and authority in the academic world.

He had long been the travelling secretary of the German Christian Students' Union. In 1900, during the Boer War, he had taken part in an exciting student conference, in which the conflict between the

English and the Dutch had created a highly charged atmosphere. Equally stirring was his work among students in Riga and St Petersburg, just a few years before the Russian revolution. He had many ecumenical connections and a thorough knowledge of world religions, especially Buddhism.

It is hard to describe how much he meant to the students of those days. His lectures on ethics had to be held in a great banqueting hall, and even that was too small. There were students from every faculty sitting or standing and listening with breathless attention. For Heim took up all the problems of the day without fear, and seemed to ponder over them as he placed them into the light of God's Word.

Our little group of friends sometimes skipped lectures that were boring. One of us would be detailed to attend, and we took down the most important points from his notes. But when Karl Heim was lecturing on dogmatics, no one was absent. Those were very special lectures. We really learned to *think*. And more! The whole point of our existence was thoroughly examined; and then it became clear that the gospel gives the only way to have real, meaningful life.

Karl Heim began one lecture by speaking of the silent companion who is always at our side, namely death. We never know, he told us, when this companion will put his hand on our shoulder. Then life is finished, and the question is, has the purpose of our life been fulfilled?

And now he asked about the meaning of life. He investigated in many lectures whether philosophy, or science, or mathematics, or the religions or anything else could answer this burning question. He went into all the ramifications, and at the end we came back empty. We stood in front of a heap of rubble. No one can answer the question of the meaning of life.

Student days

We were quietly pondering the answer: 'Perhaps life is meaningless! It is probably pointless to ask for its meaning!'

And then Heim took the words out of our mouth: 'And now what if we live our life as if it were meaningless — and then find that it does have a meaning after all? If we miss this meaning, then our whole life has been squandered.'

Four years in the battles of the First World War did not make me so desperate to find the meaning of life as did these hours with Heim. It was as if the ground was swaying under our feet. What stillness there was in the auditorium when he now said, 'No man can answer this question for us. It can only be answered by the Creator through revelation.' And then he went to the Bible: 'Here is the answer to the question as to the meaning of life: "God made man in his own image ... so that we should be for the praise of his glory."'

We were like people who have long wandered through a thick jungle and are suddenly standing on a mountain top with a panoramic view. The meaning of the Bible became clear to us, and the meaning of the revelation of God in Jesus! And we began to grasp in a new way what faith was.

All this was not coming from a speaker overwhelming us with oratory. Heim had a quiet, penetrating way of speaking that betrayed no enthusiasm. Although we were shaken to the depths of our being, it was always by his clear thinking.

These lectures gave character to my time in Tübingen and made it beautiful.

The years after the First World War were a time of very deep poverty. We were hungry and cold. We went around in old, tattered uniforms. But that didn't matter. We were happy. We were learning.

Our friends who were not theology students took us with them into the medicine lectures, or to hear a famous economist. The world was opening to us.

Often we had a celebration. Then we would get a whole bucket of soup from a soup kitchen. Everyone brought along whatever food he had just received from home. And then we had a meal that was more festive than any state banquet today in Paris or Bonn.

The inn called the *Blue Cross* became very significant for us. The students nicknamed it the '*Blue Monkey*'. This little inn served a hundred portions of fried potatoes every evening at seven o'clock on the dot. But sadly there were always at least six hundred people waiting for these hundred portions. In those days the Mensa, by which present day students are provided for, was not yet known.

So everything depended on being at the *Blue Monkey* before seven o'clock. But Heim's ethics lecture finished exactly at seven. When we rushed off for the fried potatoes, they were already sold out.

Professor Heim had enough good humour to allow us to negotiate with him. He now began and finished his lectures ten minutes earlier. Hardly had he closed when everyone rushed off. But — Oh no! — there were still hundreds already waiting there. They had all been sitting under Heim.

Yes, it was a time of great poverty. Yet all the poverty could not take away the endless beauty of those days.

Visits to my grandmother

Grandmother outlived her husband Johannes Kullen by many years. When I was studying in Tübingen I often spent the weekend at the old school house, which had passed into the family's possession after a new, modern schoolhouse was built in Hülben.

I always found my grandmother, now totally blind, in a deep armchair next to the huge cast iron range. There the dear old lady sat, constantly at work with her spinning wheel. Today you see such spinning wheels only in museums! But only a few decades ago Grandmother herself spun all the linen needed by the family.

When I entered the room and had greeted all present, I was first offered a substantial 'snack'. In the time of poverty after the First World War I was always hungry, so the meal in the room over the cattle stall was a real treat! But hardly had I wiped my mouth when Grandmother was already calling: 'Right! Now read to me the *Messenger to the heathen!*' I fetched the Basel Mission paper from the desk. I was always astonished at the glowing enthusiasm with which the old lady followed the conquering paths of Jesus in the wide world. She was blind and just sat by the oven; but her vision was wider than that of many today who rush senselessly through different countries in their cars, and don't really experience much more than breakdowns…

Baron von Kottwitz and prayer

I first came across this man in my student days. I had made a worrying discovery at that time: I couldn't pray at all.

When I was converted to the Lord Jesus and gave my life to him, then I prayed. That was right! In that matter you can't manage without a 'conversation of the heart' with him. But later on prayer seemed so unnecessary. What is the point of bringing things before God that he already knows about? It says in the Bible, 'Your heavenly Father knows what you need' (Matthew 6:32). And

Christ or Hitler?

I found the verse, 'Before they call, I will answer' (Isaiah 65:24). Doesn't that make prayer superfluous?

That was how I convinced myself. But deep down I knew: I just can't pray. My parents could pray; I knew that for sure. But I — no, I couldn't do it. And so I looked for reasons to justify living a Christian life without prayer.

At that time I read a story about Baron von Kottwitz. I had heard his name before: I had a vague idea that he was a friend of the poor in Berlin, perhaps some sort of a Christian social reformer.

Then I came across this story:

> In Berlin at that time — beginning of the 19th century — the philosopher Professor Fichte was at work. One day he got into a conversation with Baron Kottwitz. The professor made a rather lofty pronouncement as if from a teacher to a pupil: 'The child prays; but the man wills.'
>
> Very earnestly Kottwitz replied: 'Professor, I have six hundred people to care for, and often don't know where I can get bread for them. Sometimes I don't know what I can do except pray.'
>
> There was silence for a few seconds. Then Fichte observed: 'Baron, my philosophy doesn't reach that far.'

This little story made a deep impression on me. I realized that our heavenly Father doesn't need our prayer. But we need prayer in all the problems, needs and guilt of our lives.

In those days I began to learn that we can unload our burdens in prayer, and that we can pour out the joy of our hearts in worship and thanksgiving. I recognized the privilege of prayer as a wonderful gift from God to us.

Father's closing days and after

We children totally loved and admired our father. When I was a young pastor I wrote his biography, which is now long since out of print. When the book appeared, a friend asked me: 'Judging by your book I suppose your father had no faults at all?' I could only answer: 'As his son I never noticed any in him.'

Because of that an experience at his death bed made a strong impression on me. He was only fifty-three when, after a few days of illness, he was facing eternity.

One night while watching at his side I said, 'Father, you have had such a rich life as a pastor. Your congregation really loves you! And you have achieved so much! That must be a really satisfying feeling.'

At that he gave me an indescribable look and replied: 'Oh my dear Wilhelm! When you stand at the gates of eternity and know that you must soon appear before the holy God, then you will only see omissions, mistakes and sins. And therefore I am glad that I have a Saviour who makes sinners blessed for ever.'

I have cited these words from memory; I cannot give them exactly. But I can still hear the voice and remember how it gripped me that the grace of Jesus Christ is so real and is such a glorious comfort when dying.

When my father's coffin was carried out of the house, and we brothers and sisters — a flock now unprovided for — stood around weeping, my mother called with a strong voice: 'Children, if we had no Saviour, then we would have to cry till Frankfurt was filled with our laments. But — we have a Saviour!'

And she lived that before us, when her path led through terrible poverty during the inflation years and through the trials of having to find somewhere to live.

'We have a Saviour!' That enabled her to make an incredibly beautiful and happy home for us children in the good, rich days while my father was still alive. Looking back I think with amazement, 'How could one woman achieve all that?' Certainly in those days there were plenty of servants. And the aunts, my mother's sisters, often came to help when things got too stormy. And yet, eight lively children! A pastorate that flooded through the house! And guests! Looking through our visitors' book we found that during one summer sixty guests had been staying in our large vicarage.

One morning I came down to breakfast really annoyed and declared: 'From now on our house is called the *Wild Lamb Inn*!'

'Why "Wild Lamb"?' asked Mother.

I replied angrily: 'Because even a lamb would get wild with all this coming and going. When I came home late last night there was a strange man lying in my bed. I had to find a place to sleep on the sofa.'

Mother just smiled and rebuked me with the Bible saying, 'Use hospitality to one another without grudging' (1 Peter 4:9).

The picture on my wall shows her at fifty-three, still a beautiful woman, shortly after my father's home call. The face shows the peace that she enjoyed as a true child of God.

Student days

The letter from home

The little train rattled its way towards the mountains. In a very crowded compartment I was sitting next to my mother and wondering whether I should tell her what was pressing on my mind. She had met me in Tübingen where I was studying theology, and now we were travelling together to the Swabian mountains.

At last I came out with it. 'You know, Mama, I don't get much joy from the Bible any more. I find so many difficult things in it. There are contradictions and things you can't grasp that make this book not enjoyable for a modern person.'

My mother laughed out loud: 'That comes from the fact that you are reading the Bible in a completely wrong way.'

A bit offended I started up, so that the man next to us let his paper drop in astonishment. 'Well, how am I supposed to read it then? I read it in the Hebrew and Greek original text. I read commentaries. I hear lectures...'

Mother put her hand soothingly on my arm. 'I will give you an example. You know how in the war you spent almost two years on the field without a furlough? I used to write to you regularly about what was happening at home. And then one day came a letter from you that I have never forgotten.

'You wrote: "I read in your letters about food rationing cards, about hamsters, about standing in queues. I don't understand all that. Has everything changed with you so much?..." And then came the sentence which moved me so much: "How long and how far have I been away from you, that I cannot understand the letters from home any more at all!"'

Christ or Hitler?

I nodded. 'Yes, yes, I remember. But what has that got to do with the Bible?'

'Do you see?' Mother continues. 'You didn't say then, "My mother's letters are not enjoyable for me, a modern person." Nor did you say, "My mother's letters contain contradictions and nonsensical things." You just simply said, "How long and how far from home have I been, that I cannot understand the letters from home any more!"'

I began to grasp what Mother was saying. Eagerly I listened further:

'The Bible is also a letter, my dear son. It is a letter of the living God from the eternal home — written to you. If you can't understand this letter any more, you mustn't put the blame on the letter. You must say, "How shockingly far have I come away from my heavenly Father, that I cannot understand his letter any more! Now I am going to get really absorbed in it, and I will specially ask for the Holy Spirit, so that I learn to understand the letter from home."'

From then on there was silence between us, till the little train stopped in Urach. But I didn't forget my mother's advice. It showed me the way into the Bible.

For me as a young theology student she became a real teacher of God's Word. I remember how I once spoke critically about the cross of Jesus and about the blood atonement at Golgotha. I had been walking a whole night in the Swabian Mountains to get clarity of mind on the cross of Jesus. But it had just become even darker within me.

Then I said to her: 'Why should God have wanted his Son to die? Is that not an antiquated idea of sacrifice?'

At that she looked at me seriously, and then became almost angry. 'So!' she cried, 'Is that nothing … "*Who forgives all your sins*"? Is that nothing?'

That was not really an answer to my question. And yet — when she said that, the cross of Jesus suddenly stood bright and clear before my eyes. I recognized the One on whom God had cast our guilt and sin, and I grasped the greatness of redemption.

5.

Bielefeld and pastoral work

How I came to Bielefeld

After my course at Tübingen was finished and I had taken my first theological exam there were wonderful summer days in the Herborn Castle, where the preachers' seminary was accommodated. We were just a small group of seminarians, had all been in the war, and had just one wish: after the rigours of war and after hard studying, to have a bit of rest. Glorious walks through the Westerwald! Precious fellowship in the circle of friends!

After that I found I had to spend another half year as a trainee pastor in Gellershagen near Schildesche. At first that did not suit me at all, but afterwards it became a blessing. For here I found the best of all dear wives. What would I have done without her?

From the window of my room in Gellershagen I saw the rectory, a pretty little house surrounded by greenery. What particularly impressed me about it was a proverb set into the wall:

Give shelter for a little time
for pilgrims to eternity.

That attracted me, and I soon felt at home in the rectory. One day I saw a pocket Bible lying on the piano. Many passages in it had been marked, and dates were written next to many of the texts. Only someone with great independence of thought could treat a Bible like that.

'Whose is that?' I asked.

'That belongs to our Emmi,' answered her little sister.

From then on I looked at Emmi more carefully; and I liked what I saw.

But I was really smitten when I once saw her in the garden, standing on a ladder. Crowding round her were children from the neighbourhood, and Emmi was cutting lovely bunches of flowers for them from a snowball tree. (It reminded me of something Goethe tells of his meeting with Lotte in Wetzlar.) The royal way in which the girl was giving away blossoms — that was charming and beautiful.

So she became my wife. We experienced good and bad days together. When we had been married for forty years I said to her: 'If I had to do it all over again, I would run after you to the end of the world.' At that she laughed and said she felt exactly the same way.

I find that hard to understand, because I know myself. But — she must know what she is doing!

She is not only a good housewife and the mother of my children, but also — as the Bible says — 'a help, to be around him'. How many manuscripts of sermons, books and essays she must have corrected, criticized and proof-read!

Bielefeld and pastoral work

In short, she is the best and dearest wife I could possibly have.

At the end of this half year in Gellershagen I took my exam in Münster. It was quite a festive occasion! For me the most important part was a discussion with Zöllner about the meaning of 'works' in Romans and in the epistle of James. Paul emphasizes in Romans that Abraham was justified before God 'without the works of the law,' through faith alone. But James says, 'Was not our father Abraham justified through works?' Zöllner questioned me, then he contradicted my answer; the other members of the exam commission got involved and it grew into a lively debate. The outcome was that I got a good mark.

Then they sent me as assistant preacher to an eastern suburb of Bielefeld, to the St Peter's congregation. In the middle of the district was a small temporary church hall, above which was my flat.

Bielefeld was populated entirely by workers, who were consciously social democrats and trade unionists. As a junior pastor I had to reap the bitter fruits sown by decades of wrong attitudes on the part of the church, which had long stood in its unhappy defence of 'throne and altar' against the legitimate demands of the rising workers. I remember a time in my childhood when my father came home and told us with indignation that an instruction had been given to refuse assistance at any funeral if the colour red was shown in any wreaths or flags. My father had never followed this instruction.

And how staggered I was when a worker told me he had been thrown out of a church-based club because he belonged to a union.

After just seven days I could see what the situation was in my district: the workers were united in their stand against pastor and church.

Going to the service was a comfortless experience: there in the small church hall sat an old man, a faithful young girl and a few women from the Women's Union. Yes, the Women's Union was the only part of church life to be found; but even that was more a social club than anything spiritual.

I began visiting from door to door every morning and every afternoon. Soon however I heard that the men were mocking: 'The parson only comes to our wives, when the men are not there!' So I rescheduled my visits to the evenings, met the men and got talking to them.

Then I experienced for the first time how much people had given up thinking for themselves in favour of adopting schemes and slogans. It was tiring to keep hearing the same phrases about 'the misery of the masses,' of 'the guilt of the church' when it 'blessed the weapons' and 'kept quiet about the plundering', or how 'churchgoers are worse than others.' My heart cried out with longing to hear something that had come from the speaker's own thinking and from the heart. Sometimes it seemed to me as if people's brains had been removed and replaced by gramophone records which can only produce certain catchphrases…

Living with high inflation

If a man from today's affluent circumstances had visited our home then, he would have turned up his nose at it. The best piece of furniture was a little cupboard that we had bought for sixty million marks. By the time we installed it, it was already worth two hundred million marks. That was how it was in those days of inflation and devaluation.

Instead of kitchen furniture we had boxes covered with cheap brightly coloured fabric. I had inherited a table. And apart from the cheap chairs there was some fragile basket furniture. Our circumstances in the little flat were very modest, but we were so happy. And the words of Matthias Claudias were true for me: 'A man should rejoice as soon as he can see the gable of his house from afar.'

Among the most beautiful things was the friendship with Pastor Kortmann, my brother in the ministry. I shall never be able to recount all the good that he and his wife did for me.

When I was still a bachelor I was welcomed as guest to all the meals in the vicarage. And when I married and the first child came, the Kortmanns shared with us so lovingly that my heart is warmed just to think of it.

It was a lovely time, like paradise: the new marriage, the first child, the spiritual awakening in the district, the growing attendance at the church services! And a brother minister who never once carpeted his young assistant, but instead rejoiced with him in all that he did.

But we had dark hours even in those days. There was the shocking inflation: money lost value daily. A sum that would buy a lunch on one day would not be enough to buy a roll the next day. Businessmen bartered with goods. Anyone who had an allotment was well off. But as I was dependent on my salary, whose value melted like a snowball in my hand, I had to go through real poverty with my young wife.

Shortly before my wedding an old uncle had warned me that I was only an assistant preacher, so not yet entitled to a pension. It was very irresponsible to marry under such uncertain circumstances. And then there was inflation. Perhaps the church would no longer be in a position to pay salaries. What would happen then to me and my wife?

Christ or Hitler?

He spoke in a very concerned and sensible way.

When he had finished his well-meant speech, I replied: 'I have just read in the Bible how the prophet Elijah was so remarkably nourished during a famine. The Lord his God said to him: "I have commanded the ravens to feed you…" And then it says: "The ravens brought him bread and meat in the morning and in the evening."'

At this the dear old uncle got angry: 'Oh, those are just old stories! There are no ravens like that flying around nowadays!' But I was of a different opinion: 'Yes, that's an interesting question: do the ravens still fly today like they did in Elijah's time? Or don't such things happen any more? I am sure that they still fly!'

So now we young people had to suffer hunger. We stood there with the worthless money in our hands and didn't know what to live on. Now we would have to see 'whether the ravens still fly.'

And they flew! However, these ravens were not black. And they didn't come flying, they walked to us on two legs. They were the wives of our workers, the ones who at first had met us with such enmity. They were now comparatively well off. They had gardens in which they grew vegetables. And they got their pay every day in the factory, so the money still had some buying power.

They had spoken often of the 'misery of the masses.' When they now discovered that the only poor person in the district was the young pastor, they sent their wives with the 'fruits of their field.' Some brought beans, others a pumpkin. Suddenly so much help was coming my way that I could say cheerfully to the old uncle: 'The ravens are still flying. Our heavenly Father has not left us in the lurch.'

This resulted in the bonding together of the young pastor and his congregation in a new and special way. And while we didn't exactly live it up, at least we never starved.

There was a really dark time when my wartime back injury made itself felt. I was quite paralysed, and had to move with my wife to Bad Oeynhausen, where the strong baths healed me so that I could learn to walk again, though at first only on crutches.

We didn't know from one day to another how we would get through the devaluation of the money. By the time I got my salary, the money was worthless. Then my kind father-in-law, the rector of Gellershagen, made a daily journey into town and drew a day's pay from the Bielefeld congregational office. That way he got my salary in his hand and could send it in time, so that before midday when the new rate was announced my wife could run to the baker and butcher to pay them in advance or in arrears.

Meanwhile I sat in my wheelchair in the spa gardens and envied everyone who could walk properly.

But what were these shadows in comparison with the joys of those two years in the St Peter's district?

How I first came to do youth work

'This afternoon the new assistant pastor will go on an excursion with the members of the Youth League! Meet at 14.00 hours at the vicarage.'

When the pastor made this announcement after the sermon, many inquisitive eyes looked across to me.

Christ or Hitler?

'Oh horrors!' I thought, and looked round desperately in the small chapel. 'How do I do that — an excursion with the Youth League? And — wherever do we go?'

It was only the day before that I had arrived in the rural suburb of Bielefeld. And now straight away I was to lead an excursion. I was scared, especially as I had rather indistinct ideas about youth leagues.

And the reality was worse than my fears…

Ten minutes before the announced time I stood in front of the vicarage on the big road that lay still and deserted in the bright summer sunshine. There was not a trace of the Youth League to be seen.

Five minutes passed — ten minutes — then I saw a young man coming. With the friendliest possible expression I went towards him. Perhaps I could find out from him how such an excursion was carried out. But — what a disappointment for me! — he went past me and set his course unmistakably towards the public house that was opposite the vicarage. There he disappeared from view — and I was alone again…

At this point my war wound also began to hurt. The French had fired a piece of iron into my back some years before. If I stood for a long time my leg would begin to hurt. So I sat down in the grass on the side of the road and waited.

It was now 14:15 but no one had as yet appeared. Then yes! There were two coming! Hooray! They even had horns with them, trombones that glittered brightly in the summer sun!

But — these two also went past — I followed them with my eyes — into the pub!

Bielefeld and pastoral work

I carried on sitting abandoned at the roadside. Now I was no longer worried about how to run the excursion. I would manage that somehow. But — what if absolutely nobody appeared? What if I was to spend the whole afternoon in this desolation?!

Men did indeed keep coming, both old and young — but they went to the pub. At last I asked one what was going on there. He laughed and said, 'We are the fire service!' And his companion made a movement with his hand to his mouth: 'We are putting out internal fires.'

So now I knew. Obviously the fire service was flourishing here much more than the Youth League, of which there was still nothing to be seen.

In the pub, things began to get lively. The musicians played a cheerful march, but that didn't cheer me up. Then the windows flew open. The valiant firemen appeared with beer glasses in their hands, toasted my health and asked what had happened to my Youth League.

Well, I didn't know that either! Evidently it had died out long ago.

When the men saw how wretched I was they comforted me mockingly and advised me to come into the cool bar. In the end all the windows were occupied and I was the target of general derision.

Yes — there I sat, feeling wretched. Should I not just give up the whole thing and go back to my flat?

But at the sight of the scornfully laughing faces in the pub windows I was seized with fury: was this pathetic Youth League not a disgrace for the kingdom of God? Would not the honour of my King Jesus be dragged into the dust if his messenger now shamefully retreated in the face of these tipplers?

Christ or Hitler?

And suddenly it was clear to me what I had to do: if no Christian youth group came here, then I must gather one myself.

So without further ado I stood up and wandered off along the long, hot road leading to the town.

In those days there was still little motor traffic, so the road was very quiet. It didn't look as if I was going to have much success.

But then I came to a little bridge. On the parapet sat three young lads of about sixteen, trying with cigarettes and big talk to make themselves look like men.

I stopped and asked if I could sit down with them. They had no problem with that. I swung myself onto the parapet, and slowly a conversation developed: What were they planning to do? — Nothing! They had no money for any adult pleasures... Pause! It was clear: they were bored.

So I ventured a suggestion: 'Shall we go into the mountains for a bit?'

Silence. Then one asked: 'And?'

'Well,' I answered tentatively, 'we could play something, maybe cops and robbers.'

At this it suddenly became clear that the boys had lost interest in being grown men. They threw away their cigarette ends. Two ran off and fetched three further friends. They were all keen as mustard. So now I set off with these six boys into the mountains and woods.

It was a glorious afternoon. My war injury still hurt, and I have to admit that because of that I always hid quickly in a ditch and covered myself with leaves so that no one ever found me. But, above and around me raged the battle between cops and robbers in a way you can hardly imagine. The young men had become boys again.

When the sun set, we sat down on the mountain slope, took in the view of the glorious country and… Well, what now?

'Boys!' I tried. 'We could sing a song. Do you know one?'

'Oh yes, we know:

> I went in thirsty
> To the *Green Wreathed Jug*…

Well fine! So — we sang that song resoundingly. When we had finished, I said that I knew an even more beautiful one. It was called: 'Most lovely Lord Jesus…'

Well, they didn't know that. But — they could learn it. And they liked it. It could be sung with variations, some soft, some louder. Soon they had grasped it. Then the conversation turned of its own accord to the Lord Jesus. I told them stories about him, and they enjoyed hearing them.

We went home singing. It was a bit strange how alternately the song of the '*Green Wreathed Jug*' and the quite different song, 'Most lovely Lord Jesus', sounded out. And it was just as well that no critical spirit met us on the way. But my boys were happy in their hearts; and so was I.

When we arrived in front of the vicarage, my mettle was roused. Now these tipplers across the way should see that I did have a Youth League. The boys needed no explanations of what was in my mind; perhaps their fathers were in there as well.

Christ or Hitler?

So we stood up in front of the vicarage and sang to end a beautiful day; we sang once more loudly, cheerfully and from the bottom of our hearts:

> Most lovely Lord Jesus,
> who rules all the earth.

As soon as the first notes sounded, the windows in the bar were fully occupied. But none of the men had a word more to say. They listened reverently. You could see in their faces that they were in quite a solemn mood…

This day was the beginning of a rich, blessed and flourishing youth work in that place…

Oh — does the reader want to know what happened to the actual Youth League? Dear reader, I don't know that either…

Strife front and back

Very soon different families invited me, as a young pastor, to their homes. When we had had plenty of good food to eat — then it started. Then came the tittle-tattle!

And I discovered that people's lives were filled with endless disputes. Sometimes I didn't know whether to laugh or to cry. Meiers were at odds with Schulzes, and Müllers with Krauses.

The worst row however, as I gradually found out, was the quarrel that had broken out in a family with many connections. Several married siblings from this family lived in the town. Each of these invited me and gave me loving hospitality. In return I had to listen patiently to detailed accounts of the misdeeds of all the in-laws and nieces.

Bielefeld and pastoral work

I was young and full of glowing idealism in those days; so not surprisingly I decided to step in as a rescuing angel. I invited all involved to a discussion in a big garden bower just outside the town on a lovely summer evening. And they came, they really came!

It was a magical evening. The sun sank slowly behind the mountains. An unending peace seemed to lie over the world. In my bower, however, I was fighting a fierce battle. What a strife that was! They were falling on each other with their heaped up reproaches. Often they were all talking at the same time, and I had a job to prevent them from coming to blows.

But eventually the flow of words began to dry up even from the most talkative. I was able to intervene, persuade, reconcile. And at last — after a great deal of talk I had achieved it: they shook hands with each other, sang a tranquil evening song together, and then all went peaceably to their own homes.

My heart was so full! I was so happy! As if on wings I went home through the cobbled streets…

The next morning saw me going past the market, where I met one of the women who had been involved. Gladly I hurried to meet her. But before I could say a word, she was on the attack: 'Have you heard what my sister-in-law said on the way home last night?' And then followed a lengthy tirade.

I felt dizzy: 'But listen! We agreed on peace, didn't we?'

'Peace?' she screeched. And then she laughed scornfully: 'It's only now that it's really beginning!'

With that she turned to the market stall: 'How much are the carrots?'

Christ or Hitler?

So there I stood, poor dupe that I was. Oh yes! It was only now that it was really beginning. The woman was right.

And I experienced my first disappointment as a young Christian. At that time I learned that the world's misery cannot be eradicated with a few good words, but that things only become new where Jesus enters, who has said, 'Behold, I make all things new.'

My friend Karl was a miner and constantly at odds with his neighbour down the corridor. How often I had already mediated and settled disputes!

One Sunday evening I met Karl: 'Where have you been?'

'Oh you should have been there!' he called out full of enthusiasm 'We had a great demonstration in the North Park Hall!'

'A demonstration? What was that about then?'

'We were protesting against the exploitation of the coolies in Shanghai.'

'Well, I never! You're even interested in the coolies in Shanghai?'

'Aren't we just,' called Karl excitedly. 'We really have solidarity with them. Complete solidarity, they're all our brothers!' You could still feel the stormy atmosphere of that glorious demonstration.

'All your brothers,' I called out joyfully. 'Then, Karl, you'll go to your neighbour this evening, shake his hand and call him Brother.'

At that the glow disappeared and his face darkened.

'What, that fellow, that rogue? Do you know what he's just done again? But I'm going to smack him one!'

'All our brothers?' I thought, and went away.

And once again it became clear to me what a great thing it is that the Bible says, 'Love your neighbour.' To love someone far away is not difficult; but the neighbour! There's the rub!

The cracked bell

Truly it would make your heart bleed to see the sight: in utter despair the young man sat with me on the sofa. The way his shoulders hung down, the sad expression on his face, the slumped posture — everything expressed sheer misery. And yet he was a giant of a man, big and strong, with bushy black hair. But now even his hair was hanging mournfully in his face.

At last he plucked up courage again and continued: 'Yes, you will hardly believe what ideals we had when we married. We looked down with such contempt on all the dreary mediocre marriages. We loved each other so much…'

A deep sigh interrupted his speech.

'And then?' I encouraged him.

He looked at me: 'Not so fast! When I think back on the first time, then … Oh, I just cannot describe what happiness I had. You know, my wife is a pretty woman, and clever! We wanted to show people what a real marriage looks like. Yes, that we did…'

Once again he sank into silent brooding. To get the traffic moving I prodded him again: 'What happened then?'

Irritably he started up: 'What is there to say much about? The day before yesterday it came to the point — I forgot myself and hit her

103

… she was being so cheeky after all. Yes, I hit her … then she ran away … the child she took with her, it was ill … and yesterday I received information that the child had died… Now it's all over!'

Long silence. Then I dared to ask quietly: 'Did you pray together?'

Incomprehensibly he gawped at me.

So I continued: 'So it was a marriage without God! Nothing surprises me now. That can't go any other way!'

Wildly he looked at me: 'And our idealism?'

I shrugged: 'Man! Idealism breaks up in the face of life. Living without God means running into unhappiness.'

And now some of the episodes of the same story:

The funeral of the child. It was dreadful. In the middle the little coffin. On the right stood the young woman with her relatives. Her eyes were red with weeping. On the left he stood alone and defiant. The two did not look at each other.

The Bible study: In a small, dingy hall I was expounding the Bible. In front of me sat the young man with hungry eyes drinking in every word, as I spoke of Jesus, who saves the broken idealists and sinners. Afterwards he asked me for a Bible. And then began the wrestling of a young man with God: 'I will not let you go, unless you bless me!' (Genesis 32:26).

Back on my sofa again: The young man sat before me completely changed: 'Pastor, now Jesus has found me. I know that through his death he has reconciled me also to God. I have peace with God!…' His eyes shone. Then he continued:

'Until now there was no way I was going back to my wife. But this morning I read in my Bible how Jesus says: Whoever divorces his wife commits adultery. — Now I know that I must sort things out with my wife. Would you help me?'

Gladly I promised to do so.

The young wife: Nervously and excitably she started up: 'Back to him? Never! The fellow hit me! Leave me alone…' Hysterically she began to weep.

I gave her time. Then I said: 'You are a nervous wreck. I am going to send you to a farmer in the country, so that you can recover. I'll tell you now: the farmer is a Christian; and his household is run on Christian lines!'

The thought of escaping from everything to a quiet, country community revived her. Joyfully she agreed…

The young man: He was very depressed. 'It's not going to come to anything!' he lamented. 'It was once a beautiful bell, and made a lovely sound. But now it's hopelessly cracked.'

I comforted him: 'Trust in Jesus and tell him your predicament. He can also heal a hopelessly cracked bell so that it makes a lovely sound.'

'Do you really believe that?'

'Yes.'

A letter from the farmer: '…and as for the young woman — well, you certainly sent me a nice city plant there! At first she kept asking if there wasn't a cinema here. Now she is quieter and listens when we have worship and read the Bible. But people from the city are dreadfully nervous!…'

A card from the young woman: '…and today is Good Friday. My whole life has died. But I suppose it has to be that way! Today I heard in the sermon that Jesus died for us. If only I could grasp that…!'

Another card from the young woman: '…Easter is today! Yes, really — resurrection! Jesus lives, and I live with Him! I am so tremendously glad! Now I know Jesus! How I thank my dear hosts, that they have showed me the way to life. I have risen with Jesus to a new life … and now I want to go home, to my husband! Now everything must of course become different, because now we know our marriage will have Jesus in it… Please ask my husband to come and collect me. I am looking forward to seeing him…'

End of the story? No! Now it is really beginning. Jesus has healed the cracked bell. And it makes a new sound.

The bad and the good mother-in-law

'Pastor, you must have a serious talk with my daughter some time!' lamented the woman.

She sat before me wringing her hands. I didn't know her at all; I had never seen her at any of my services. Her talkative manner did not make a good impression on me.

'So? Your daughter is into bad ways? What has she done then?'

'Oh, you must have a serious talk with her! Every evening she stands at the front door with a young man.'

Bielefeld and pastoral work

I had to laugh. 'That is the way of the world. I think one day you're going to bring the young man into your flat and...'

I got no further. She jumped up as if a tarantula had bitten her and cried out: 'Never will that fellow be allowed to come into the flat! I'm glad to be rid of him!'

I was astonished: 'You know the young man?'

'But of course! My daughter was married to him, wasn't she?'

'Your daughter was married to him? And now she stands with him in the evenings at the front door? I don't understand that!'

'Yes, of course my daughter is divorced from him. I said to my daughter straight away when she first brought him here: "He is not the one for you!"'

'And then your daughter married him all the same?'

'Unfortunately!' the woman lamented. 'I kept warning her.'

'But if your daughter is married to him, surely she doesn't need to stand outside the front door with him.'

'Well, you've got to understand! After that she did divorce him!'

'Oh I see! She divorced him, because you wanted that. And now it's becoming clear that the two really love each other very much. And now the divorced couple are meeting like a pair of secret lovers? Is that how it is?'

The woman nodded.

Christ or Hitler?

That really was an odd story! I still had to get things a bit clearer. So I asked: 'Why didn't you like the young man? Is he lazy? Does he drink? Does he abuse his wife? Does he spend money like water?'

She shook her head. 'No, it's not that. He is simply just a miner. And my daughter is pretty. She could do better for herself.'

That put an end to my composure. Now I gave the woman a real telling off, till she felt quite small. And then I went with her to the daughter. I found a pleasant young woman. And then I found out how much she loved her husband, but that under her mother's influence she had arranged the divorce. Yet now — yet now it turned out that she and her husband greatly regretted that. And they didn't know what they should do.

In short, I saw to it that the two found their own flat and escaped from the mother's influence. They got married again and were very happy together.

Anyone who could find out the reasons behind the many divorces would be shocked to see how the devil often uses the nearest relatives to drive married couples apart. They stir things up and needle away until some poor little wife believes she has been cheated, or some poor husband imagines that he got tied up with the wrong wife.

Therefore I praise the worthy woman whom I now want to talk about.

In Frankfurt there lived a widow who was struggling to make ends meet with her growing children.

One day a telegram brought excitement into the home. The oldest son, who was far away, sent the news: 'Have got engaged. Coming day after tomorrow with my fiancée.'

108

The first reaction was an embarrassing silence. Should this son not be caring for his mother and his siblings? And how did she come to be his fiancée? Nobody knew her. Feeling a little uneasy they went to bed that evening.

The mother however was a real Christian. In the night she poured out her heart to the Lord. And the next morning she gathered them all around herself and said: 'I am giving you a strict command. You are only to rejoice with your brother, and receive the new sister with love. And now the most important thing: I want us all to see only the good things about the girl. In case one of you discovers a fault in her, then you are not to talk about it with anyone, but to tell it only to God.'

Meanwhile the engaged couple were sitting in the train. The girl was feeling heavy-hearted: how would she survive the critical looks of her future sisters-in-law, about whom her beloved had been able to tell her so many good things?

But from the joyful greeting onwards all worries flew away. She was surrounded with such love and heart-felt warmth that she opened her heart fully and especially came to trust completely in her fiancé's mother.

Love and peace reigned. And have done ever since, for over thirty years!

Why should I keep quiet about it? The widow, who acted so lovingly and wisely, was my mother.

6.

Serving miners in Essen

Early impressions

In 1924 I came to Essen, to the big *Altstadt* (Old Town) congregation. I'll never forget how, on a dull November day, I took my first walk round the district. Blackened walls surrounded the three coalmines. Huge tenement blocks provided the accommodation for countless families. In between were streets with little sooty houses that were still standing from former days.

I saw men staggering out of the pubs. I heard angry shrieks from nearby flats. I saw children digging up paving stones in order to find a little sand to play with. I saw young lads standing in groups on the street corners swapping dirty jokes.

It was unspeakably wretched.

I did have a wonderful helper: the indomitable Sister Louise had already been working in the district for a long time. She knew all the people and had had great success in gathering a flock of women. But apart from that the doors and hearts were closed to the gospel. These were not pagans who were to hear the gospel for the first time. This was really a post-Christian world; the people seemed to have left Christianity behind.

Also the district was so big it was impossible to oversee it. Some six or seven thousand people! And it had as many Catholics and two thousand dissenters! If I did five house visits a day, it would take me years to get through them all. And yet — house visits were the only way to get contact with the people.

It was clear to me that the only thing I could do was to ask God for authority and love. And then get in there — according to the words of Jesus: 'See, I am sending you as sheep in the midst of wolves' (Matthew 10:16).

I made a start and went from door to door, visiting every flat. Mostly they tried to shut the door in my face and spat out: 'We don't need any parsons!' But I had already put my foot in the door, and said, 'It's true: you don't need a parson, but you need a Saviour!' At that they were astonished and opened the door. After a year, if I just went and stood in the street, the men and women came to me with their needs and worries — and also with their sins.

It soon became apparent that 'the wolves' were not so dangerous after all. In time the people came to trust me. Often I didn't get as far as making the visits that I had planned, because I kept being stopped on the street, so that I was doing pastoral counselling for hours surrounded by noisy traffic.

How I rejoiced when one day a policeman said to me almost crossly, 'The people used to call us when there was a rumpus. Now they call the pastor.'

Yes, 'the wolves' were not nearly as wild as they made themselves out to be when they were at the huge political demonstrations. I remember for instance a meeting in a home. One of those present was just about to take his jacket off. I stopped and asked: 'Do you want to make yourself really comfortable? Then perhaps you had better go into the room next door.'

He replied: 'I just wanted to show that I am against this thing. I am an atheist!'

'Good,' I said, 'we have taken note. Now you can put your jacket on again.' He did so and was satisfied.

When we drank coffee afterwards I sat next to him. He then made a little declaration of friendship to me: 'You know, when the revolution comes, the parsons will be hanged from the street lamps. I'm afraid I can't help you there. But as a man you seem very kind to me. As a man no one will do anything to you. No one!'

I have long wondered how that will be, when they string up Pastor Busch from a lamp post, but let the man Wilhelm Busch go free.

Another funny incident was with the old fighter against the 'parsons' who declared to all the people in his house: 'I hear that Busch is visiting the houses. If he should come to me, he'll be flying down the stairs.' This proud utterance was of course immediately reported back to me — perhaps in the hope of seeing me 'flying down the stairs'!

So I went to the old man. He was a widower, and I found him in an indescribably filthy kitchen. I felt sorry for the old man, so I greeted him heartily. The man was so touched that he offered me a chair. And then we talked about how the Lord Jesus died also for him, and how he was seeking the lonely man. Afterwards I visited all the other people in the house and mentioned in passing that I had been with the old man.

In the evening the people were standing around on the street waiting for the old man. At last he appeared, and they were all on his back. 'You didn't throw the pastor down the stairs after all!' The old man nodded thoughtfully and declared: 'Yes, this time I managed to restrain myself. But if he comes back, he will be flying.'

There were serious situations, too. The years between the two world wars were full of political passions. I was once performing a marriage in a home. The bride's father was a Communist while the bridegroom was a steel helmet man, a National Socialist or Nazi. I was shocked when suddenly the bride's father rushed at me with a bread knife. I thought it was all over for me. But then the bridegroom intervened, and as he was younger he came out on top in the rumpus. Wildly wrestling, they both disappeared through the door. And the housewife said soothingly, 'Have another cup of coffee!'

Through all this struggling and caring about people I won more and more trust. It may have helped that I said nothing against the men's political and trade union conflicts, because their living conditions were really unbearable. We can't imagine the like today. I often said to the men: 'I cannot understand why your leaders do not demand what is right in the name of God. Why do you combine a just cause with atheism?'

But politics was not my calling. I wanted to make known the name of Jesus. And it did become known.

I nearly got beaten up

'Free-thinkers' meeting at the Kesselbrink. Come all of you! The word is... Free speech!' That was the call on the red posters on every wall and corner. Those were agitated days around the year

1925. Political meetings, which were actually 'saloon battles', began to be held. And now there was to be one about world views!

It was clear to me, an assistant preacher in a totally Marxist district, that there at the Kesselbrink I would find all the men that I looked for in vain in the church on Sundays. So I just had to go there!

A huge hall filled to overflowing, tobacco smoke, a hum of anticipation! I pressed right to the front and found to my astonishment that there was still a chair free in the front row. The men around me looked like prominent men in the free-thinking movement; they gave me some odd looks. Daniel in the lions' den must have felt rather as I did.

Then the chairman rang a bell. The speaker gave a long lecture which had nothing new, only the usual claims that when people didn't know the secrets of nature, they explained everything strange by saying it was the gods. When there was thunder and lightning, that was the gods at work. But now we are enlightened. We can do without the scaffolding of faith. The church is to blame for trying to keep people tied to the mental state of the Stone Age.

There was restlessness in the hall; everybody knew these wise sayings already. But then came the discussion, and things got interesting. Feelings were running high. More and more came the sound of heckling, furious bellows or resounding laughter.

I had prepared a little address. Again and again I put my hand up. My written application had long since been put on the chairman's table. But I was simply passed over.

And then it happened: an old freethinker began to speak. He was better; he didn't just come out with the usual worn-out phrases. He had evidently heard something of the gospel, and had his own rather cumbersome thoughts about it. That made the gathering even more restless.

Then he called: 'The whole of Christendom is just full of contradictions! These Christians keep saying they are sinners. And then again they declare that they have a particularly good relationship with their God. Surely only one of those can be true...'

A few young lads howled, 'Stop!' From somewhere came guffaws of laughter. The chairman rang his bell and called, 'Quiet!'

That was the moment when something exploded inside me. The anger about all the stupid lectures and especially the blasphemies! The annoyance that now they were laughing at a man who had grasped the decisive question of the gospel, namely how one can be a sinner and yet a child of God! My disgruntlement at the fact that they hadn't let me speak — all this led to an internal explosion. I jumped up and cried as loud as I could: 'The blood of Jesus Christ, God's Son, makes us clean from all sin!' So now at last the previous speaker had his answer.

But I didn't have time to be glad about that, for in a moment the whole hall had turned into a raging pandemonium. I looked into gaping mouths, saw swinging fists, heard mad shrieks. A wild man leapt towards me and lifted up his arms to strike... Everything happened so quickly, my heart missed a beat with shock. Then — yes, then something remarkable happened. I felt a strong man pulling me into his arms. I wanted to defend myself, but he whispered into my ear: 'Just stay still; don't make a sound!' Then he had no more time to speak to me. He was literally covering me with his own body, while he sternly commanded the man who was storming at me to leave me alone.

Only afterwards did I discover that he was a big man among the free-thinkers, and clearly a clever one, who said to himself: 'If this little pastor gets beaten up here, then that is a good advertisement for him, but a bad one for us.'

For a long time he held me pressed to him, until things got quieter again; then he let me go. Somewhat dazed I left the hall.

It says in the Bible, 'He has commanded his angels about you, that they carry you in their hands and you do not hit your foot against a stone' (Psalm 91:11-12). I have always believed that. But that my Lord can even make leading atheists to be his angels — that, I have to say, I didn't learn until that evening.

Father Bläsing and my meeting hall

As I began to feel at home in my district, it became clear that to get further I needed a room in which I could gather the people around the Word of God. What use to me was a church or hall far from my district?

And then God heard my cries. The wonder happened! Father Bläsing — that's how we all came to know him later — came to see me. There he was, sitting in my study and telling me a strange story!

'You know the Elisenplatz?'

Who would not know it? This desolate place was right in the middle of my district. The town council had once tried to plant some trees and place some benches there. But in the next winter the benches were taken away for firewood, and the little trees had already been pulled up or broken by fellows who regarded anything beautiful as an annoyance.

Father Bläsing went on: 'There is a small two-storey house in which only the top floor has been fully developed.'

'Yes, I know that. It borders the colliery yard at the back.'

'Well, some years ago a believing miner called Brepohl lived in this house. He used to hold meetings in his living room, where a little flock gathered around God's Word. When Brepohl died, the meetings finished. I myself did not have the courage to continue them. But one thing I did: I went to the church congregation and asked them to rent Brepohl's living room. Perhaps one day someone would be found to resume the meetings.

'The presbytery agreed, probably because the coalmine only wanted five marks for the room. These five marks were included in the budget year after year. Apart from that no one bothered about the room. For years I kept the key and waited to see if anyone would come who could use it. Now I have been watching you. I have observed that you love the Lord Jesus and want to win souls for him. So you are the man to whom I want to entrust the key. Perhaps this room will be what you need.'

I almost fell on Father Bläsing's neck. Immediately I went to the little house on the Elisenplatz. Father Bläsing beamed when he saw how happy I was to see it.

Now there was work to be done! First I begged and got twenty chairs together. More would not have fitted into my 'meeting hall.' Then I had 10,000 bright red leaflets printed: 'We invite you to the Bible hour on Monday at 19.30 in the meeting hall in the Elisenplatz.' Above that was the text 'Jesus Christ has come to seek and to save the lost.'

These 10,000 leaflets I distributed myself on the streets and at the coalmine gates — with the result that about ten women and one man came to the first meeting. On top of that Father Bläsing, my wife and I were there. Jesus said, 'Where two or three are gathered in my name, I am in the midst' (Matthew 18:20). The minimum number had already been exceeded.

It was a beginning. The Lord Jesus also said that the kingdom of God is like a mustard seed: 'It is the smallest of seeds, but when it grows it becomes a tree, so that the birds of heaven come and live under its branches' (Matthew 13:32).

The real work of the kingdom of God begins small and quiet. But then it grows. After a year the little 'hall' was really too small. The Bible hours and men's evenings were crowded out.

And then I formed a bold plan. With beating heart I went to Herr Spindler, the General Director of the mine that owned the building. I cannot express how afraid I was of the great man. But he was friendliness itself. He had to laugh when I described our little hall to him. At the end his promise was: 'I'll rehouse the residents in the ground floor flat in the little house, and then you can make the whole into a hall which we will put at your disposal.'

How happily I went back home! How full of joy was my little congregation when I told them the good news! And the people who had to leave the flat were happiest of all. The General Director had ordered that they should get a fine apartment, so that there would be no ill feeling as a result.

One of my men got hold of a builder who would do the job cheaply and allow me to pay when I had the money. Oh yes! Money was something I didn't have at all.

But now the real problems began. The building control department refused authorization, because the ceiling was not high enough. Oh, those people had no idea how little air we could manage with! When I had at last got the building control department to promise authorization, the housing office created difficulties: a dwelling could not be converted into a commercial room! As if we were running a business! I ran from pillar to post but the thing went no further. At last the coalmine administration came back to me and said, 'If you don't convert the property we will put people into it again!'

And now let me confess! We did something forbidden: we just built without authorization; we hoped that in our wretched region no one would be interested in our building anyway.

But — on the last day, when all was ready, a painter left a cart standing in front of the little house. An official saw it, went inside and discovered the whole thing. And now the cat was among the pigeons!

I came home to meet my wife in tears. All the offices had telephoned one after another. The mine didn't want any difficulties, the housing office demanded restoration to the original state, at my expense. The building authority was even hinting at severe penalties.

I felt as if the sky had fallen in.

And then I experienced what the real wrath of a man can accomplish. I rushed to the housing office and raved like a wild man. All came running together: 'Pastor, calm down!' No! I would not calm down. I threatened to make the whole thing public. 'I am now going to inform the press,' and so on.

And what happened? After an hour I had all the authorizations in my hand.

'The wrath of man does not do what is right before God,' says the Bible. And so let it be. But the heavenly Father understood his poor tormented servant. And what he then had to reproach him with in a secret hour was no business of either the housing office or the building authority.

Now the work began happily. Seventy chairs were in our little hall. The youngsters sat on the window sills, and the older ones discovered that three people can sit on two chairs. My wife played the harmonium and started a male voice choir. Those were rough miners' voices. But with love and delight the choruses and revival hymns were sounded out.

You dear little hall! The place of my greatest conflicts and defeats! Place of the glorious victories of our risen Lord, who 'spoiled the strong man's goods' (Matthew 12:29).

And Father Bläsing? He was there with us. That was all! He had only stepped forward once in the decisive hour. From then on he was quietly there, said little — and prayed for the work.

Recently I went through the district again. How everything has changed today! The tenement buildings had been destroyed by bombs. The miners are socially better provided for and no longer so wretched. In the middle of the district there stands a church hall, a congregation house and a vicarage. Father Bläsing has long since gone into eternity. But his picture still hangs in my study and must always have a place of honour.

Thugs lying in wait

'We should have cancelled the men's evening,' called my friend Ernst as I entered our little hall. Thirty men were standing close to each other, and a lively discussion was in progress.

Christo or Hitler?

'Cancel? Whatever for?' I asked astonished.

Ernst turned to me: 'Today it's going to get fraught. Two of the miners in Beust have arranged to lie in wait for you.'

'And then?'

'Don't act stupid! They want to beat you up!'

It may seem strange to the reader that these miners talked in such a familiar way to their pastor. But that's how it was. There stood Ernst. Not so long ago he had been a wild free-thinker and a fiery communist. But now the Lord Jesus had met him and had won his heart. That was how it was with all these men. They were all beginners in the faith, and already they were finding that there is unrest and trouble when Jesus gathers his people. But such conflicts brought us all together into a close fellowship, so that the familiarity was quite natural.

'Is that how it is? They want to lie in wait for me?' Ernst must know what he was talking about, for he worked at the *Graf Beust* mine himself. I laughed: 'Oh nonsense, they have often threatened me; and nothing has ever come of it!'

Several others who also worked on *Graf Beust* chipped in: 'Look, it's true what Ernst says. That Czermis is in on it, and he's a real thug.'

'All the more reason for us now to look at God's Word!' I cried. But I felt quite bad myself. The men here were not timid. Their hard labour had made them tough. If they were so worried then it must be getting really dangerous.

We sat down round the table, sang our songs of Jesus and read and talked about a Bible passage. That quietened our hearts. We

122

had turned to a chapter from Acts in which the Lord says to Paul, 'I am with you and no one will dare to harm you' (Acts 18:10). The choice of text had not been planned, but in this threatening situation it seemed to be the right one.

At the end a few men prayed. And now…?

'We're going with you!' they all declared.

I thought about it. If they all came with me there would be a wild brawl. That was surely not the will of the Lord. And what passions would be awakened in my men! No — better not!

'Brothers!' I exclaimed. 'Now you must really give me the chance to prove my faith. I want to put my trust not in your fists, but in the Lord.'

They understood that. The Lord Jesus was very real to us all.

So off I went. Totally alone! And yet not alone. He has said, 'I am with you always…' I really wanted to believe that now.

I went across the dimly lit Elisenplatz. As I turned a corner I saw them on the darkened street: about twenty men.

What happened now was as if I was not acting on my own volition, but under the guidance of another. I stepped rapidly into the middle of the group and said cheerfully, 'You want to beat me up? Here I am, at your disposal!'

Boundless embarrassment! Then a mumbling: 'Oh rubbish! Nobody will do anything to you! No one is thinking of such a thing!' So they went on confused and in a muddle.

Christ or Hitler?

A big fellow wanted to rescue the situation. He held out a *Schnapps* bottle towards me: 'There! Have a drink with us!'

I took the bottle, smashed it on the ground and said, 'This cursed *Schnapps* is just bad news for you!'

Now things became ominous: 'What a cheek!' 'That expensive *Schnapps*!' 'You'll have to pay for that!' were the calls from all directions.

I took out my purse: 'Whose is the bottle? I'll pay for it. I don't want anyone to suffer loss on my account. But you'd do better to buy bread for your children with it! Come on then! Whose is it?'

No one answered. I put my purse back in my pocket. 'Men,' I called, 'what have you got against me?'

'You want to make the people stupid!'

'No! The *Schnapps* makes you stupid, not the gospel! You just don't know it! I'm going to explain it to you…'

A few crept away. The others listened as I told them about Jesus who saves those that are lost.

It turned out well. The men accompanied me to my house. And in the following week two of them came to our men's evening.

'Go away, Daddy!'

The two of us were lying in the grass on the edge of the wood. Around us was the stillness of a hot summer's afternoon. How beautiful that is! The green leaves, the deep blue sky with little white clouds, the humming of insects…

Serving miners in Essen

We had wandered out of the grey industrial city and were now lying here. But you don't get rid of the city that easily; it was still with us in our thoughts and hearts. So my companion, a miner, was talking about his daily life. He spoke of the gruff works manager and the warm-hearted foreman, of minor accidents and of the hard daily grind, of the heat of the tunnel and the loneliness at the coal face.

'Hey!' I interrupted him. 'How did you actually come to be in the pit? You weren't always a miner, were you?'

This question was followed by a long silence.

'Hey you!'

'Yes, what?'

'How you came to be a miner, that's what I asked.'

At that he raised himself up, slung his arms round his drawn-up knees and looked at me almost as if shocked. 'Yes,' he said, 'that is a fearfully solemn story. But since you ask me, I'll tell you…

'So, you're right, I wasn't always a miner. Before that I was a brewer's drayman. Man, what a different life that was: all day on the move, up on the box, with two fine horses in harness…

'But the job was my undoing. We had to drive from one pub to another. We stopped at each one, and drank a glass here and a glass there. So I became addicted to drink without even noticing it. The pubs became my home.

'Well of course, my wife was sitting at home with our child, our little daughter. They were just irksome to me in those days. I couldn't bear to see their eyes so sad when I came home drunk.

Christ or Hitler?

'One evening I was sitting in the pub again. The door opened just a little. In came my little daughter. My little one in that pub so full of commotion!

'She was not in the least bit afraid. Slowly she made her way through the noisy, smoking, drinking, card-playing men. She looked around searching and checking each one.

'Then she found me. A little hesitantly she came towards me, tugged my sleeve and whispered: "Daddy, do come home! Mummy's waiting for you. It's so cosy at home. Do come!"

'That was so indescribably charming, just irresistible — the child in the chaotic pub — that I stood up to go with her. At that moment I felt how all eyes were on me. The pub had gone completely quiet. I saw mocking faces, heard malicious remarks.

'Then it got to me — I don't know myself just what it was — annoyance about being taken by surprise like this; fear of being seen as a henpecked husband by my companions; perhaps also rage about myself and my wretched condition. In short, I shouted furiously at my child, pulled her up hard by one arm, so that she whimpered and began to cry, dragged her through the pub and threw her roughly and violently out of the door.

'Then I drank myself senseless.

'The next few days I did the same. The week passed in a dull haze of compulsive drinking and dizziness.

'One day I came home to lunch. Roughly I tore open the door. At that my wife lifted her hand, shocked and beseeching.

'"What's the matter then?" I blabbered out.

'She pointed to the bench in our kitchen/living room. "Our child is ill, she's dying. I beg you…"'

'True enough, there among the pillows lay my little daughter, her face hot with fever.'

'"Really bad?" I asked, shocked. My wife nodded silently.'

'Man, I just can't tell you how I felt. My child! You haven't lost one yet, have you? No? Then you can't understand what that's like. I hurried towards the bench: "My little girl!" and wanted to stroke her forehead with my hand. At that, an awful dread came into her eyes, as she braced her arm against my hand: "Go away, Daddy!"'

'Shocked to death I stood there. "My child!"'

'But agitatedly she waved me away. "Do go away, Daddy!" And she gave me no rest till I was standing at the door again.'

'Yes, that's where I stood for two hours. Oh, what am I saying? It was an eternity I stood there. I saw how my wife gave the desperately ill child a drink, saw how she supported her, settled her in bed, stroked her, heard how she prayed with her.'

'But whenever I tried to take a step nearer, the child cried agitatedly: "Away, Daddy, go away!"'

'Then I gave up and stayed standing at the door. I stayed standing, till my child died.'

'In those two hours my wasted life came before me in all its horrifying reality. In those two hours I was reaping what I had sown. In those two hours the ground opened up under my feet; I experienced hell. In those two hours God was speaking to me…'

Thus far he told his story. Now we were surrounded again with the silence of a hot summer's day. High above us small white clouds sailed in the clear blue sky.

'And then?' I said, at last interrupting the silence.

'The rest is quickly told. I gave up my job and became a miner. I began to go to church again with my wife; for without God's Word nothing would have come of my new life in the end.'

I nodded. You have a good understanding of each other, when you have spent some hours sitting together around God's Word…

And then we got up and wandered together into the glorious sunshine.

Peace on earth

'Pastor, you're going into competition with us,' said the stout copper, giving me a friendly slap on the shoulder. 'When there's trouble the people don't come to the police station, they come to you!'

I laughed. He must have heard the story about the housing department. That was a story! It was late at night when the doorbell rang, and I put on just enough to go and answer it. At the door was a young woman with high hopes that I could help her. I knew her well; she lived with her husband in a huge tenement block, a dreadful home. Forty families lived there, and the landlord once complained to me: 'Every winter the banisters are chopped up for firewood.'

Now the young woman was standing there looking distraught. At first I couldn't understand what it was all about. Then I understood:

they had got into a dispute with a brother-in-law who had no flat and was claiming the young couple's room. Now the brother-in-law had gathered a gang of fellow miners like a private army. 'They want to stab my husband and throw me out!' the woman shrieked hysterically.

'OK, I'll come right away,' I said. 'I'll just get dressed properly first. You go ahead and tell them I'm coming.'

Half an hour later I was climbing the dark stairs. The banister was missing again, so it was quite scary going up.

I reached the third floor and went down the long corridor. Suddenly a voice bellowed: 'Stop! Murder!' It was for real: there stood the young husband in the doorway behind a real barricade of furniture, holding a massive cudgel in his hand.

'Calm down!' I called. 'The pastor is coming now.'

'Oh, is that so? I thought they were coming — the others.'

'Man! Just let me in please!'

The barricade was pushed to one side. There was only a small lantern burning in the room; the lamp had been smashed to pieces during the previous struggle. The floor was slippery; that was from the evening meal, which they had thrown at each other's heads to start with. Bits of broken china crunched under my shoes.

'So where are the others?' The wife lay whimpering at the back of the room, where hardly any light penetrated.

'The others are sitting in the flat upstairs plotting how they can throw me out of here.'

Christ or Hitler?

There was nothing for it — I had to go up to the attackers. So, up the banister-less stairs again! On the fourth floor I could hear straight away where the hostile force was gathered. I wondered how the many other people who lived on this floor could sleep with all that noise. Perhaps they were awake but didn't dare to complain.

I kicked the door open to reveal a bare room. Two *Schnapps* bottles were on the table. Men and women were sitting around. Because there were not enough chairs some sat on the floor leaning against the wall, their legs in the general tangle of limbs.

When I entered there was silence; everyone thought the police had come. Then they realized it was only the pastor. 'The black thrush!' one of them called out contemptuously into the silence. The mood became dangerous; I got really scared. And my heart cried out, unheard by the people around, to my heavenly Father for help: 'Lord! You who shut the mouths of the lions for Daniel, tame these wild people too!'

'Men!' I then said. 'It is good that you are all gathered together. We must talk about this matter calmly.'

A woman screeched out rudely.

'Hold your tongue!' I said sharply. 'This is a men's matter.' I was glad to hear a general murmur of approval. Clearly they were pleased to see the impudent one shut up.

'So, what is the matter? First we've got to clear up what is going on. But just one person is to talk at a time!' With that I sat down on the floor, in the only vacant place left. The men shifted a bit and thus accepted me into the group.

Now the negotiations began. It was a complicated legal claim, which I could not sort out. So I said, 'Now we'll do two things.

First, a deputation will go down to the disputed flat and say that they can take down the barricade; the war is over for tonight. And secondly, tomorrow morning everyone who is not on a morning shift is to meet here at nine o'clock, and I will go with you to the housing department. I will vouch for the fact that this brother-in-law will get a room.'

That was agreed to.

'Well, now you can go home!' said the man sitting next to me on the floor.

I laughed. 'Now you want to get rid of me so that you can go on boozing! That won't do any good. No, I'm going to see you all home. Who will take the homeless brother-in-law for the night?'

A man volunteered.

'Good! Now let's go!'

They all set off. In spite of my tiredness I couldn't rest until I had brought the last one to his front door.

And then came the next morning! There I was at the head of about twelve wild fellows going to the housing department. I don't know whether it was sympathy that had brought them all here. Perhaps it was more curiosity and the hope that the pastor would suffer defeat at the housing department. Yes, I was feeling bad; I had promised to get a room. What if I couldn't do it?

Secretly I folded my hands: 'Lord, you can help!'

The department was housed in a long barrack. So the officials could see clearly through their low windows as the dangerous troop approached. They had worried faces. There was after all a lot of unrest in those days.

And then what astonishment as they detected the hesitant pastor in the middle of the column! That was strange! In a moment, lots of officials gathered together. I pretended to be fierce and demanded to see the chief.

Soon I was seated opposite him, while the ominous murmurings of my wild companions could be heard outside the door. But — how glad I felt when I saw a thoughtful face that looked at me in a friendly way behind spectacles. Then I poured out my heart. The chief laughed at first, then wiped his eyes — and in the end he was prepared to help.

That was a great moment, when in front of the barrack I made known to my followers that the whole problem was wonderfully solved.

'Now we'll go for a drink!' cried the wildest one, who was actually least concerned about the matter.

I smiled at him: 'No way! Now we'll help the brother-in-law move in. And every one look at home to see whether they have a plate or a lamp to spare for the poor couple whose things you smashed to bits last night!'

They could see the sense in that. There was good will all round! Wearily I crept home through dusty streets. In my heart two voices were disputing.

One said, 'That's what you study theology for in the end, to fight such battles. If only our learned professors knew what problems we have to face at the front!' That was a gloomy voice.

But the other voice was really joyful. It kept on singing: 'Peace on earth! Peace on earth! And whoever helps to that end is a messenger of the Prince of Peace!' Then I decided to listen only to this second voice. And so I was happy to be in my calling.

'The cobblestones are smiling at me!'

Dreadful! How this man blasphemed, mocked and cursed! And his comrades threw the cards down and cursed with him. The *Schnapps* bottle had central place on the table. What darkness there was in this heart! With cold eyes the man stared at me.

'No thanks,' he said, 'we have no need of God. He should have been there when I had my accident. Now I can spend the rest of my life sitting in this d..d wheelchair.'

Angrily he hit the sides of his wretched vehicle.

I already knew about his accident. He had been a miner. One day at work the end of the overhang fell down. They pulled him alive out of the rubble, but his spine was broken. Now he was paralysed, in the prime of life, with no hope of recovery.

Oh the despair! Oh the bitterness! Oh the deep night in his heart!

To be sure, his fellow miners visited him, played cards with him and brought him *Schnapps*. They meant well; but that didn't bring light to a darkened heart and a life of despair.

On the evening after my first visit I was sitting in my men's group. We explored the Bible together. We talked about our daily needs and conflicts. There were lots of miners here who found life was a struggle to survive; it was not easy for them to serve Jesus in their surroundings.

I told them about this unhappy man. 'Aha,' they said, 'that man needs help.'

The following week, when I was about to begin the men's evening again, the door clattered open and the wheelchair was pushed in. The man was snarling and growling a bit. He grumbled: 'They just took me with them, and I can't defend myself.' But you could already tell that deep down he was thankful that they had taken him out of his 'lair.' I think he had some inkling of the love behind the rather rough treatment.

We sang our beautiful hymns again, 'There is a fountain filled with blood drawn from Immanuel's veins,' 'I worship the might of love.' We looked at God's Word together. We spoke of our needs and brought all in prayer before God.

This hour together must have done the man good, for when my friends came to collect him the next week he was already expecting them.

From then on he was there at all our meetings. God's Word did its glorious work in his darkened heart. The man recognized that the greatest disaster of his life was his lost state as a sinner. He began to seek peace with God, met Jesus at the cross and found the blissful relief of the forgiveness of sins through Jesus' blood.

Now everything became new. His house became tidy instead of chaotic. Old friends were annoyed and stayed away, but others came instead. Songs to Jesus sounded out where only quarrelling and swearing had once been heard. The *Schnapps* bottle went and the Bible lay on the table. His wife and children revived. In short: Jesus made all things new.

One day I visited him. His wheelchair was on the edge of the road in front of his house, where the sun came through a little between the grey houses. I sat down next to him on the front steps.

'Pastor,' he said, 'when once I stand in eternity before the throne of God, then I will thank him for the fact that — he broke — my back.'

I was shocked. 'That's a big thing to say.'

'Yes, you see, if God had just left me to run on as I was, then I would have gone straight to hell. I didn't want to listen to him at all. So in his rescuing love he had to grab me hard to bring me to conversion. And that's why one day I am going to thank him for it.'

I was deeply moved. But he continued: 'You just don't know how happy my heart is. From the time that I knew that I belong to Jesus, the whole world looks at me in a different light. Everything is so happy. Yes, Pastor,' he pointed to the grey street, 'even the cobblestones are smiling at me!'

7.

Youth pastor in Essen

My predecessor Wilhelm Weigle

The first time I went to preach in Essen I stayed with an elder in the church, who showed me kind hospitality and took me around this mighty industrial city with its dense masses of people. In the middle of a busy road he stopped me and said, 'That's our youth pastor Weigle over there; come on, let's say "hello" to him.'

I was staggered to see an old, gaunt-looking man. His grey beard shocked me, and so did the trembling hands. I had come from the youth movement, which put a lot of emphasis on style. This old man, with his cloth hat and strange jacket buttoned up so high, totally contradicted my mental picture of an impressive youth leader. I was really disappointed!

A few months later I was a pastor in Essen. Now I really got to know this man, whom thousands in the town remember with deep gratitude. I found that behind his unremarkable appearance lived a volatile genius, a fiery spirit hidden by a quiet collectedness, which gave him a rather unique dynamic.

Christ or Hitler?

Wilhelm Weigle was not the sort you would call the life and soul of the party. I have seldom met a man who devoted himself with such single-minded concentration to one aim: to lead the boys in Essen to Christ.

There are people who feel trapped in the circumstances where God has put them. Not so for Wilhelm Weigle: doors were open to him to work far and wide. But apart from a few articles and lectures he restricted himself to his work in Essen. It meant more to him to help a single grubby young boy than to speak at a hundred conferences and sessions about the theory of evangelical youth work.

This concentration also gave his character the tremendous dynamism that everyone who knew him could sense. I first noticed this through a relatively minor incident. I was standing one day in my confirmation classroom when there was a knock on the door. Weigle entered and said, 'You have Karl N with you in the class. He played a stupid trick on Sunday in the youth centre. Would you allow me to speak with him now?'

'Of course!' And then I called the boy. He was a big, cheeky fellow, who was causing me much trouble.

'My boy!' said Weigle. 'You have made me very sad… Do you know that you have also made Jesus sad?'

At that moment I was thinking, 'I'm glad that I am not this boy.' Anyone else could have said what Weigle said without scratching the surface of the thick-skinned rascal. But from Weigle's mouth these words made the boy completely break down.

As I went back to my flock, leaving the two alone, I was thinking frantically: 'What is the secret of this power?' and I came to realize that Weigle had prayed earnestly, wrestling with God for the heart of this one boy before talking to him. Hence his words had incredible power.

'Jesus is your best friend!' So many boys heard this sentence from him. He said it with an incredible intensity that made a deep impression.

I must tell of my first visit to the Youth Centre, today called the Weigle House. If you ask any man who was a boy in Essen between 1911 and 1933 about the Youth Centre, he'll probably tell you: 'The time that I spent there was the best time of my life.'

The Youth Centre

This huge house in the heart of Essen is a paradise for boys. It has sports halls, quiet reading rooms, table tennis rooms, a gym, shower rooms and a real boys' restaurant where for a few pfennigs you can get everything from rollmops to lollipops. There are dark rooms for photographers and a great hall with a film projector and a screen, while all around is the glorious playground. Every boy from fourteen to eighteen is constantly assured: 'This belongs to you with all that's in it.' Here they can let off steam without horrified adults warning them to mind the furniture.

This house was created by Weigle with the help of the congregation and with support from industry. He had emphatically told the directors of local firms how wrong it was to have allowed an industrial city like Essen to grow so huge without thinking of its people. Now here was an opportunity to put right some of this injustice, by providing a home to the young.

It was a Sunday afternoon when I first came to the Youth Centre. From the street I could already hear resounding singing. I had to

Christ or Hitler?

The Weigle House
Hanna Busch (Essen)

stand still for a moment in astonishment. The boys were singing a hymn! I have heard a few hymns in my time. But usually hymn singing was rather formal, and often it was frankly rather boring! This was different!

I stepped into the hall. Some 800 boys between fourteen and eighteen were sitting and singing:

> My Jesus is my life,
> My portion, my reward.
> Him only I'll exalt,
> Because I am alive…

I could understand why Weigle made all church musicians despair. Hundreds of boys were singing neither beautifully nor in tune; and they were singing a song that was not in any hymn book, one of those songs whose tune is not popular with musical experts nor with most pastors. 'Salvation Army tunes!' is what people call them with contempt.

But the boys were singing loudly and with enthusiasm. And that was just irresistible.

I was standing in the great hall and looking round. A single picture hung on the wall: the returning Lord Jesus Christ on a white horse. On another wall was a text: 'My son, give me your heart, and let my ways be good in your eyes.' Above the door the words: 'Truly he is not far from every one of us.'

And in this hall was a crowd of boys happily singing Jesus songs. Then Weigle spoke. He quietened this great wild horde by simply raising his hand. That was enough! I have had so-called youth leaders roaring 'Quiet!' without any noticeable effect. Here a lightly raised, badly trembling hand was all that was needed.

Christ or Hitler?

Weigle talked about Jesus. What else could he talk to boys about? His talk was astonishingly simple. A totally scatty city boy who can't concentrate for five minutes could easily follow it. The words were such that one forgot the old man on the platform and was placed in the presence of the risen Saviour. It struck me: here is not Christendom, but Christ. This man does not have only a Christian 'world view.' He knows the reality of the risen Lord.

The meeting finished. With an enormous din, the boys stormed out and distributed themselves over the whole place. While I wandered with Weigle through the turmoil, I realized that the apparent confusion did have a secret order.

No boys were left on their own. A host of older leaders and younger helpers were there to serve. It was like a wonderful machine, or better, a glorious boys' republic: boys gave out the books in the library, young men led the games, others were helping at the toy cupboard, at the gate, in the restaurant. Almost all of them were taking part in some way.

I must insert here a little experience from the year 1947. Together with Provost Lorenzen, whose heart burned for the people he served, I was walking through the destroyed city of Kiel.

High on a partly destroyed wall sat a boy of about sixteen laughing at the horror of the passers-by, who were worried about how long this fragile wall would still hold.

The old provost stood still and asked with a little sigh: 'Who is going to talk to a boy like that?'

I answered: 'You can't speak to him, I can't reach him either; it needs an eighteen-year-old car mechanic to speak to him.'

And that was how it was in Weigle's youth work: in every region there was an 'eighteen-year-old car mechanic' to go after the boys and call them to Jesus. This staff of labourers, artisans, schoolboys, businessmen and mechanics was organized in such a way that everyone had his district in which he worked.

'You know,' said Weigle, 'a good organisation can't create life; but a bad one can hinder life.'

Meanwhile we had finished our tour and were standing again in the big hall, now empty. My eye was drawn to the only picture: the returning Christ on a white horse! Before I could comment that this picture wasn't a great work of art, Weigle said simply, 'One of our fellow workers painted that.'

I said I thought the return of Jesus was not so interesting to the boys, and that I would have chosen a different subject if there was to be only one picture hanging here.

Then Weigle replied really seriously: 'Look, tomorrow these boys will be back in their schools, in their offices, factories and workshops. And there they have to endure a lot of mockery and hostility against Christianity. So this picture is telling them every Sunday:

The victory of Jesus is certain for ever,
The whole world shall surely be His.

Since then, that picture is dearer to me than any other.

How I began to work with Weigle

I had been in Essen for several years, but had not been able to get closely involved with Weigle's youth work. I noticed that Weigle was keeping me away from it. The reason for this he told me himself later:

> I knew that you had come out of the idealistic youth movement, and there is nothing I fear more than the mixing of idealism and the gospel.

However, one day he asked me to speak about the Bible to his fellow workers during a Bible course.

So there I stood in front of 150 young men. When I discovered among them many sixth formers, I recalled the pathetic religious instruction that I had to put up with at school. So I said something like this:

> The worst enemies of the Bible are not those who keep attacking it. Much more dangerous are those who want to speak positively about it, but have never heard God's Word in the words.

Then I told them how our teacher always said, 'Of course the Bible is not a geography book! Of course it is not a history book! Of course it is not a science book!...' And we mocked him among ourselves, saying, 'He knows what the Bible is *not*. But what it really *is*, he doesn't know any more than we do.'

Then I explained to the young people how it pleases the living God to speak to us through this book; and how it is only here that we can come to know both our own lost heart and the glorious salvation accomplished through Jesus.

The next day Weigle said to me, 'Dear brother, I have much to ask your pardon for. We belong together.' Later I spent thirty years as his successor in the work.

How I became youth pastor in Essen

I was very happily engaged in my work among the miners in the 13th district of the Essen-Altstadt congregation. One day Weigle called me over to himself and said, 'I am old and ill. I am going to have to give up the youth work. But I can't just go. I owe it to my faithful fellow workers to look for the right successor...'

There was a long pause. Then he said in passing: 'You certainly can't be my successor. After all, you're no good at organizing. And youth work involves a good deal of organizing...'

I had to smile a bit, because I so heartily enjoyed being among the miners, that I did not feel any desire to leave the 13th district. And also the man knew me only too well: 'After all, you're no good at organizing!'

Soon after that Weigle's health broke down completely. In his extremity, he sent for me and insisted: 'Now you must take on my work, in spite of all my misgivings!' In vain I countered with the fact that I had begun a work among the miners, whom I could not let down; that I was no good at organizing, that I..., that I... It was all of no use.

This trembling, sick old man overpowered me. So I said, 'Yes.'

Then a year passed. A dreadful year! My miners were sad that I had left them. And the work in the youth centre didn't go well. The fellow workers were against me, for no apparent reason. They were just missing their old friend. Then the house had to be renovated, but money was short. Weigle had many friends, who could give enough money. But — they didn't know me.

I was in dire straits in every way.

Christ or Hitler?

And in a quiet hour of the night it dawned on me, why this was. I had allowed Weigle to overpower me, without asking my Lord and Saviour. To be quite honest, I had to confess: I ran into this work in disobedience, against God's will. I had come here without clear leading from God. And that was why he was against me.

It was a hellish time! In every hour with the boys came the nagging doubt: What do you think you are doing? Your Lord cannot bless you, because he doesn't want you in this place at all.

Then I tried again to convince myself that everything was all right. Everybody wanted it this way: Weigle, the presbytery and also the church leadership. And then — you are after all the youngest pastor! You are really quite suited to the work!

But that could not satisfy my doubts. What did it all mean, if God said, 'No!'?

How many men have made shipwreck because they ran after their own will and did not ask for God's leading!

In the end I couldn't bear it any more. At a Tersteegen's Rest conference I plucked up the courage to speak to a brother minister, Alfred Christlieb: I had a personal need, and would he be so kind as to listen to me?

I can still see in my mind's eye the red iron tables under the chestnut trees in the garden where I told this brother that I was not at all sure that I was on the right path in my youth pastorate. I had not asked God in prayer. But there was no way back either: my previous post was now occupied, and I had moved into the youth pastor's house. Back I could not go. But to go on without the certainty of the blessing of my Lord — that I could not do either. What was I to do?

Christlieb listened in silence. Then he said that it was a difficult matter; I must give him a day to think about it. And if I had no objection he wanted to discuss it with a brother minister. That was all right with me. Off I went, already feeling somewhat relieved.

The next day I sat opposite the two men. With fear, but also with great trust, I waited to hear what they would say about my muddled situation.

And then came something so unbelievably simple, clear and illuminating, that it could only have come from God. Christlieb asked me: 'Have you already confessed your hasty step as sin to your Saviour?'

'No!' I stammered. 'I kept wanting to justify myself to myself!'

'Well. Go into a quiet place, confess the thing to him as sin, and then believe that Jesus takes away this sin as well with his blood.'

There was a great silence between us. We could only hear from the distance the lively conversation of the conference guests under the shade of the chestnut trees.

Then Christlieb began again: 'And ask the Saviour to bless the wrong way. If you cannot now go back, then he can change the wrong way into blessing.'

I did according to his counsel. And my Lord in his mercy took the burden away from me, and blessed my path so much that, if I had five more lives, I would still only want to be youth pastor in Essen.

But that was not the end of our conversation. Christlieb added another sentence: 'Note this for all time: if you are faced with a decision and have no clarity about it, then mark time on the spot until you have clarity. And if someone urges you, then think: only the devil is in a hurry. Wait till God tells you to go. He has said, "I will guide you with my eye."'

Soon I was to have good use for Christlieb's final counsel. When Hitler came to power and everything was shaking, the word was: 'Up to such and such a date you can still join the party!' Or, 'Up to such and such a date you can still become a member of the "German Christians". Then the lists will close. Hurry!' I seemed still to hear Christlieb's voice: 'Only the devil is in a hurry. If you have no clarity...' So I let all the dates pass and remained a free man.

During the war the pastors were supposed to swear a political oath of loyalty to Hitler. Then the fight against the church was to be finished. Many took the oath. I had no clarity. The due date passed. How thankful I am to my pastor for such advice!

December 1935: in the Weigle House with Pastor Busch

Youth pastor in Essen

During the first years of Hitler's reign there was another pastoral talk between Christlieb and myself. In Salzuflen a great gathering of pastors was taking place. The address in the morning was by a man completely befogged with the great words of those days. Words like 'creation ordinance of God', 'folk' and 'race' were coming down like hail. In the discussion one man said, 'If our nation has such an aversion to the Old Testament, then let's just put it aside. What really matters is only the New Testament.'

My blood was boiling. And when it was my turn to speak in the afternoon, I spoke freely what was on my mind: that we must confess the whole of God's Word! And that we could not know much about God's creation ordinance, because we lived in a world ruined by the Fall! And then I said, 'I know no other revelation of God but that in Jesus who was crucified for us.' And I added that we had no other commission today than, as always, to preach him.

It was great to see how the gathering responded to me. Many pressed my hand in gratitude. But then came Christlieb, who took me by the arm and said, 'Let's go into the garden for a bit.' There he began: 'Dear brother! Everything you said could have come from my own heart. I can underline it word for word. But — '

A long pause! I suppose it was difficult for him to express what he meant.

'But — while you were speaking, there was something about your mouth that betrayed in what spirit you were speaking. There was anger, lack of love, pride and self-satisfaction. You must repent of giving room to a bad spirit.'

I was struck deep in my conscience. Christlieb was right! Just as Jesus had said to his disciples, 'Don't you know of what spirit you are?' So now he asked me this in the quiet garden.

Christ or Hitler?

What a true pastor and friend was Christlieb! To avoid giving an unbalanced picture, I must tell another anecdote. Christlieb could also be hard. He told me once about a gathering of pastors in which a colleague was giving a long and totally unprofitable talk. 'So then,' said Christlieb, 'I folded my hands under the table and cried to the Lord: "Lord! Stop his mouth!"'

The old man smiled as he continued: 'And the Lord heard me. Suddenly the man could not go on any longer, and he ended his talk.'

Confession after thirty-five years

'Please take a seat!' I said. Silently the man sat down. I could tell that he wanted to say something, but couldn't find the right words. At last he reached into his jacket pocket, pulled out a worn wallet and began to rummage through it.

Meanwhile I looked at him. I could see that he was a miner working at the coal face. He had scars on his face and hands. He seemed to be about fifty years old. I had never seen him before, either in church or in any other Christian gathering.

He now found what he had been looking for. With emphasis he banged a 100-mark note in front of me on the table and explained: 'That belongs to your youth work!'

I looked at him in astonishment. In my poor miners' district I was not used to such big gifts. It all seemed rather suspicious. What was going on? So I hesitated to accept the note; it lay there between us on the table.

Then the man realized that he had to say something. And so he began his account. I can't recount it word for word, but with many interruptions and silent pauses a staggering story came to light.

As a fifteen-year-old boy he had belonged to a youth group run by my predecessor Wilhelm Weigle. Because he seemed keen he had been given a small position of trust. He was allowed to distribute the newspapers and collect the money; but he had used some to buy himself 'students' feed'.

'Students' feed?' I asked.

'Well yes, that's a sort of sweet stuff. And you know that boys are sometimes dead keen on sweet things.'

It was about one mark altogether that he had misappropriated.

A long silence followed. Then it came out: 'This one mark ruined my life! I didn't want to go to any church any more. I said to myself: I can't possibly appear before God as a thief. So I stayed away and became a careless man of the world. For years I forgot the one mark. But then I got married. My wife wanted us to have a church wedding. But I resisted her. Was I to stand there and pray? And me a thief?'

Again he was silent for a long time. Then he continued: 'See, that's when the misery began. I know well that God lives. But I had to run away from him — because of that one mark! When the children came, my wife prayed with them. Inside me I screamed: "You can't pray. There's no way a thief can pray…"'

It turned into a long account. He closed by saying, 'For thirty-five years this one mark has been pursuing me. I can't take any more. Even if you despise me — I've got to confess at last and put things right. So, here are 100 marks. Take them! Then at last I can pray again!'

Christis or Hitler?

'Why 100 marks? You only took one!'

Agitatedly he cried: 'With interest and interest on the interest! I want to have peace at last! Is that all right now?'

'No!' I said. 'No!'

He looked at me, horrified: 'Why ever not?'

'It is good that you have confessed at last. And it's right that you have restored the stolen money. I will put it into the literature account. But — the most important thing has not happened yet. Do you know whether God has forgiven you?'

'I've made it good now, haven't I?'

'Can we do that, make something good again? The bad deed has been done. Can that be wiped out? And doesn't the fact remain that you betrayed the trust of the old pastor? He is dead now. How will you make that good again?'

He groaned aloud. So I continued, while he listened intently to every word:

'Before God we cannot undo a bad deed. But — there is one who has already made everything good again: Jesus, the Son of God.'

And then I spoke to him slowly that great word from the Bible: 'The blood of Jesus Christ, God's Son, cleanses us from all sin' (1 John 1:7).

At that he buried his head in his arms. And I knew that now I had nothing more to say, because the Saviour of sinners himself had come to a wounded conscience to bring healing.

Youth pastor in Essen

'Oh Theo!'

It was twelve o'clock when I left the shop. There was a huge crush of people in the high street. Slowly the crowd pushed its way past the shop windows. Impatiently I tried to work my way through. It was impossible!

Bump! I had collided heavily with a woman who was obviously in a hurry. Embarrassed, I started to apologize. At that a radiant joy spread over the woman's face. 'Oh, Pastor Busch! Theo will be really pleased that we've met each other!'

I had to smile. After all the 'meeting' had been anything but gentle. And anyway — who was this woman?

A little unsure of myself I said I couldn't exactly remember who she was. Would she please help my poor memory?

'Oh well,' she said cheerfully, 'you actually don't know me at all. I am Theo's mother.'

This Theo again! I was still no wiser. Who was Theo?

'Dear Madam,' I explained, as we tried to stay together in the press, 'I know quite a lot of Theos. Which one do you mean?'

'Well, the big one — with the blonde hair — who keeps coming to your youth centre. Who recently lost his wallet. Didn't you then…?'

Now light dawned. 'So, you are the mother of *that* Theo? Well, then I can really congratulate you. He is a fantastic fellow!'

This Theo had often come to my notice among the hundreds of boys at the Youth Centre in Essen. In the Bible studies he sat facing me with eager and focused attention. And when we sang, his face shone in a way that no one could fail to notice. He was singing not just with his mouth, but with his whole heart. And he was especially keen when it came to outreach and visiting.

'Yes,' I declared again, 'that Theo, he is a very fine young man.'

Now I have often seen a mother's face shining when I praise her son. And therefore I was surprised when this mother suddenly became very serious.

Then she said quietly, 'You have no idea what he is really like.'

By now we had reached a quieter street. So I heard these words distinctly, although they did not seem to be directed to me at all.

I became curious. 'There must be some secret behind this. Dear lady, I would be very grateful if you could let me into it. I do want to get to know my boys really well.'

For a moment the woman reflected. Then it all came out. 'Yes, I must tell you about that. You see, we were a completely godless family. My husband still doesn't want to know anything about Christianity. He has a real dislike for it. And so we all lived totally without God...'

The woman interrupted herself. We had to cross the road. And — yes, we were long past just having a chat. This was serious. That meant she had to collect herself fully. So now I turned with her into a quiet side street. And there she continued:

'It was about the time Theo reached seventeen that I noticed he was so different. When there was a row, he stayed quiet. And he was always trying to make me happy. He was so patient with his little sister. It was as if through Theo another spirit came into our family.

'And one day he told us quite openly that he was going to your youth circle. A few friends had taken him along. He had come to know the Lord Jesus; and his life now belonged to the Lord.'

Again the woman paused. I sensed the strong emotion in her. It was gripping to hear that she had to tell me that this disclosure had only drawn an angry growl from her husband. She herself however had been strangely animated by her son's testimony. Her heart had become quite restless as a result.

'Yes, so since then I have been going with Theo to your services.' And then her face shone. 'Now I also belong to the Lord Jesus. That is like a wonderful secret that my Theo and I share together. And every day I read a little in the Bible. There are some things I don't understand … and…'

Now she was really red with embarrassment: 'Then I ask my boy. He understands much more. It's a shame that I, mother that I am, have to learn from my boy. But Theo is not haughty at all. He can explain things to me so well.'

The way the woman said that brought tears to my eyes. And through my mind went the ancient prophecy of Malachi, that the hearts of the parents should be turned to the children.

'And your husband?' I just had to ask.

She smiled: 'Oh, he still doesn't want to know anything about all that! But Theo and I — we pray for him every day. We do love him. He is a good father. One day he will also … if we pray for him like that. Then it cannot be otherwise…!'

There was a long silence. Then she began hesitantly: 'It really is strange that a mother through her son…' The rest of the sentence was missing. But I understood her.

In the evening I met Theo in the youth centre. He was just playing table tennis with a few young lads he had brought in. I pressed his hand: 'Oh Theo!' And he answered me with a happy laugh.

Gottfried Dühr

When I first knew Gottfried I found him very annoying. He sometimes came to my sixth formers' Bible Circle and played the role of the critical intellect. He knew all there was to know about Christianity and the church, for he came from a godly family. His father was a faithful member of an academic circle that often met in my flat.

Gottfried used to come in, tall, slim and good-looking with a cynical smile on his lips. His whole expression said, 'Ok, let's hear what the good old pastor has to put before us today.' And because the others in the circle had the same attitude, these hours were often a real trial for me.

In other parts of my youth work there were young men who worked with me, looked after boys, led excursions and wanted to serve Jesus. They often said, 'Why don't you give up this intellectual club? It won't come to anything real. You are wasting time and energy!'

But I could not bring myself to do that. 'They still come!' I answered. 'I think Jesus will be able to overcome even these mocking hearts.'

And so it turned out. Gottfried Dühr was one of the first to have his heart won by Jesus. This is how it happened.

Youth pastor in Essen

The Third Reich had begun. Everywhere in Essen the flags fluttered, the loudspeakers droned, the columns marched. One Saturday evening, on a hill with the charming name Secret Love, there was to be a mighty (what was not 'mighty' in those days?) joy and propaganda bonfire lit by the Hitler Youth. I went out as well, because as youth pastor I had to take an interest in what was moving the young people.

The whole thing made me unhappy. Raving hordes of boys! Empty speeches in which Hitler was celebrated like a god! Wild threats against all who were now 'still out of line'!

Sadly I turned to go home. The young people were not being inspired to great goals. They were being turned into fanatics and stirred up against — yes, really against all and sundry: against Christianity, against the church, against the middle class, against other countries, against Capitalists, against Marxists, against Communists and Socialists, against the older generation, against the past, against other youth organizations, against…

I went away. Behind me sounded the bellowing denunciations of the speaker.

Then in the darkness I saw Gottfried Dühr.

'You are going?' he asked. 'May I accompany you?'

He stumbled along next to me through the darkness, till we came to a street and a tram. We got in. The whole time I was airing my resentment against this movement that was fooling around with young hearts.

Gottfried had also left early, and had not the slightest intention of joining the Hitler Youth. But he had to get some fun out of contradicting me. So we argued in whispers in the fully occupied tram.

Suddenly the thought came to me: 'Have you got nothing better to tell this young man than your resentment?' So I abruptly changed the subject and asked — without any forethought at all: 'Where do you really stand with Jesus?'

Long silence…

Then Gottfried said, 'I think we had better get off! We can't discuss that in the tram!'

So we got off and strolled along to a quiet, dark wood. And here the young man opened to me his heart:

'You see, I know everything about the gospel from my parents. I also believe it all! I have no doubt that what the New Testament witnesses is true. But — I am dead. The gospel moves nothing in me. Perhaps I have heard too much of it from my youth up. I don't know. Anyway, I would like to be able to rejoice in Jesus like you! But he only bores me!'

'Oh, Gottfried!' I replied. 'How wrong I've been about you! I thought all you could do was scoff at everything. And now a longing heart is showing itself. I'll tell you what the matter is: you are doing nothing for Jesus! I am going to put you into Section 1 of my youth organization. The leader there is a young businessman who I'm sure will make good use of you. You'll work together with him in Segeroth. Do you know Segeroth?'

He shook his head indignantly: 'Of course I have heard of it, but I have never been there. Why should I go there?'

I laughed and hummed quietly the home song of that notorious district:

> Where bones crack and splinter
> And dark flows the blood,
> That's where my home is,
> That's Segeroth!

Gottfried was a bit annoyed: 'What am I supposed to do there?'

It was clear to me that the best thing was to throw the spoilt young man straight in at the deep end, so that he would learn to swim. 'Tomorrow is Sunday,' I said. 'You'll be at the service in the Market Church at half past eight. Go to the left side of the gallery; that's where the boys from Section 1 sit.'

'What? At half past eight in the Market Church?' cried Gottfried. 'That's the time when I am most enjoying my sleep!'

'Well, that is now going to stop. At half past eight in the church. Following that we have a prayer meeting…'

At this Gottfried smiled in the way I knew so well. But I didn't let that disturb me any more. 'And then you will do house visits with Paul Dorr in Segeroth. There you will see how people's lives are destroyed, how youngsters are led astray and how insecure their hearts are. You'll learn to wrestle for people, you'll learn to weep and to rejoice. And above all you'll learn to pray; and your pride will go, and you'll really learn to believe!'

'Out of the question!' declared Gottfried. 'I'm to run around in Segeroth and help young fellows from depraved families? Completely out of the question!'

Christ or Hitler?

'All right,' I said. 'You've still got a night to sleep on it! And look — there's the tram again. I'm going home now.'

Next morning the first hymn was just beginning in the packed Market Church. The boys from the youth centre were sitting in the gallery and singing to make the walls shake. Professor Rendtorff from Kiel once heard this singing and said, 'That's not singing; that's a roar to God!'

But above this 'roar to God' could be heard a clattering on the wooden stairs. And look! In came Gottfried making his way to Section 1.

He soon became one of my best helpers. For years he worked with loyal faithfulness in Segeroth. Later the whole area went up in flames under a carpet of bombs. And today there is nothing left of the old dire poverty, nor of the old romance of this infamous district.

And Gottfried fell in the same war that destroyed Segeroth.

But old Segeroth and Gottfried Dühr belonged together. Every Sunday after the service he went through the houses where there were boys of fourteen and over and invited them to the Youth Centre. Everybody got to know him. In one flat he was thrown out with swear words, in another he became a sort of consultant on parenting.

He liked to recount an experience he had in the Menage, a huge dreary brick building which had a family living in each room. Often a room housed two or three families, when the children married and moved in with their parents. These days it is hardly possible to imagine such dreadful overcrowding.

Every Sunday morning, when Gottfried came to one of these Menage families, there was trouble. The head of the family, a rock solid old free-thinker, sprang out of one of the well-filled beds and bellowed: 'Get out! Immediately!' Gottfried didn't let himself be put off. Among the swarms of partially dressed people he looked for the boy he had come to see and talked to him.

One day Gottfried had a great surprise. The whole family were sitting around, properly dressed. The room had been tidied up. And as Gottfried arrived, the old man politely offered him a seat. And then he began to ask: 'Tell me honestly: what does the parson pay you for bothering about my boy? You don't only visit him. When he comes to the Youth Centre in the afternoon, you care for him in a touching way. I just can't believe that a well-dressed businessman like you is doing that just for fun. What does the parson pay you for it?'

Gottfried laughed: 'Nothing!'

'I don't believe you!'

'Then just leave it!'

'Yes, but why are you doing it?'

Now Gottfried told the listening gathering of young women, men and children about Jesus. Oh yes! Now he could give his testimony. For meanwhile the living Lord had met him in the fellowship of young Christians and in service. He spoke of his own experience; and he led these people to the cross of Jesus and showed them how God loved them too, so much that he gave his Son.

When he had finished, the old man turned to the whole family and declared solemnly: 'If Christianity can make such a modern young man care about my child, then there is something in it. And from now on the whole family is going together on Sunday mornings to the Market Church.' And that is what actually happened.

After leaving school Gottfried became a businessman in industry. He took to his job with great joy and lively interest. And sometimes I was worried and said to him, 'Now your profession is going to make such demands on you that you will have no more time for youth work.'

But Gottfried just laughed away such worries. For him the service of the young was not a hobby but a calling. And he knew that the Lord, who had put him into this service, did not demand success, but faithfulness. Gottfried's faithfulness in fact often put us to shame.

Our work was becoming more difficult because of the pressure from the Nazi regime. The army took in many of our fellow workers. Gottfried became more and more indispensable to me. It was not so simple for him either, for his company sent him to a branch in Dortmund. He didn't want to give up living with his parents and working in the Youth Centre. So he commuted by train on a daily basis.

At that time I went through the Youth Centre one evening. I could hear loud singing from one room:

> I want to sing of my Jesus,
> Of his faithfulness, love and grace…

Quietly I opened the door to see which section was meeting here. There sat Gottfried, the well-dressed businessman, with a small, rather unwashed boy from Segeroth.

My heart was moved. There comes this young man, after a full day's work, straight from the station to the section meeting. And the gang let him down badly: just one turns up. But Gottfried is pleased to see this single boy, and spends a well-prepared hour with him. If only we could always have such fellow workers in our evangelical youth work!

I thought of this story when later, as youth pastor of the synod, I once dismissed a youth work secretary. She was supposed to be gathering a group in a remote part of the town. When I asked one day how things were going she told me: 'I let the group disband. Recently only three came. That wasn't worth the effort, so I gave up the whole thing.'

I got angry. 'Madam,' I said, 'what terrific girls they must have been to come when no one else did! You could have had a lovely hour with them; they would have been full of joy and invited others next time. Instead of that you sent them away. Madam, I cannot use you on the difficult battlefield of our youth work.'

The longer Gottfried Dühr was in the work, the more he grew into the life of fellowship with those who had their spiritual home in the Youth Centre.

Tour in the Baltic lands

In 1938 I did a lecture tour in the Baltic lands, and Gottfried accompanied me as travel manager through the glorious cities of Riga, Reval (now Tallinn) and Mitau (now Jelgava). I was glad to have his company.

Those were priceless days full of rich experiences, but also full of enormous tensions.

The German-speaking Baltic people, though Latvian and Estonian nationals, were full of enthusiasm about Hitler and wanted to hear about Germany. But the native Latvians and Estonians were afraid of Germany and eyed my lectures with suspicion. There were both the spies from Nazi Germany and the listeners from the Latvian police sitting in the audience. I was so glad that Gottfried and I could pray earnestly together every morning. And if I was in danger of making a careless remark during a lecture, Gottfried's tall figure was there at the back, his face so full of anxiety and warning that I got back immediately to my real matter, the gospel.

Just once we had a bit of a row with each other. That was when we had to hurry to the airfield at Reval one morning. Many friends had come to say goodbye to us, and in all the tumult it happened that we spoke sharply to each other.

Then we sat as the only passengers in the Lufthansa plane flying over the bay of Riga — silent and annoyed with each other. Till Gottfried suddenly said, 'Do you know why things went wrong this morning? We haven't had our morning worship yet.'

I had to admit he was right. And now up there in the sky we opened our Bibles and prayed together. Then the sunshine of God's grace broke through, and it was a glorious day. So Gottfried became a pastor to his pastor.

Then came the war! Gottfried was eventually called up. Near the end of the war he was in a radio car with a young man from Düsseldorf, whom Gottfried had been able to lead to the Lord. The two must have had precious fellowship together in that radio car.

When the Americans had overrun the little village of Heng near Neumarkt, and the shocked inhabitants came out of their cellars again, they found an overturned radio car at the edge of the village and next to it the dead bodies of the two young men. The Catholic chaplain took charge of their papers. Later he told the parents that it had shaken him to see from all their diaries and letters how much the two had set their hope on the Lord Jesus Christ.

Apparently they had not been killed by the Americans, but by marauding bands who were wandering around shooting and plundering. Even the funeral, so said the chaplain, was disturbed by such shooting.

Now Gottfried's picture is hanging in my study. I often look at it: the gaunt, slim face with the prominent, sharp nose and the laughing eyes. Gottfried was a good businessman who followed his profession wholeheartedly. But he was also like the businessman in the parable of Jesus who sought and found a precious pearl. And eternity will reveal how many young people he was able to lead to such riches.

The university for the unwaged

In 1930 the great depression began in Germany. It's hard to imagine now what that was like. I remember, when wandering through the Sauerland in the spring of 1931, how shaken I was to see the usually busy factories and businesses still and deserted. Thousands thronged the dole queues.

One day a young man sat in front of me. 'Look,' he said, 'if I were to jump into the river, no one would miss me. My father would be glad to get rid of a mouth to feed, and the state would be glad to see one less person drawing the dole. It's a pointless existence!'

I couldn't put that out of my mind. At last I had an idea. There is one sort of people that don't produce anything, and yet don't have the desperate feeling of worthlessness: students! I could save the best of the young people from their despair if I transformed the unemployed into students.

The Youth Centre was empty in the mornings. Here were enough rooms to start a 'university.' So I made an announcement in the newspapers inviting young men to the UfA (*Universität für Arbeitslose*, University for the Unemployed).

The first result was that the film production company UfA threatened me with legal action for stealing their name. It took a lot of effort and humility to pacify the great gentlemen. I renamed my enterprise UfE (*Universität für Erwerbslose*, University for the Unwaged). To this day I am grateful to the real universities that they didn't threaten such action. Obviously the professors had more of a sense of humour than the film people.

The first lecturers were some secondary school teachers who willingly offered up their free periods. But soon the lecturing staff increased. An unemployed engineer contacted me and asked if he could become a student. 'No!' I said. 'But you will teach higher mathematics.' And it worked — he gathered a group of intelligent young men.

An agriculturalist appeared and asked if I had anything for people working on the land. I said to him, 'You can be our lecturer on farming.' Young men who wanted to emigrate to Canada or Australia came to him and got an introduction to farming. The Berlitz School provided English and French language courses. An unemployed decorator taught how to decorate shop windows. I taught geography and literature. An unemployed musician formed an orchestra. The German Jiu-Jitsu champion offered to teach this Japanese sport. A lawyer lectured on legal issues. To sum up, after half a year we were able to offer a programme of lectures in a great variety of subjects.

It worried me more and more to see the young men so hungry! So I began to beg, in order to be able to offer each student breakfast every morning. Our valiant caretaker and his family had their hands full preparing rolls with cold meat and coffee for five hundred young men. He deserved praise, our caretaker 'Uncle Hermann'!

In 1932 the political contrasts in Germany grew sharper. The National Socialists (Nazis) wore SA-uniforms (SA, *Sturm Abteil*, Storm Section). That aroused the Communists present, and they appeared in Red Front fighter uniforms. Now the saloon battles that were being fought everywhere began among us also.

Then I strode between the quarrelling fellows and roared 'Quiet!' so mightily that there was silence. And I declared to them: 'This is a university! Only mental weapons are used for fighting here! Shame on anyone who breaks the civil peace! Here everyone can have his own views!'

And then it became peaceful again and even happy. The grim, desperate look disappeared from many faces. Life had some content to it again. You had to get up early to be in 'college' on time. You made new friends. You learned to understand other points of view. You had homework to do.

We had glorious two-day excursions in the summer. What outings they were! When I went through the Sauerland or the mountain country with my hundreds of young fellows — some in SA uniforms, others in Red Front fighting kit, others again in scruffy old clothes — then the shopkeepers pulled down the blinds and the farmers drove their cattle out of the meadow, because they thought this was the revolution starting.

It was great! But sometimes I lay awake at night and tormented myself. I had been called to be a messenger of the gospel. Was I not leaving my real calling now? Was this social service really my work? Was it not for people in other professions? More and more the American YMCA came before my mind. Had they not ventured, as I was now doing, into social work, and in so doing slipped away from their real service of telling young men the gospel?

I was determined not to let that happen. And so one day I dared, with much inward trepidation, to announce to the students: 'Next term there will be a lesson on "world views" once a week for all students. Free discussion will be guaranteed!'

And it turned out that this very lesson became the intellectual and spiritual centre of the UfE. I would speak first for ten or twenty minutes about the message of the Bible. Then came the discussion, in which a lot of authority was needed to get the young men to listen to each other. In the last quarter of an hour I responded to all the questions that had been raised.

Oh, those discussions! The English rightly observe that we Germans are bad at discussing something. That is our strength and also our weakness: we lack cool objectivity. These young men argued with passion and trembling excitement. There were young Communists, Nazis in their brown uniforms, steel helmets and Socialist falcons, there were Nihilists and Christians, fools and wise men, fanatics and cynics, atheists and disciples of Jesus, sectarians and idealists.

Often the hall became a raging battleground, and I had to jump in like a lion tamer and make it clear to the excited men that they were now students, so they were not to fight with chair legs, but only with weapons of the mind. Then the tension would dissolve in cheerful laughter.

But there was one thing in which almost all were united: their response to the gospel. The gospel? That was swept off the table in the first three minutes. Oh well, the pastor had to speak like that! But this old fashioned dogma had no serious significance now. Then came the political ideologies: the teaching of Lenin! The teaching of Hitler! The economic doctrine of Silvio Gesell! Karl Marx! It was teeming with technical terms, great ideas, economic solutions! And I stood there so small and stupid with my simple gospel about the Saviour of sinners. What use was that to this crowd? Every one of them had the recipe for the world's salvation ready in his pocket!

And so things might have gone on indefinitely, had it not been for the matter of the bread rolls. That came about like this.

Ideologies and bread rolls

One day we decided to do a two-day excursion to the Sauerland. The weather was very uncertain on the morning we left, so only a hundred and fifty diehards came along.

That was an unforgettable journey!

I cannot remember ever having such constant rain. But we had made up our minds to carry on regardless, so on we went. The glorious Dechen Cave provided shelter, so its strange stalactite/stalagmite formations were all we got to see that day. Everything else disappeared in mist and water.

At last we arrived at a youth hostel, singing and soaked to the skin. Every seasoned traveller knows what that was like: a cheerful milling crowd! Clothes were dried in front of ovens, and after supper we sat, cosy but tired, around the fire. I was just going to tell them about a journey to America, when a baker's apprentice appeared:

Christo or Hitler?

Greetings from the baker! And would any of the gentlemen like to order rolls for the morning? There are four for ten pfennig.

My companions sat and thought. I could read it on their faces: ten pfennig! A lot of money for someone out of work! You could get three cigarettes for that: Ecksteins at three and a third pfennig each! But such fresh, crisp rolls! True! But — there was going to be bread for breakfast anyway.

In the end about fifty men decided to order the rolls.

So, now I could tell my story! Afterwards I could even hold evening worship, the mood was so friendly.

When I knew that they were all in bed, I breathed a sigh of relief. Now the Communist was sleeping peacefully next to the Nazi, the expert scout next to the city gent who had set out with immaculate creases in his trousers — though sadly the creases had long since disappeared.

I went to my room and fell into a deep sleep. Then I dreamt that I had got into a popular uprising. Roaring masses thronged the streets. I started up. I was wide awake!

It was daytime already. I had overslept. But — what was that? The popular uprising of my dream was shocking reality: I heard angry cries, wild fighting…

Just as I was, in my pyjamas, I rushed out and surveyed the scene. The sweet peace of the evening was completely gone. A raging battle was taking place.

With difficulty I found out what had happened. That morning the baker had appeared with two hundred bread rolls. Those fresh rolls had such an inviting aroma. And anyway the whole thing now appeared in a different light. So the cigarette lovers of the night before had just rushed at the precious wares and torn them from the baker's hand. And many of those who had ordered the night before came away empty-handed. Of course they were not going to stand for that. That was when the row started. And because they were now in a ding-dong battle, many other tensions surfaced as well. All the scores were going to be settled once and for all.

With a determination born of desperation, astonishing even to myself, I gradually gained attention and at last got a hearing. I made the categorical demand: 'First all the rolls are to be given to me.' There was an inward fight, silent conflict in young men's hearts, friendly words from me — and then a mountain of rolls lay in front of me.

Then the question: 'Now who actually wants rolls?' They all did.

I issued my instructions like a commander: 'To begin with, everyone gets one. And then get me the baker!'

The deeply shocked man was found somehow. Before the gathered company I asked the decisive question: 'Are you able to deliver another four hundred rolls within half an hour?' He was able! Praise be to the valiant man!

Oh, the peaceful breakfast that followed! And then we discovered with delight that a glorious day had begun. The sun shone, the flowers were blooming and the trees rustled. How beautiful the world was!

Under an old lime tree we gathered for morning worship. My rough companions no doubt regarded this as an eccentricity of their pastor. But still, the man made so much effort! And so, why should one not listen to him? After all, one was not inhuman.

Christ or Hitler?

Poor chaps! They had no idea of what was coming!

I spoke on the words: 'See, I make all things new' (Rev. 21:5).

'Friends,' I said, 'we are all united in demanding one thing: the world must change. Yes, indeed it must! For half a year now I keep hearing in every "world views" lesson how each of you has a political or economic recipe to rescue the world. Oh, I was astonished at what big ideas you had! But now I am disappointed. You, who think you can save the world with your ideas, cannot even share out two hundred rolls in peace! What can I say to that? This morning here was like the world at large: there was enough food for all to share. With good will everybody could be satisfied. And what happened? Fighting and screaming! Don't take this badly: but I don't believe in your ideologies any more. What use are they, if they fail so dismally on such a small scale?'

The young men sat in silence. They were really shaken. No one dared to say anything.

So I went on: 'And why was it like that? Because each of you thought only of himself. Your evil and selfish hearts spoilt everything.'

I could see in their faces that they knew I was right. Still they stayed silent.

'You have always made out that the Bible is a stupid book, long since overtaken by modern knowledge. Now I am telling you that the Bible is right! For it says that things will only change when our heart changes, when you and I become new, when we are set free from our terrible selfishness!'

It was a glorious service. The summer breeze murmured in the old lime tree, and the bird song did not disturb us; it only emphasized the quietness. The best thing, however, was the congregation: young men, who had become aware of the uselessness of their ideologies, that they had thought would solve all the world's problems.

'Friends,' I called, deeply moved, 'you are mistaken if you think the Bible has been overtaken by modern knowledge! Here we are shown how hearts are made new. Here we find the Man sent by God, who through his blood and his Spirit completely transforms us and makes us new — Jesus Christ!'

The sun shone so brilliantly, but what was its radiance compared to the glory of the Son of God, which rose over these poor young men?

From then on the University for the Unwaged began to listen to the message of the Bible.

The 'world views' lessons became weighty. That came from the gospel of Jesus Christ, through which hearts were moved and consciences struck.

Let me finish with just one example. A militant atheist kept wanting to speak and at last complained that he could not get his turn. So I gave him a promise: 'Next time you can give the introductory speech.'

The 'world views' lesson began the next Wednesday. The crowded hall was silent in anticipation. The atheist was called to speak, but didn't respond. At last it became clear: he had not turned up!

Then his friend volunteered the information: 'He has been struck! He doesn't believe in his unbelief any more. But — he cannot talk about it yet!'

Great stillness! Everyone sensed something of the overcoming power of the risen Lord Jesus.

The former atheist is now my friend; we are united in heart. It was gripping when one day he gave testimony before the gathered students to the faith he now had in the Lord Jesus Christ.

8.

Family and friends

My brothers

My brothers studied theology, as I did. The first to lose his life was my youngest brother Friedrich. After Hitler's Gestapo had forcibly closed down a seminary in which he was a lecturer, he became director of a preachers' school in East Prussia, while he was still young.

Friedrich was a great theologian. He had obtained a doctorate under Professor Schniewind, and it was his heart's desire to bring together scientific theology and the vital East Prussian fellowship circles, of which he was the chairman. So he brought Professors Iwand and Schniewind to the great fellowship days in Königsberg; and these distinguished theologians were glad to attend.

Fritz (short for Friedrich) fell in the Second World War somewhere in Russia. When I was preaching some time ago, a man came to me afterwards and said, 'I was in your brother's company. We tormented him with our ungodliness — it pains me now to think of it. But the fact that I am here in church is a fruit of his life. The way he was, and the things he said, had a lasting effect on many of us.'

Christ or Hitler?

The next one to go was my middle brother Johannes. On a dark January night in 1956, when he was travelling to Trier for a young men's day, he was hit by a drunk driver during carnival celebrations. His own driver was killed outright. He himself suffered a long time before going home to his rest.

He had been the Federal Director of the West German YMCA and a youth pastor in Westphalia. It was gripping to see thousands of young men accompany him on his last journey. That showed something of a blessed life that had been consumed in service. I keep meeting people who owe to him what is most important in their lives.

We three brothers were united in deep love and cordial fellowship. Now and then we went on rambles together. That was just marvellous. Theological battles were fought. Together we enjoyed the scenery, people and our fellowship.

How much we belonged together became clear through a striking event during the Hitler regime.

It was a beautiful summer's day. Our respective wives and children had already arrived for the holidays in Hülben, and were sitting and chatting happily together under the old beech trees in the garden. The men still had service to do somewhere. Suddenly the garden gate opened, and in came Johannes. He brought the news that he had been dismissed in Witten and was out of work. Now he just wanted to take a few days to distance himself from the event.

The next day they were sitting and chatting again under the beeches, when the garden gate opened and Fritz arrived unexpectedly. 'We thought you were in Dantzig!' they called to him. He explained how, in scandalous circumstances and with much harassment, he had been expelled from Dantzig. Now the second one had come.

On the third day brother Wilhelm appeared. He should really have been at an evangelistic week in Stuttgart. He said, 'This morning I was summoned by the Gestapo and told that I am not allowed to speak publicly in Württemberg any more. I must immediately leave Stuttgart. So I've sadly come to the Swabian Alp to see Mother.'

So now the three brothers sat there together, all three outlawed and rejected, yet so happy; for they were of one spirit.

And Mother was radiant.

Stories for children

I never thought of that!

It was a really nice situation, when early morning in the bedroom I was getting dressed.

My three children 'Little man,' Hanna and 'Chubby' were sitting on the laundry chest like swallows on a telephone wire.

As a young father, I enjoyed telling them Bible stories. I am still convinced that this is better than all the pedagogical tricks.

But because my day was very full, the time when I dressed in the morning had to be used for this. And why not?! Did not the French 'sun king' Louis XIV hold his receptions while dressing in the morning? The *lever du roi* (the king's getting up) was famous. Why not a *lever du père* (father's getting up)?

So I was telling the story of David and Goliath. The children on the laundry chest were listening with bated breath.

Christ or Hitler?

While I put on my shoes I imitated the blasphemous mocking cries of Goliath. Trembling on the laundry chest!

Then I was interrupted. The situation had to be made completely clear. 'Daddy! Was Goliath as big as our house?'

'Something like that.'

'Oh, something like that. Carry on!'

I tied my tie and told of the faith and courage of young David. How he, with nothing but a sling in his hand, faced the dreadful Goliath.

The tie was not on properly. I tore it off my neck irritably. And then I found that it was just what I needed to represent a sling. 'That's how little David swung his sling!'

While I tied it all over again — this time successfully — I recounted the exchange between the two warriors; the mockery of the wild Goliath and the confession of faith by brave David.

I put on my jacket. Meanwhile I let the stone whiz through the air to kill Goliath, and, with David triumphant, I finished my story and was fully dressed.

My boy was not triumphing, however. Sadly he asked: 'Daddy, what did Goliath's aunt say then?' I looked at him, shocked: 'I don't know!' Then I went into my study.

'What did Goliath's aunt say then?' Boy, oh boy! That's something I have really never thought about! Yes, whatever would she have said? She must surely have wept dreadfully when the news came: your strong man is dead! Surely her world must have just collapsed in that moment.

No! I had never thought about that. How perceptive children are towards the deep sorrow of a fallen world!

Bump!

Again my three children were sitting on the laundry chest. This time the story was about the storm on the lake.

Because it all got highly dramatic towards the end, I had to stop getting dressed. There I was standing in shirt sleeves, without a collar or shoes on, telling the story.

The three pairs of eyes reflected the terror of the disciples as the storm got wilder and wilder, till finally, in bewilderment and panic, they shook the Lord awake: 'Lord, help us! We are perishing!'

And then their faces shone when the Lord Jesus stepped over the swaying deck. I put my heart and soul and everything I had into the story:

'There stood the Saviour. The storm tore at his clothes and dragged at his hair. But then he stretched out his hand and cried with a mighty voice: Silence! Be still! — and then...'

Bump! My 'little man' jumped off the laundry chest and said in a confident and matter of fact way: 'And then the thunder was broken to bits!'

Satisfied with that, he trotted off into the nursery.

For him the whole thing was completely clear: if the Lord Jesus engaged himself in the matter, it could only end in the way it did. 'Oh boy!' I had to think. 'If only I could always have such unquestioning faith!'

Christ or Hitler?

Friedrich von Bodelschwingh and family tragedies

I want to tell how this great pastor, who lived from 1831 to 1910 and is famous for his 'Bethel' institution work with thousands of epileptics, handicapped and other disadvantaged people, became important in a special way to me personally.

There was a point in Bodelschwingh's life when God broke him, and when he became a man of compassion. 'At that time,' he said later, 'I first noticed how hard God can be against men, and through that I became compassionate towards others.'

In 1869 Bodelschwingh had already spent several years in happy pastoral work in the little village of Dellwig. There was blossoming and growth all around him. The congregation was awakened; the people came in droves to hear his powerful sermons. Old quarrels among the farmers were buried. New life was also springing up in the little vicarage: a lively bunch of children were the joy of the young couple.

And then in a very short time four children were torn away from the parents.

Bodelschwingh wrote an account: 'Of the life and death of four blessed children.' It is gripping to read how the deepest pain was illuminated by the hope of eternal life.

One can feel the heart-rending lament when he says about the dying of little Friedrich:

> Then the eyes break, and we are already saying farewell. But no, once again he opens them, bright and friendly and begs: 'Mama, lap!' Mother takes him on her lap, the tears flowing down her cheeks. The child can still see that, and lifts his

little hands, as he has so often done, to wipe away the tears. It is his last service of love. The little head falls forward, and in less than a quarter of a minute the final difficult breaths are over.

But always the light of eternity shines into the sadness. Thus the father writes about the home call of his little son Ernst:

Our little Ernst always specially enjoyed seeing the sunrise from his bed; he often sat up to admire its beautiful radiance. Even on his deathbed a beam of joy came over him when the sun's first rays fell on his pale face after a fearful night of pain. How much more we now understood the morning hymn that we sang together several times by his bed at his request:

Eternity, your morning glow,
light from uncreated light,
Send us in this morning now
rays to shine upon our sight.

Through your power drive away
all the darkness of our night!
Light our way into that world,
you transfigured Sun of grace.

Lead us through the vale of tears
to the land of sweetest bliss,
Where the pleasures that exalt
never, never pass away.

It is sobering to see how unsentimental the parents were at the death of such children. Bodelschwingh writes of his Ernst:

When someone expressed the view that Friedrich had gone to heaven because he had always been so kind, this sounded a discordant note to Ernst, and he reminded us that his little brother had sometimes been very stubborn. I could see how it calmed him when I said to him, 'You well know why we go to heaven; it's because the Saviour has died for us and has forgiven us our sins.' He nodded with deep agreement.

Every Sunday he learned from his mother a weekly passage from the Bible. When he came to Psalm 103:1-3 and Mother asked him, 'So what good things has the Lord done to you?' he answered without needing to stop for thought, 'He died for me.' 'And what else, my son?' 'He has forgiven all my sins.' Then he himself, from the many prayers he knew by heart, chose quite definitely for his last days the little prayer:

> The blood and righteousness of Christ
> my robe of honour is.
> With that before God's throne I'll stand,
> when up to heav'n I go.

Dreadful days! And yet — days full of the 'morning glow of eternity.'

At that time the pastor was broken. Not just by the sorrow. He grasped the fact that God goes into judgement with those he particularly loves. The fact that things hidden to us were passing between Bodelschwingh and his God appears from what he wrote at that time to his mother:

> The sense of the *judicial*, which was part of this affliction, has given way to the sense of assurance that God has thoughts only of peace with us and our little child. Oh that we might only go on and on observing his holy ways with care, so that he can also fulfil these thoughts of peace in us.

Family and friends

I keep being drawn to the picture on my wall. And then it seems to me as if I could speak to the old man myself:

> Father Bodelschwingh! Do tell me whether the pain over your children left you one day. Or did it stay with you the whole of your life? See, a few metres to your left where there is the picture of my eighteen-year-old son. It is twenty years since he was torn from me. But often the pain attacks me so strongly that I think I must take the picture away, because I can hardly bear to look at the boy's serious face. Father Bodelschwingh, was it like that with you?

He doesn't answer me. That's how it is: the hardest things are those that each must endure for himself; no man can help him there.

And now I come to the place in *my* life, for the sake of which I love Bodelschwingh as a father who went through such deep sorrow.

When I was married in that month of bliss May 1923 I said to my young wife: 'I'd really like to have six sons, and they must all play the trombone. That will be glorious, to have our own trombone choir!'

Well, I was not really being serious, and when our heavenly Father gave us two sons and four daughters I was tremendously happy particularly about the girls.

But now I am concerned with the two sons. The Lord took them both away...

We already had four children when our little Eberhard was born. I cannot describe the joy that he brought to us all. Sometimes I think my memory may be playing tricks on me: but whenever I think of this child, it is as if I see nothing but bright sunshine.

Busch family in summer 1931 (Hanna Busch on left in front)

One evening, when we were going to bed late, my wife took the fourteen-month-old boy out of his cot. I was deeply shocked when he, apparently fast asleep, let his head fall to the side. I can still hear to this day — sometimes I dream of it — how my wife, at first laughing and then more and more fearfully spoke to the child, 'Eberhard, wake up! Come, laugh at Papa!'

I cried out: 'The child must be dead!' I tore him out of my wife's arms and ran off to the nearby hospital. Oh, those dreadful moments, when I ran through the night with my beloved dead child!

In the hospital they tried to resuscitate him. In vain!

Family and friends

It was like a bad dream when I was told: 'The police has provisionally confiscated the body, because this is an unusual, unexplained death.'

The doctors then presumed a thymus death, caused by a gland failure. Well, that told me nothing. A holy God had taken away from me my child. And I could so well understand Friedrich von Bodelschwingh when he wrote after the death of his children: 'The sense of the *judicial*, that was also included in this affliction...'

My work demanded me. And yet I was as if numbed. Many came to comfort us. I experienced then that one man cannot comfort another. Nothing that people said to me could reach down to the abyss of my pain.

But Jesus can comfort. I heard his word: 'My peace I give to you' (John 14:27). And he made good his word.

At such times one faces anew the question, whether one is really serious about the hope that Jesus gives. I answered that myself when I had the words 'In the Shepherd's arm and bosom' engraved in the little marble cross in the Essen East cemetery.

I know that my child is safe with Jesus. Not with the dead, but with the living, my heart seeks also my other boy, our oldest, our Wilhelm.

He was musical; from the early years of life he found his greatest joy in music. I can't forget how one day as a sixteen-year-old he said to me: 'I want to be a musician.'

'O my dear boy,' I answered, 'there are a hundred thousand coffee house musicians [a profession that has almost died out today] and only one Furtwängler [the great conductor of those days, whom he so much admired]. And you don't know if you're going to make it to be a Furtwängler.'

He didn't take long to think it over, but declared: 'And if I become a coffee house violinist — I will stay with music.'

What could I say?

'Good, agreed! You could after all become quite famous one day. Then I don't want to appear in the story of your life as the father who didn't understand. One thing I ask: finish your schooling; then you can study music.'

He agreed to that, even though he found the early years of secondary school hard going. But when he reached the senior classes, it was as if a spell had been broken. His spirit began to unfold and spread its wings. It was a joy for me to see this.

Busch family in 1936/37

l to r: Margarete, mother Emmi and father Wilhelm, Elisabeth, Hanna and Wilhelm jr, with Renate seated in front

Family and friends

The difficult times drove us together, so that we never noticed any generation gap. The boy suffered greatly under the Nazi regime. I remember how once, after spending several weeks in prison, I went to his headmaster and asked him: 'I want to leave Essen completely for a few days, to get back my equilibrium. Please give my boy some time off so that he can come with me.'

The man was very understanding: 'I am not really supposed to do it. But I can see how much the boy is suffering too.'

And then we both had some unforgettably beautiful days in a remote part of the Sauerland.

When my son reached the senior classes in the grammar school he himself wanted to resist the ungodly repression of those days. He chose his friends from the Bible Circle that I was leading. This work had already been so defamed that only a handful of young people had the courage to swim against the tide and keep coming.

His friends decided one day to disobey the command of the Hitler Youth (to which all young people without exception then had to belong) to assemble on Sundays during the time of the church service. That stirred things up.

The Hitler Youth leader summoned me and gave a threatening talk. I explained to him: 'The boys have done this of their own accord.'

'What's made them do that?' he bellowed.

'Because it says in God's command: "You shall hallow the holy day."'

'We will cut those boys down to size!'

Christus oder Hitler?

'Try it! But it won't give a good impression of your cause if you make martyrs of the youngsters.'

After that the Hitler Youth overlooked the matter in silence.

However, the young people were not enduring these battles with grim faces. They knew how to laugh. Their fellowship came from God's Word. Those were precious hours for me, when on Tuesday evenings we would meet and open up the Bible together.

I never commanded my son to enter my youth work; he just grew into it of his own accord.

Such fellowship, based on God's Word, is strengthened by doing things together: hikes, camps and sport. But all of this was forbidden by the Gestapo, the Secret State Police.

My Bible Circle members found a lovely way round this. My boy decided to do a bicycle tour. He invited his friends. And in the end he said it would be nice if his father came as well.

These touring days are still unforgettable for me. The happy, radiant youths with their glorious *joie de vivre*, with their questions and their frequent, wonderful laughter!

Now and then a patrol would stop us with a threatening look. 'Halt! What kind of youth group is that?'

My boy: 'Am I not allowed to have a ride on my bicycle?'

'Yes; but there is an older person as well. Who are you?'

'A pastor.'

'Aha! A forbidden church youth group!'

My boy: 'Nah, that's just my father! He's coming to make sure we don't do anything stupid.'

'And the others?'

'Those are my friends; I invited them.'

Then we cycled on and left the fellow trying to work out whether we were actually a church youth group or just a harmless family outing. Meanwhile we looked for a quiet place where we could have our Bible study.

On one of the tours we made a discovery that shocked us. My boy had a nose bleed which just would not stop. We took him to a hospital and eventually were told: 'This boy has haemophilia; his blood can't coagulate.'

And yet later they conscripted him for the war in Russia. I ran to see the army doctor who examined him. But a pastor who belonged to the 'Confessing Church' and was not 'standing without reserve behind our beloved Führer' did not get a hearing.

I can still see the little troop standing on the station. Destination Russia! They were just children, eighteen years old. I could have screamed when I saw my child marching away, looking so pale. What did this tender artistic soul have to do with an unjust war? He had been caught in a pitiless machine.

Then somewhere in Russia he bled to death. Abandoned and alone!

No! Not alone! In his wallet was found a bloodstained scrap of paper with the words: 'The Lord is my Shepherd; I shall not want... And though I walk in the dark valley, I fear no evil; for you are with me.'

Song in chaos: my son's last letter

My heart throbs when I think of my boy. He was almost a child still when they fetched him away to be a soldier. Somewhere near Leningrad the Russians shot him dead. What did a human life mean to the mighty ones in those days? Like a grain of wheat crushed between hard millstones — that was how the end of his life seems to me.

He was not at all suited to the hardness of war. He wanted to be a musician. His soul lived in music. And when we talked with him we often had the impression that his spirit was far away listening to some tones that we could not hear.

Shortly after Christmas of 1944 came the news that he had fallen: a cold, heartless communication full of empty verbiage! But a few days before the end he had written a letter, in which he told us how he experienced Christmas. This account shows so powerfully the rawness of the time, the loneliness of the young boy and the glory of the gospel, that I must overcome my reluctance and share it.

'Listen!' said the captain to the very young soldier. 'We are going to spend the festival here in this little Russian town. I'm sure we could arrange a nice Christmas celebration for the company, don't you think?'

'Yes, Sir!'

'I have heard that you are a musician. That's quite something! A funny sort of trade! But never mind; you are obviously the right man to take this sort of thing in hand. What do you think?'

'Yes, Sir!'

'You can do that just how you like. We have a hall with a piano. Make up a choir, practise something nice — something a bit Christmassy — you know what I mean! I am leaving it all to you. Do you understand?'

'Yes, Sir!'

The boy was overjoyed. What a lovely commission in the dreadfully monotonous existence at this base! His joy carried the dull comrades with him. Their souls, which were suffocating in the repetitive cycle of drill, unclean male conversation and alcohol, began to stir.

When Christmas Eve came the company had a simply beautiful celebration. The lovely gospel of the Son of God who became poor and lay in the crib, of the angels who sang on Bethlehem's field, and of the shepherds who heard the message with astonishment and joy, was at the centre. Even the roughest fellows became quiet and were moved. Their souls, which had been as if buried alive, seemed to be silently pressing towards the light.

The celebration finished. A deep stillness lay over the hall.

But this was suddenly interrupted by a shout from the captain. The doors flew open. Orderlies appeared, laden with *Schnapps* and wine bottles.

Christ or Hitler?

Then it was as if all the dirt and debris poured clattering over the souls again. Shrieks and howls! The first dirty joke erupted in the hall. Laughter! And then the orgy of drinking began, in which the men drowned all their sorrows, their yearnings, their homesickness…

Sadly the boy stole away. Christmas Eve. Before his mind's eye was the picture of home, his parents, his sisters. How lovely, how heavenly it would be if he could celebrate Christmas there…!

He crept away like a wounded animal between the blankets of his hard bed and went to sleep.

Grey morning light filtered into the dormitory when he awoke. The comrades were coming back. Drunk, staggering! Laughing stupidly! Dirty talk fouled the air.

The boy threw back his blankets and went out in silence. His heart was torn with homesickness. Oh how mean, how grubby, how low all this was! And this was Christmas!

Busch family about 1943, when Wilhelm's brother was leaving for the army on the Russian front where he fell a year later

Family and friends

Without much thought he went to the hall where the celebration was held. What a sight! The chairs were broken, the tables overturned. Everywhere the floor was covered with disgusting puddles of drink and vomit.

But — there was still the piano — undamaged! Not till a few days later, at the New Year celebration, did a pair of drunks throw that out of the window.

On that Christmas morning it was still standing there. The young soldier rushed towards it and...

Yes, now he held his own Christmas celebration. There sat the lonely boy in the devastated hall, where he played and sang:

> Praise be to you, Lord Jesus Christ
> That you were born as man,
> The offspring of a virgin true
> For this are angels glad.

One song after another came into his mind. How good, that all these beautiful hymns had been learned by heart at home!

> He brings you all the blessedness
> That God the Father has prepared.

At the end he pulled out his little Testament and read quietly and with full attention once again the wondrous story, as it is recounted in the second chapter of Luke's Gospel. '...See, I bring you good tidings of great joy, which shall be to all peoples; for to you is born today the Saviour... And the shepherds returned again, praising God for everything they had heard and seen, as it had been said to them.' His heart became so glad about this that now he could only worship and praise. And so he went back again to his beloved piano and sang through all the carols once more. They sounded through the cold morning — some Russian peasant may have stood still with astonishment under the window:

> See what the Lord our God has given:
> For us his only Son.
> He lifts us up from all our woe
> Into the joy of heaven.

Did it dawn on him that only a few weeks later this would happen to him:

> …from all our woe
> Into the joy of heaven?

There he sat, alone, forsaken, yet comforted in a strange land, in a bestially destroyed hall, singing the praises of the child in the crib. And suddenly he had to break off in the middle of his playing; for a great light had dawned on him. He wrote home about that:

> Is that not the situation of the assembly of Jesus Christ in all ages? In the middle of the chaos of this world she sings, joyful and free of care, the songs of praise to her Redeemer and Saviour.

Now he is no longer alone. He stands in the great congregation, which — defying the devil — sings and praises:

> Joy above all earthly joy;
> Christ has vanquished every grief.

Sometimes in my sense of loss I have turned to the verse that Paul Gerhardt wrote in the Thirty Years' War, when a child was torn away from him:

Family and friends

Oh could I but stand far away
And hear you as you speak,
When deeply moved your feelings rise
To honour God's own name,
Which holy, holy, holy is
And makes you holy too;
I know that then I'd be constrained
To pour forth tears of joy.

Yes! Christians do have consolations! And yet — the pain is still there.

I once complained secretly to a dear old friend: 'I cannot get over the fact that I have been allowed to devote my life to young men, and that my own sons were torn away from me.' He replied with the short sentence: 'If you cannot get over a fact, then you must just stay under it.'

And now my questioning look falls on the picture of old Bodelschwingh: 'Did you also have to stay under it?' Then it seems as if he nods and says, 'Yes, stay under. You know, dear brother, that the word which in our New Testament is translated "patience" is in Greek "*hypomone*" which literally means "staying under".'

But I can add this: God does not just take away, he also gives. He has given me three sons-in-law, and I cannot tell which is dearest to me. And one is even a musician — and not a coffee house violinist, either.

The fellowship

My father once gave me, when grown up, the following advice: 'Always keep together with the "quiet in the land". That's where you'll find strength and support. You know, some like to find fault with the fellowship people. The world is glad when it can find faults in believing Christians, but don't let any of that put you off. Where the Cross and Jesus are honoured and served, you must think: "This is my place! I want to keep close to them."

Father often advised both young and older theologians: 'You must learn more and more to go through thick and thin with God's people.'

He not only gave this advice, but followed it himself. He sought fellowship with the 'Brothers'. He was always there at the great fellowship conferences.

Once when he was talking about an evangelistic campaign he said, 'I don't go up to preach until I've gathered some brothers for fellowship in prayer.' Father also had a small fellowship circle in his own congregation in Frankfurt. Sometimes not many were there; the sexton and the dignified bank manager Bansa, a few old ladies and a teacher, two or three labourers and the guests and family from the vicarage. They sang, read God's Word and talked about it, and here at times my father gained strength for his arduous service.

Father sought and nurtured such fellowship everywhere. He specially loved the Swabian mountains where his wife came from. Every year he went on holiday there with the whole family, and we enjoyed not only the glorious countryside, but also the delightful fellowship with the brothers. One who was there gave this account:

Today is the monthly meeting in Württingen! Early in the morning a cart pulls up, and in a moment every seat is taken: the whole family, great and small, some men and women who want to come too, a few aunts and uncles, if they can arrange to be free. And now the delightful drive into the laughing summer's day takes us through the green wood down the steep slope, through the neat little town of Urach, up again onto the white country road. Slowly the road begins to rise. 'That'll be too much for the horses,' says Father and gets out, along with everyone else that can walk. Then off the road and uphill we go through glorious forest tracks. The birds sing, and the sky above is radiant. How lovely is the wide, wide world! At the top we meet the cart again, and on we go at a merry trot. Now there is hearty singing, and soon Württingen comes into view.

There they stand ready at the entrance to the village, those who are eagerly expecting us: Farmer So-and-so, little Dor, Widow R and whatever they are all called. 'Come with us!' is the call from all sides, and with so much hospitality it is a problem to know where to go. Then the company is divided up: 'You go here, you there and you to those,' and so on, and full of joy the hosts return with their guests to their homes, where the good noodle soup is steaming on the table in the low-ceiling living room. Other dear guests are already sitting there, who have come from Reutlingen, from Holzelfingen and from all other '–ingens' and all directions of the compass.

It is one o'clock. The sun is beating down, but in the church it is nice and cool. Here they all come together now. Soon every place is taken by the women below and the men above, and at the front the leading brothers sitting on chairs on the altar steps. The two hours fly by, because each one speaks briefly and grippingly in his own dialect. Those are not empty words; they are speaking about the realities of our faith. Often then they sing from the heart:

Christ or Hitler?

Hallelujah, Oh the heights,
Oh the depths of richest grace,
This we see within the heart
Of Him who loved us so…

I particularly remember one of these monthly meetings. After days of rain this Saturday had begun with brilliant sunshine. That was a strong temptation for many of the farming brothers to gather the hay rather than go to the monthly meeting. Yet their spiritual longings and the love to their brothers exerted a stronger pull, so that they came together.

But when the meeting began, some distractedness was evident. In spirit the farmers were with their hay. So the leader, an old farmer, stood up and said smiling, 'O brothers! Just put your hay heaps away to make room for the Saviour!'

They laughed, realizing that they had been found out, and they 'put their hay heaps away.' It was a blessed meeting; and the following week saw such radiant sunshine that all their worries about the harvest were blown away.

9.

Christ or Hitler?

Encounters with the Gestapo

The guilt of my generation

Have you heard of Rolf Hochhuth? He wrote a play called *The Representative*, referring to the pope's claim to be God's representative on earth. The play is about the way that the church kept quiet when the Jews were transported to Auschwitz before their very eyes. It ends gruesomely at the incinerating ovens, whose fires flicker throughout the last act.

In many towns the Catholic Church demonstrated vigorously against the performance of this play. I most deeply regret that. It must have been the less intelligent Catholics who objected, because it's quite obvious what Hochhuth wants to say: it was not just the pope, but your churches that kept quiet when the Jews were taken away to the ovens before your eyes. As one who lived through that time I can only say that this charge against us is justified. I think it would have been much better if the churches, instead of demonstrating against the play, had said, 'Yes, we failed terribly.'

Christ or Hitler?

If I myself had spoken out then, as today I know I should have done, I wouldn't be standing here now; I would have been condemned to death in Plötzensee. And if someone of my generation tells you, 'I knew nothing; I'm completely innocent,' then don't believe him. Ours is a guilty generation.

I belong to the church that shares in this guilt. At that time the thing that concerned us most was trying to rescue our own little projects. And in the turmoil of those days we didn't know how to do it. In fact we did hide and rescue Jews here and there — and the pope did that as well.

To show you how difficult that was, here is a little example. A doctor from my home town of Essen wanted to flee to America via Switzerland. There was disagreement with the escape centres about whether he should take his assets with him. They didn't want to let him enter Switzerland without money. I happened to be in Switzerland at the time, and — from the public telephone booth in the Zurich railway station — I phoned the escape centre that piloted out Jewish people. I said they must get Dr H from Essen out even if he wasn't able to take his money, as he was in great danger.

They successfully got him out. But six months later the Gestapo placed this conversation, which I had made in Zurich from a public call box, word for word in front of me. So they were tapping telephone calls from Switzerland.

It was a difficult time! Here and there we said and did things to help the victims. But I want to say this quite clearly and openly. We didn't cry out, as we should have cried out, 'This is genocide!', and that makes us guilty. Do you understand? How a person of my generation can live without the forgiveness of sins is a mystery to me.

Christ or Hitler? Encounters with the Gestapo

The influence of the Gestapo

It's hard to imagine now what that was like, the Gestapo, meaning secret state police. That's the remarkable thing about totalitarian states: the normal machinery of justice using police, courts and prison is not enough any more, so that a second structure develops — secret state police, Gestapo prison, concentration camps. This state police was a giant organization, which monitored the whole of life in Germany.

We often asked ourselves whether the Gestapo were omniscient or not? They liked to spread the aura of 'We know all.' They knew a lot. If I spoke a sentence without careful thought, then that could be reported to the state police. At that time we learned the so-called 'German look'. When people spoke, they looked round to see if anybody was listening. Yes, the Gestapo knew a lot. They had created so much mistrust that when two were talking together each could never be sure whether the other wouldn't report some silly sentence. So everyone hid his real thoughts and only said things that the state police were allowed to know. The people became a nation of hypocrites. That produced gruesome complexes and warped mentalities, and gave my generation soul-wounds that are still not healed.

We had extraordinary experiences with the state police. One Sunday pastors in the Confessing Church were going to read out a declaration from the pulpits against euthanasia, that is, the idea of killing mentally weak and epileptic people. The declaration was also to be distributed to the congregations in leaflet form.

The state police got wind of it. On Saturday came two gentlemen; they always came in pairs. One was the companion, who stayed standing at the door, and the other sat down on a chair in my study. There on the table were the leaflets, a great stack of them.

The officer laid his arm on the stack and asked: 'Have you got the leaflets?'

I said, 'I'm not obliged to give you any information as to that.'

'Then I must do a search of the house.'

I said, 'I can't stop you. Have a search. Here are big bookcases, each one of them could have leaflets behind it. I can't stop you.'

The man stood up, went furiously through the whole house, then sat down again on the chair, laid his arm on the stack of leaflets and said, 'There don't seem to be any.'

I would like to believe that he was a friendly man, who didn't want to see anything; but I knew the fellow. If he had found the leaflets, he would have taken them with him. That was the uncanny thing. When the people started the fight against us, they were starting a fight with the living Lord. We read in the Bible that people had 'their eyes restrained' (Luke 24:16). Surely that man's eyes were restrained. He simply didn't see what was there under his arm. But it didn't always go so well!

God's Word as a weapon

I often asked myself: 'Why do they hate us and persecute us so terribly?' They hated it when a clear biblical message was being proclaimed. For it became more and more evident to us that every word of the Bible stood in contradiction to all that those people believed. My brother Johannes was once arrested and expelled from Stuttgart after he had held a lecture about Jesus. They had nothing against that, until the lecture closed with the words: 'My confidence is in you, in you alone, and apart from you I have none.'

The state police latched on to that. Our confidence is in the Führer! And you say: I don't have confidence in any but Jesus? Unheard of! That was a blow right at the central teaching of the Third Reich, and of every totalitarian state.

I once spoke in a huge hall in Wuppertal together with the old pastor Niemöller, the father of Martin Niemöller. Shortly before the beginning the state police came and said,

'Niemöller, you are not allowed to speak, that's been forbidden from Berlin. Pastor Busch is allowed to speak, but not you. The only thing that you are allowed to do is read from the Bible.'

'Good,' says old Niemöller in his deep voice. 'First we'll sing, then we'll pray, then I'll go to the front.'

'Here is a word from Psalm 73.' I can still hear his voice today:

> For I was envious of the boastful when I saw the prosperity of the ungodly... They stand fast like a palace, therefore their defiance must be regarded as a precious thing and their wrongdoing must be called well done. They boast themselves like a fat paunch, they do whatever they think. They regard everything as nothing and talk evil about it and slander with a high mien. What they talk must have been spoken from heaven; what they say, that has to count on earth. Therefore the masses run to them, they run to them in heaps like water.

At this the two state policemen began to rummage in their briefcases, for they had a Bible in there and of course they had to check. They looked over Niemöller's shoulder. Does it say that in the Bible? 'Therefore the masses run towards them.' Then they found the place: it actually does say that in the Bible.

Then it became still, deathly silent, while Niemöller continued:

> Until I went into the sanctuary and considered their end.
> How do they suddenly become nothing! Like a dream when
> one awakes, so you, Lord, make their picture to be mocked
> in the street.

At this even the state policemen shuddered. 'If they're right then
we're lost!' You understand: they had no problem with a general
'field, wood, and meadow Christianity.' They had nothing against
that; they even supported it. The Führer said in his talks: 'May the
Highest bless us and Providence be with us.'

But the Bible speaks of the fact that we are lost sinners before
God. The Führer, a sinner? The Aryan man, a sinner under God's
judgement? No salvation except in Jesus? This they could not stand.

Faith and authority in the factory yard

When my friend Hennes gives you a handshake, you know what
you are getting, both in the handshake and in the man himself.

Hennes sometimes says with emphasis, 'I am only a simple worker.'
But I really wish that all the 'educated' people had the vision and
the inner freedom that Hennes has.

'Hennes' is an abbreviation for Johannes (or, John in English) —
the Rhenish abbreviation! And he is a real cheerful Rhinelander,
too.

I feel very close to him. He comes into my vestry every Sunday
morning before the service, along with a few other men. Then we
call on our heavenly Father to make his Word mighty in the service.

In the year 1934, Germanic religious ideas were sprouting everywhere like grass after rain. Professors, *Gauleiters*, Hitler Youth leaders, all were competing with each other to present their abstruse notions as Nordic religion. The poor people just waited to see which of the many directions would be chosen by the Führer. Only one thing was clear: biblical Christianity was dismissed!

One day Hennes was standing talking with a great crowd of workers in the Krupp factory yard during a break. Soon the talk turned to religion.

One of the other workers took himself very seriously. He spoke great words, and then he poured out his scorn on Hennes for still going to church. He was sure that would soon finish.

Hennes answered as best he could. The discussion quickly became heated. More and more workers started to crowd around the two.

Then Hennes said, 'I have the impression that we are talking past each other. Now let each of us declare just what he actually believes, so that it's clear where we stand. I'll start, and then you say what you believe.'

And then Hennes began loud and clear: 'I believe in God the Father Almighty, Maker of heaven and earth. And in Jesus Christ, his only Son our Lord...'

Suddenly everyone was quiet. In the church — yes, this *Apostles' Creed* had often been spoken there... But here in the factory yard? Among rough men in working clothes?

Hennes left nothing out: '...the forgiveness of sins, the resurrection of the body and the life everlasting. Amen! — So, that is my confession of faith. And now it's your turn. Tell us what you believe!'

Christ or Hitler?

The other began to stutter: 'Listen, … pay attention!…'

But now Hennes was ice cold. 'Never mind "Pay attention!" You are to tell us what you believe.'

Again the other man began to stutter: 'So, regarding Christianity — that is after all — that doesn't work…'

Hennes was relentless: 'You are not to tell us what is wrong with Christianity. We already know that you are against us. You are to tell us quite positively what you *do* believe. Come on, get on with it!'

With bated breath the people round them listened to the battle of words. Then came encouraging voices. 'Come on, Karl! Just say it!' He stood there with a bright red face. At last it came out of him: 'What I believe? What I believe? Well, that hasn't quite come out yet! They're still working on that in Berlin!'

Laughter erupted. And into the noise and guffaws the poor man cried out angrily: 'But when it's out, then I'll believe it. You can rely on that!'

No one doubted him any more…

I have often thought that we should do it more like Hennes. We should ask the opponents of the gospel about their own belief. Then we'd soon see that most of them are big on negatives, but when it comes to producing something positive they are very, very poor.

O Hennes! I would give you a chair in practical theology!

State power and youth work

I soon came into conflict with the Gestapo because I was youth pastor in Essen. I had a big club house for hundreds of young people aged between fourteen and twenty. On Sunday afternoons there were 700-800 young men under God's Word. There was also a big programme of other activities, but everyone quickly became aware of my conviction that a life without Jesus is not life but death. And that of course was annoying to the authorities — a work like that! If a pastor had a little Mothers' Union, then the Nazis said, 'Let him get on with it; that will die out of its own accord.' But here hundreds of young men were gathering. To them that was a bad thing.

In the first year the state police had not been fully developed. At that time the Nazis didn't know exactly how far they could go in infringing people's rights and how far the people would tolerate the government operating 'a little outside the law.' But even before we had anything to do with the Gestapo there were dangerous frictions between my work and the party. Where did these come from? They came from the fundamental question of that time: who really has jurisdiction over our conscience? The young men who came into my Youth Centre had learned that our conscience must be tied to God's Word. Luther had said at the Diet of Worms, 'My conscience is captive to God's Word.'

We all have a conscience. We know that there is good and evil. But who decides what is good and what is evil? Who has authority over your conscience — perhaps in sexual matters or in dealing with money or with truth and lying? Is it public opinion? Your colleagues at work? Who has the say about what is good and evil? Luther said, 'My conscience is captive to God's Word.' My young people learned that 'the Lord Jesus must have authority over my conscience'.

Christ or Hitler?

Now along came the state with the Nazi party and declared: 'We say what is good and evil.' Right from the beginning there was an attack on the innermost being of the person. The party determined what was good. That inevitably produced all kinds of conflict.

For example, my young men went to church on Sunday mornings, for it is God's command, 'You shall hallow the holy day.' I said to them, 'You don't need to come to my youth group. That's not God's command. But the service of God on Sunday, that is God's command.' And so they came.

The school might arrange a march with the *Hitler Jugend* for Sunday morning at 8.00am. The young men stood up and declared: 'Sorry, we're going to church.'

'Nonsense, this is service for the Führer!'

But they stood firm: 'My conscience is tied to God's Word.' So the poor headmaster, a highly qualified teacher who didn't really know which way the whole thing was going to go, tore his thinning hair out, trying to decide in this conflict. It really struck me at the time how my young lads already grasped the principle that one must be obedient to God from the beginning.

Another example occurred at the school's country house. The senior pupils went there. The *Hitler Jugend* immediately took over its running. There was a grace before meals that went like this:

> Dear Lord Jesus, stay from us far;
> We'll gladly eat just as we are.

That was the *Hitler Jugend*'s prayer. What was one to do? Here and there young men stood up and said, 'Sorry, but we're not coming until after this prayer. We're not going to listen to this blasphemy.'

'But it's your duty to be here.'

In such small issues clashes soon developed.

So that produced the first big conflict, the question of the conscience. And the second thing that we learned in the first year under Hitler was, how unprepared we were for such a time, how helplessly we stood before the question of what really was to be done. I want to tell you something about that.

Paul Humburg's leadership

1933 was the year in which Hitler seized power. And now the dreadful movement called 'German Christians' broke into the church and the church struggle began. Paul Humburg soon stepped forward as one of the leaders of the Confessing Church. Not for love of church politics, but, as he often said, 'for Jesus' sake.' The Confessing Synod in the Rheinland chose him as their president.

It meant so much for the Confessing Church to have such a man as leader in its hard struggle. His clear stand is expressed by something he often said, 'If it does not concern the Lord Jesus, then let us leave it alone.'

Enormous burdens and responsibilities weighed down his soul. It oppressed him when members of the Confessing Church were imprisoned. He entrusted the education of young theologians into the hand of the Confessing Church. That meant putting these young men in great danger. We will never forget a theological exam that had to be interrupted because the Gestapo appeared. The exam was continued in another place. Yet again both examiner and examinees — Oh, we were all being tested! — had to flee.

Humburg had to suffer a great amount of deprivation in his life. When he once complained of this to an old Christian woman, she said to him, 'When the pastor is in the press, the congregation gets the oil from it.' We experienced that. He became a pastor and communicator of God's grace, both in preaching and in personal conversation.

My wife also experienced that once. I was in prison in Essen, with little prospect of an early release. That left my wife in great need. And the children also were receiving strange looks from their school fellows because their father was in prison.

And then one day Humburg came to visit my wife. It seemed incredible that this man, burdened in so many ways, should concern himself about an individual. He was glad to see that my wife was standing wholeheartedly behind her husband, was suffering the deprivation bravely and not complaining.

When he left, Humburg gave her a word from the Bible, a word that would not have occurred to anyone else in the circumstances. It was just the little sentence from Psalm 23: 'My cup runs over.'

My wife told me later how in that moment all the riches that we have in Christ Jesus had been given to her. And because of that the deprivation had become quite small.

I was once with Humburg at the funeral of a fellow worker, where he just said quietly, 'Brother, we did love you.' So now I want to say over his grave: 'Brother Humburg, we did love you.'

How Karl Barth helped us then

The story of my picture of Karl Barth seems improbable; but it really happened, and the whole thing was quite a bit of fun.

Christ or Hitler? Encounters with the Gestapo

This photograph of the famous theologian from Basel dates from around 1925. Someone gave it to me as a present, and I put it in a drawer in my desk. I didn't want to hang it up; for Professor Barth had spoken and written in such a conspicuous and unfriendly way about pietism that I thought my pictures of the Great Awakening preachers known for their piety, like Zinzendorf, Wesley, Hofacker, Herrnhöfer, Michael Hahn and Spurgeon, would fall off the wall if I hung their opponent Karl Barth among them.

So the picture remained in my drawer, though I have to confess that it really deserved better treatment, since Barth had had a powerful effect on me, as shown by the much used 1923 edition of his Romans in my bookcase. I had taken in Barth's main emphasis: that real theology means having God at the centre of our thinking. And I understood his suspicion about my fathers in the faith, that with them the 'pious man' is in the centre.

But I am convinced that Barth misjudged them. And that was why I put the picture in the drawer. His books however were in my bookcase and spoke to me.

And then came the time, after all, when I took out the picture of Barth, had it framed and hung it on my wall. That was when Hitler came to power and with him the great confusion about the church. From all sides we were being persuaded that this great 'emergence of the German nation' must be encouraged by the preachers in the churches.

And the state used police pressure to reinforce this encouragement. Without meaning any harm I said at the end of a sermon that a rumour was circulating to the effect that I had joined the Nazi church movement called the 'German Christians', and that this was not true! Two hours later the police president put me under house arrest. Mind you, it was comparatively harmless, because the Third Reich was still in its early stages.

Christ or Hitler?

Being under house arrest I had the opportunity to see from my window the endless mass of so-called Christians that were streaming to a Nazi-ecclesiastical demonstration on the Burgplatz in Essen. Then I asked myself: 'Am I in the right way?'

And when in 1933 the number of those who were unwilling to take part in the dangerous game of 'Germanising Christianity' got smaller and smaller, reason often said fearfully: 'You're getting extreme and putting your youth work at risk! Is that perhaps just stubbornness? Could it be that you are just incapable of understanding the greatness of the times?'

And then Karl Barth wrote a short article, *Theological Existence Today*, in which he called on us to 'preach on as if nothing had happened! You are to proclaim the great works of God, which he has done in Jesus! This message is not affected by the passing events of the time!'

That was so liberating — pointing out the direction — that suddenly I could see my way most clearly. I can well understand why the authorities drove Karl Barth out of Germany soon after that. He went back to his native Switzerland.

But he had shown us the way to go. He had pointed to the living God and his acts. From then on we could say 'No!' to all evil and unreasonable demands and pressures, and we knew that this was what we had to do.

I was deeply grateful to him, and hence decided to hang his picture on my wall.

The question was: Where?

Just then I noticed an engraving that hung almost a little ashamed in a corner: the portrait of Friedrich Schleiermacher, a professor

212

and preacher in Trinity Church in Berlin from about 1810 onwards.

I have to admit that his picture was not hanging there because he had taught me very much. On the contrary! This Romantic had brewed up a theology that mixed idealistic philosophy with some hardly recognizable remains of the pietism of the Herrnhut Moravians.

The picture was hanging there because it was an enchanting engraving. And because the head which it shows is so handsome. The long fine hair, the sensitive mouth, the narrow aquiline nose, the thoughtful eyes — all this results in a truly 'romantic' face.

So there I stood with a picture of Barth in my hand, which was so completely different, showing an aggressive, strong bright face. My eyes went to and fro between the pictures.

And then I had to laugh.

For Schleiermacher was really the exact opposite of Karl Barth. Barth's theology says that what matters is the objective, the holy God and his great works in Jesus. In Jesus he has revealed himself. In Jesus he has reconciled the world. These are the objective facts, whose truth does not depend in any way on us.

Schleiermacher taught exactly the opposite. He put it like this: 'Piety is neither knowing nor doing but a certainty of *feeling*. It is the *feeling* of total dependence.' So here everything was based on the subjective, so that the revelation of God in the cross and the resurrection of Jesus almost completely disappeared.

And now I hope that the great theologians will forgive me for trying to present such a serious theological problem here in such a simple way. Yes, may they especially forgive me for having some fun; for I decided to hang the two pictures next to each other on the wall. Then my fathers in the faith would presumably be satisfied, since their way led through the middle between the two. They were convinced that the objective salvation of Golgotha must be grasped in personal life and subjective experience. That was what they taught, and that was how they lived. That was also what I found in the New Testament and believed myself.

As I was standing on a ladder and hanging up the two pictures, I said laughing to my wife, 'I just wonder which of the two will fall from the wall first. Because I don't think they can bear being next to each other.'

And what happened? Schleiermacher fell down! One morning his picture had disappeared. It had slipped behind the wall of books. It was impossible to get it out of there except by moving each book case.

My friends, all influenced to a greater or lesser extent by Karl Barth, were very pleased with Schleiermacher's disappearance.

Not until my house was almost completely destroyed in a bombing raid in 1943, and I took the rescued library away from the rubble, did the picture of Schleiermacher come to light again.

Getting on — yes! God's Word — no!

It's terrible to see a man crying! What could reduce a real man to tears? It was sorrow about his own son; that can shake a man to the depths. But the sorrow was especially bitter because the man knew he had only himself to blame.

I first got to know this son as a little fourteen-year-old. He was coming to the Bible studies that we had arranged for boys of his age.

He loved coming. His heart was open, like freshly ploughed earth, to the good seed of God's Word. As the sunflower turns to the light, so the boy was reaching out for Jesus and his salvation.

Then came the time of the Third Reich when Bible studies became a target for the enemies of the truth. They said that it was unnatural for lively boys to gather for Bible studies. And the boys who still came were mocked and laughed at, or even threatened. The boys bore that bravely; they knew that they had to reckon with conflict for the sake of Jesus and the truth.

But many parents became fearful, including the father of our young friend. He maintained that 'you can be a Christian anyway without that.'

'No,' we said to him, 'there is no Christianity without fellowship under God's Word.'

'Yes, but what if my boy becomes conspicuous that way, if people think he is backward or stupid? And he's got to get on! He must get on whatever happens. You have to trim the sail according to the wind.'

'My dear sir,' the leader of our youth group said to him, 'of course we want your boy to get on! And he will; he is a capable fellow. But if you stop him coming to the Bible study, you will take away his anchor...'

'So what? He must have the anchor inside him.'

'No, you are mistaken. We have no anchor in ourselves. Only when a boy knows the Lord Jesus does he have an anchor.'

But the father insisted, and he got his way. He succeeded in persuading his own son to keep away from the Bible studies. The others who still came kept inviting him, but they didn't know what had happened. They were sad that their friend didn't come any more and were at a loss to explain why.

The result was that the boy avoided his old friends and kept out of their way as much as he could. It was not long before he found new friends, for whom the boys' Bible study had long been a source of annoyance.

They were overjoyed to see one of the pious boys now coming over to them. 'We'll teach him the way!' was the word. And they did teach him the way. The father noticed it the first time on Good Friday, when the whole family was about to go to church.

'I'm not going!' the boy declared cheekily.

'You're not? Why ever not?' asked the astonished father.

'Oh, that's all rubbish!' the boy blurted out.

'We have to be patient,' thought the man and left the boy at home. But a few days later the mother complained: 'Our boy is getting so rude. I can't tell him anything any more. He immediately contradicts me.'

The father was staggered. His son? He had always been so proud of his obedient son. So straight away he gave him a good talking to. But the boy rebelled. The father was furious and gave the rascal a strong clip round the ear.

From then on the relationship between father and son was broken. It would take too long to tell the full tale of woes that followed. The boy just did as he liked. He would come home late, he smoke endlessly, sit in the cinema evening after evening, and so on…

No punishment and no warning helped; it just made things worse. And one day came the crunch. The boss to whom the boy was apprenticed turned up, and a really bad story came to light.

That was when the man sat before me with tears flowing from his eyes. Of course, getting on — yes, yes, yes! But hearing God's Word — no way! The price had been too high for him.

It comes down to this, that nothing else helps if we neglect the most important thing: bringing our young people to Jesus. For 'What shall it profit a man, if he gains the whole world and loses his own soul?' (Mark 8:36).

Conflict with the Hitler Youth

Soon after Hitler came to power the Hitler Youth began to fight against all other youth organizations. The state could of course have forbidden all the others and commanded all young people to join the Hitler Youth. But the leaders had the optimistic idea that young people would voluntarily leave their organizations and come in droves to join the *Hitler Jugend*. They were disappointed when that didn't happen! So then they began to exert first a gentle and then an increasingly persistent pressure.

That worked. One after another the youth organizations closed. Some voluntarily affiliated themselves to the Hitler Youth. Others were dissolved. Some small idealist groups went underground and then slowly died off for lack of new members.

The Hitler Youth sent its spies into all the youth hostels and along all the ramblers' paths. Woe to the young people who were suspected of perpetuating disbanded organizations!

Christ or Hitler?

By the end of 1933 only the denominational organizations remained determined and intact on the battlefield. They refused to agree to voluntary dissolution.

At the beginning of 1934 the pressure increased. The work at the Youth Centre grew all the more. Many of the young people from the disbanded clubs came to us, and spiritual life flourished as seldom before. It was particularly those boys who had newly joined us that came to realize how true freedom comes from the gospel.

Now we were forbidden to go on any rambles. We responded by arranging 'Missionary festivals', to which of course we had to walk, as we had no money for the train.

The distinctive ramble shirts were forbidden, so the boys dressed in mufti. Sheath knives were banned. The Hitler Youth spies even searched our boys for penknives. Sport was forbidden. Soon there seemed to be nothing that was not forbidden.

But it was like with the people of Israel in Egypt: 'The more they oppressed them, the more they multiplied and spread' (Exodus 1:12).

Meanwhile Hitler's favourite, Pastor Ludwig Müller, had been appointed Bishop for the Reich. And I had become youth pastor for the whole Synod of Essen.

One day the newspapers had front-page headlines over the story that the Reich Bishop Müller had affiliated the evangelical youth to the Hitler Youth. We sent him a telegram in which we said very clearly that he had acted without any right to do so and that we could not be bound by his agreement.

In response to that I was relieved of my post. But the youth work went on. We said, 'The Bishop has sold something which doesn't belong to him at all.' The next step followed logically: the Hitler Youth began to use force. As was usual in the Third Reich, the police received instructions not to intervene under any circumstances. Thus we were outlawed and deprived of all right to protection.

When our boys kept being attacked and beaten up on the streets, we resorted to self defence. We applied for permission for a demonstration to be held at the Essen water tower. It was clear to everyone that this was provoking a battle.

We received permission. When the demonstration was finished, hordes of Hitler Youth fellows in civvies fell on us. They had dressed in civvies instead of their uniforms so that the whole thing could be described as a 'spontaneous eruption of the wrath of the people'. We had reckoned with all this. I had fifty strong young fellows ready, who now waded in. The Hitler Youth were flabbergasted at coming across resistance. They fled and called the police. These appeared after all, as things had not gone as expected. The police officer said to me in threatening tones: 'You are putting up resistance against the State Youth!'

I answered him: 'No! I see no uniforms of the Hitler Youth! So I must assume that anti-social groups have attacked us. We gave them a good thrashing!'

Nothing further came of the matter. I got a bad comment in my file. And the Hitler Youth had learned their lesson.

I will never understand why the state did not then simply prohibit our organizations. I suppose they still wanted to uphold the myth that the young had voluntarily 'come streaming in to join the Hitler Youth.'

A second battle proved to be decisive. The Hitler Youth had used two dark nights to take over and occupy two Catholic youth hostels. A law suit was started to recover the properties, but that never reached a conclusion. No judge would dare to pronounce a decision against the Hitler Youth.

It was clear to us that our beautiful clubhouse, the Youth Centre, was next in line.

So we formed a watch of a hundred young men who took it in turns to spend the night in the Youth Centre. I turned a blind eye when I noticed these lads equipping themselves with rubber tubes, knuckledusters and clubs.

And then one night it all began. The alarm bell rang in my house which was nearby; a special line had been installed. I was sorry for my poor wife, who had just brought our youngest child into the world. I had not taken her to hospital, so it turned out to be an exciting birth. Immediately I rang the police and reported: 'Some bands want to attack our Youth Centre!'

For a long time no one responded. Then a police officer whom I knew asked me to come to the nearby station and told me that he had orders that if the Hitler Youth attacked, the police were to act as if they noticed nothing.

'So you will not intervene in any circumstances?' I asked.

'I'm afraid we are not allowed to! You must understand that, Pastor.'

'All right! I'll go with that!' I replied to the man's astonishment. And then I ran to the Youth Centre. Hundreds of young fellows had gathered all round the house. I could not get in any more. So I could only watch as the hordes suddenly rushed in with a roar — and then the gates of the house flew open and fifty of my men stormed out with grim determination.

The attackers were shocked. This was not part of the plan. And then a great fight began. Fleeing Hitler Youth fellows ran to the nearby railway station. When the people there realized what was going on, they joined in. People we didn't know at all took pleasure in being able to express their resentment against all the Nazi oppression.

It was total victory. By the time the police finally appeared the battle was over.

The next morning I reported to the police superintendent, the very upright and favourably disposed SS leader Zech.

'Superintendent,' I began, 'you must now make it clear whether we are living under the rule of law or in the Wild West. If you are not prepared to defend citizens, then we have to defend ourselves as in the Wild West.'

'I don't quite understand,' he stammered. Obviously he had not heard about the whole thing. Just then there was a knock at the door and an official brought in a report of the night's events. For a long time he read it in silence. My heart was beating. 'Is he going to arrest me now, on the spot?' I asked myself.

Suddenly he laughed out loud: 'Why, that's wonderful!' he called out. 'And these Hitler Youths let themselves be beaten up by your lads? That serves them right!'

He gave me a guarantee that the police would from now on protect us, but requested that I would please disarm my troops.

The man kept his word as long as he was our police superintendent. Later he was pushed off to an insignificant post elsewhere. I suppose he was too just and honest to prosper in that system.

Christ or Hitler?

In the spring of 1934 our organizations were at last dissolved by the state. For some time the Youth Centre was sealed by the police. Later we were able to gather the young people again for Bible studies and mission events. The work went on till the bitter end of the Third Reich.

That was a bad time, when the Youth Centre was locked and sealed. Where formerly hundreds of young lads had filled the house with life on Sundays, now there was deadly silence. Yet there were still gatherings in private homes. In a worker's flat the living room was cleared out every week so that the youth hour could take place under the section leader. And none of the many residents reported it.

Meanwhile a Nazi movement had spread far and wide in the church, the so-called 'German Christians'. Because my young people were suddenly left without leadership some of them began to sabotage the meetings of the 'German Christians'.

A troop of fifty young fellows suddenly appeared during a big meeting. The speaker, a decent, unsuspecting citizen, spoke about what a gift from God Hitler was. The lads heckled him. The speaker became nervous. Then the chairman of the meeting intervened and called: 'The young people should not be hanging around at the back. If they've got what it takes, let them come to the front.'

At that the fifty came to the front, and the tumult really began in earnest. The chairman shouted in desperation: 'If our beloved Führer knew about this!'

Then one of the lads said loudly: 'The Führer said we are to take the revolution into the church!'

'But he didn't mean it like that!' called the poor, tormented chairman.

The boys laughed and retorted: 'We can't help it if the gun backfires!' The gathering dissolved in tumult and laughter.

We found another way

At that time a book called *French Protestantism* by Joseph Chambon was published by the Christian Kaiser Verlag, of Munich. The Nazis allowed the publication of this book; they probably regarded it as a harmless piece of historical writing. They only got worried when they discovered that the book sold out soon and a new edition was required.

The Nazis never grasped why it meant so much to us. Chambon described how the French Protestants (Huguenots) were persecuted dreadfully and yet survived. Cunning and force were used to try to exterminate them. And in the process the Huguenots went through all the ways in which persecuted Christians can respond to a hostile state. They suffered, and they used force. They emigrated, and they also banded together.

Here was a primer for us who were living in conflict with a state that challenged our freedom of belief. No wonder that so many young people bought the book.

For a few weeks I met with my young fellow workers, who were trying hard to gather and care for the young people whose associations had been disbanded. As we spent these hours together we felt as if we were on trial. We studied this book, and it dawned on us that we were on the wrong path when we tried to force the state to do right. Christians should not take up the weapons used by the opponent. This became especially clear to me from the case of Coligny.

Christartml...

Christ or Hitler?

And now I must speak of this brave Admiral. We are in the second half of the sixteenth century. Chambon writes:

> The first occasion of the eight consecutive wars of religion that depopulated and desolated France was the bloodbath at Vassy which the Catholic Duke of Guise instigated among the Huguenot congregations. Then came the slaughter among the evangelicals in Sens. The Protestants' answer was the victorious attacks on Rouen and Lyon. In this they departed from the Christian terrain of victory. They gave up the only Christian weapons: confession and readiness to suffer. They descended to a terrain on which in the long run their opponents would be surer than they. They took the sword by which they would perish.

How did this descent to the level of worldly thinking and acting take place?

Calvin had previously written to Admiral Coligny these famous words: 'The first drop of blood that our people shed will call forth streams of blood that will flood the whole of Europe.'

The Protestant nobility, however, held that they were called to oppose the Catholic party with force of arms. If only these Huguenots, who followed the Calvinistic direction of the Reformation, had considered what Calvin wrote in his famous *Institutes*: '...our hands ... are not charged with any duty but to obey and to suffer'!

This book had a decisive effect on my young fellow workers and on me as well. We began to read the Bible with new eyes. What new meaning we saw in the word from Revelation 12:11:

'And they overcame him by the blood of the Lamb and by the word of their testimony, and they did not love their lives, even to death.'

You may find it ridiculous for us to compare our much smaller struggles with the sufferings of the Huguenots. But with Christians it is always a matter of the fundamental attitude. And so we learned from Chambon's book that our way had to be a new one, in the footsteps of the 'Lamb that was slain': testimony, readiness to suffer and waiting on God to act.

So we, too, took the decision at that time that we would not defend ourselves any more. We would also be prepared to go to prison. But we would make the utmost use of such rights as we had.

In this way surprising and delightful things happened, of which I want to give you one example. It was not clear at the time whether we were allowed to have Bible camps or not. The Nazis had forbidden almost everything to the evangelical young people. Our boys were not allowed to wear uniform, not allowed to have a shoulder strap or pedometer, they were not allowed to engage in any sport or to swim. They even investigated among other things whether we had swimming trunks on us. Almost everything was banned. And we asked: so what is there that's still allowed? Holidays were not yet forbidden.

A camp that had to disband — in fourteen days

Of course we took care not to be too open about it. So I sent off two men, and they found a lonely mountain 1000 metres high in the *Fichtelgebirge*. There we could put up a few tents for fifty sixth formers. When we arrived, we heard that there was a big Hitler Youth camp nearby. That was embarrassing, because they always made it a matter of honour to cause trouble, and the police were too scared to intervene. So we took our tents down and stayed in a little barn.

Christ or Hitler?

In this remote place there was a mountain hut, a guesthouse where the landlord was an old Nazi from before the time they came to power. He had been hit on the head by a beer mug in a pub fight, which had probably destroyed some brain cells. So he wasn't 'all there' anymore. Still, he was a terrific chap, an original Bavarian, and we became great friends. 'Wilhelm Busch,' he said, 'if anybody wants to do something to you — I am an old fighter!'

Yes, somebody did do something to us. One day a boy came rushing up pale with shock and said, 'A gendarme is there; you are to come over to the guesthouse immediately.' Naturally my first instruction was: 'There's to be a prayer meeting during the time I go over.' And while my high school boys knelt behind the barn in the grass and talked with Jesus, I went to the guesthouse.

The gendarme, who had toiled up from the valley on foot, was waiting. I ordered a coffee and a bilberry pancake for each of us. Then I asked him: 'What's on your mind?'

He pulled out a letter from the Gestapo:

> The camp is immediately to be dissolved. Pastor Busch is to report tomorrow morning early at the land council office in Wunsiedel.

I turned pale. I went back to my young people. 'Have you prayed?'

'Yes, we're counting on the Lord hearing us.'

The next morning I started off down into the valley. As I was going, suddenly the landlord, my old fighter, was standing there with his chamois hair on his hat, and he said, 'I'm going with you. While you're with the authorities I'll go into the surrounding pubs where all the old fighters are sitting and tell them what's going on.'

'That's great! So you'll do the murmuring of the people in the background!'

And then we both walked down to a train station where there also was a guesthouse. We asked where we could buy tickets. The woman was in the laundry and called out, 'They're in the kitchen cupboard. That's where the money bowl is. Put the money in, the tickets are lying next to it.' So we bought ourselves tickets and travelled on a little train to Wunsiedel. Then we separated, and he went to look for the old fighters and drum up support.

At that time things were still very much in flux. Suddenly I was facing, not the Gestapo, but a young land councillor, a Prussian, who had ended up in this little Bavarian town.

He went for me: 'How dare you hold a camp?'

'That is not forbidden.'

'But in Bavaria it is forbidden!'

'We're a German Reich. You can't blow your own tunes in Bavaria. In any case you're obviously not a Bavarian.'

'I am not discussing things with you! Orders from Munich. The camp is immediately to be dissolved.'

'All right,' I said, 'but may I just explain something. We came with a coach and we're going back by coach. The coach has already been paid for. It's coming in two weeks. How I am to get these boys home now is a puzzle to me. I have neither money nor means to dissolve the camp. I'll send you down the fifty young lads early tomorrow morning, Councillor. God grant that you have money to pay for their journey home and means to provide for them.'

227

'Wait a minute; you just want to send them here? How is that supposed to happen?'

I said, 'They'll arrive here roaring with hunger; perhaps they'll even sing you some of our hymns. They'll get you moving all right.'

He replied: 'You can't do that!'

'Of course I won't do that. Who said I would? You did.'

'I did? Then I'll have to ask again in Munich.'

So I was not to do anything, I was to await further orders. I picked up my old fighter again and we went back to the camp. The way my sixth formers received me, full of joy that we had won the day, was glorious. The next morning we had a Bible study again under the pine trees. The sun was shining, we were a thousand metres up, and each day was a gift. Here we heard the Word of the Son of God, who saves sinners. In such surroundings the Word of God has a new glory.

That day nothing happened. We had another morning with a glorious Bible study, but then someone came rushing up: we were to come, the gendarme is there. So again I ordered bilberry pancake and coffee. But inwardly I cried to God: 'Help me not to lose my nerve!' because I was in a very lonely position of responsibility.

The gendarme pulled out a letter which said, 'The order remains that the camp is to be dissolved, but you are receiving fourteen days to break up the camp. If after that another boy is seen…'

We happily made our camp, put the tents up, pulled out a tent post again each day and did that for fourteen days.

But the most beautiful thing was that the gendarme said, 'Now I'm happy for you, that it has worked out this way.'

I asked him: 'Does that matter to you, what a Protestant pastor does? I assume you're Catholic?'

'I'd very much like to talk to you.'

'Oh,' I said, 'would you like another pancake?'

Then he started off. He was shattered. He said, 'I recently took part in a Protestant funeral. They sang a song there, which has these words at the end of each verse:

My God, my God, I pray you through Christ's blood,
Whatever happens, let my end be good!

'Pastor Busch, you know when all's said and done, we all have to die some time. That's going constantly through my head as I walk: My God, I pray you through Christ's blood, whatever happens, let my end be good. But I don't understand it. What has the blood of Jesus got to do with it?'

Then I said to him, 'You die, and then you go to God. Either you take all your sins with you, including the ones you've denied doing — and then it's dreadful to fall into the hands of the living God — or you find your way to Jesus, who has authority to say to us: "Your sins are forgiven." He can say that because he paid for us on the cross. I belong to this Jesus.' And then we talked together.

But it ended even better. After five days a boy came running and said, 'The gendarme is there again with a high ranking Hitler Youth leader.'

'Oh,' we said, 'now the Hitler Youth are at it again. The old story.' I was called, went across, bilberry pancakes, Hitler Youth leader, 'Heil Hitler' and so on. And then I almost fell off my chair, when the gendarme said, 'This is my son. He is a high ranking Hitler Youth leader and now has more power than I do. He has also become quite ungodly. Because of that, things aren't working at home any more. He has become so rude to his mother. At home I should still have the say. But that isn't working any more either. So I said to him: "My boy, up there on the mountain is a pastor who will tell us how things can come back into order. We're going to go there." Pastor Busch, you tell him yourself, what you told me about Jesus!'

So, nothing about dissolving the camp! It struck me then, what I kept noticing with the state police: whatever rank a man has, whatever he makes himself out to be, he has a troubled heart that is crying out for peace. There is so much dirt and guilt there — but 'How can I get free, how can I come into the light?' Here is a heart that's crying for Jesus. I learned that over and over again. I learned not to believe people's 'scrambled egg' and their stiff caps and all the other things they use to make themselves important. They wear medals and dress coats, constantly something new that men invent so as to look like birds of paradise. I don't believe in any of that; I believe that the man of today, exactly like the man of two thousand years ago, is a poor man, whose most urgent need is the Saviour, the Son of God who can give him peace with God.

So I said, 'My boy, isn't it working out at home?'

'No.'

'Are you the way you should be?'

'No.'

I addressed him using the familiar '*Du*' for 'you.' I said, 'You need a new life.'

'I do. But how does that happen?'

And then I told him for an hour about Jesus. I called my lads in. Then we sang songs to them.

'Ha,' said the young Hitler Youth leader, 'if only we had something like this here.'

Poor dog that I was up there, hunted and without rights, I became really happy through the gospel!

Secret ways to the pulpit

But after that things became serious. In the first year everything was being built up, and the state police was getting established. Then came the time when we didn't discuss any more, and we couldn't slip through loopholes any more, and just for conscience' sake, without union or organization, we came together around the Word of God. And this was the time in which the strong arm of the state kept finding me and throwing me into prison. I'm going to tell you about the experience that most churned me up, my first arrest. That was in Darmstadt.

At that time we had a team holding evangelistic weeks. The team included the present Bishop Lilje, Dr Humburg who is already in eternity, Eberhard Müller, myself and five to seven other people. We arranged these weeks simultaneously in Darmstadt, Kassel and Mannheim. I spoke in the afternoons in Mannheim, in the evenings in Darmstadt and the next morning in Darmstadt, afternoons in

Kassel and so on. So we hurried through the many parts of the country, for five days.

Our subjects then would probably not tempt a dog to come out from behind the oven today. For instance, in Mannheim I spoke about 'Love and honour in the evangelical training of youth'. Today you'd ask: what's that about? At that time everybody understood that there was a conflict about the highest values: Christians say *love* is the highest, but the Nazis say that *honour* is the highest value. 'Those feeble Christians?' they said. 'For them the highest value is what they call love — the love of God in Jesus, the love which they give to others. Yet love is a weakly matter. The highest value in life must be honour.'

Every thinking person was faced with the question: 'What actually is the highest value in life?' At that time this was a tremendously vital discussion. There wasn't the sluggishness that smothers all spiritual life today.

Entrance to each lecture cost two marks. The huge Christchurch in Mannheim was packed full with three thousand people. Those were conflicts, real spiritual battles in which we were always playing with our lives, because the authorities could say to every sentence: 'You have attacked the official philosophy of the party.'

I had spoken in Mannheim and towards the evening I reached Darmstadt. A friend met me by car and said, 'My dear Wilhelm, Paul's Church in Darmstadt is full, but the Gestapo have manned all the doors in order to arrest you and stop you from talking. I'll drop you in a quiet side street. You'll have to see yourself how you get in. I'll wait in the side street for you.' Then he dropped me off and said, 'I'll stay here in case you have to beat it. Now you see how you can get further.'

I went along the street and came to a large empty square. There was the great Paul's Church. A tremendous lot of people, great excitement, and in the doorways, which were illuminated, stood the state police. You could recognize them already by their faces: a mixture of bourgeois, bulldog and uniformed policeman. They were checking everybody who still wanted to go in. This was clear: I wouldn't get in there. But I wanted to give my sermon.

I looked at the surroundings. Next to the church were some railings. Behind them was a quiet court. At the other end of the court was the vicarage. The entrance to the vicarage lay in a side street. So when I looked at the surroundings from the viewpoint of an old officer from the First World War I realized that the only possibility to get in there was through the court, because that was not being watched. But I could only come into the court from the vicarage. I went round the corner; the vicarage was dark, but the door stood open. Was that just a trap? Were they standing inside and waiting for me to come? Or had the vicar wanted to open the door for me? I stood desperately alone in front of the open door. Should I go through or not?

They say that the man of today is very lonely, but I have seldom experienced such loneliness as I did then. Completely exposed! No one could make this decision for me. But I can testify that at that moment in which I felt this loneliness it seemed as if I could grasp and feel that HE, the Lord, was next to me. Jesus has said in agreement with this: 'I am with you always till the end of the world.' I became so happy that I can't describe it to you. HE has redeemed me, HE has paid with his blood, HE is alive, HE is with me. I am on the victor's side.

I went into the dark vicarage. Suddenly an arm grabbed me and someone whispered: 'Come with me!' Was this the Gestapo? I was led down the cellar stairs, through several cellars, until I noticed that I was now in the cellar that had the boiler for heating the church. That was clearly under the court. But everything was totally dark. The man who was leading me switched on the torch, pointed to a small spiral stair and said, 'Go up!' I went up, and suddenly I was in the church. It was packed full!

I threw my raincoat to the first available person. From the pulpit they never fetched anybody down. My subject was: 'Jesus Christ, the Lord.' Since I had entered the vicarage a great calm had come over me. There stood the uniformed police who wanted to take me, and I stood above and could only say, 'Let's do away with all unrest. We now want to talk about the most glorious Person that there is, the one who came to us from the eternal world, whose name is Jesus.'

Loudspeakers were installed outside because it was clear that the church was not big enough. The state police now had a great hassle to cut through the loudspeaker cables, so that the people outside wouldn't hear the 'dreadful' message. And then I spoke for a whole hour. God gave me great joy because I could simply show them what it means, that the Man of Golgotha pours streams of forgiveness and grace into my life, and that I can live with the risen One. That is something wonderful!

'Stop! You are under arrest!'

I then went down from the pulpit and grabbed my coat. People moved fast at that time. Quickly there were twenty people around me. The police came running immediately: 'Where is Pastor Busch?' But now they first had to check twenty or thirty people. In that time I had long since escaped, through the cellar into the vicarage and out. Already I was standing outside again and watched this ridiculous pantomime, how they checked everyone that was coming out. They had photographs of me. Is this him or not? Meanwhile I was standing peacefully outside and watching quietly.

But the evening wasn't finished yet.

I thought it was time I disappeared. I went to my car, which was by a street light in a quiet road, and I thought the driver had probably gone to sleep because he sat there so motionless. I said, 'Günther!' Suddenly someone came forward from behind the car and said, 'Secret state police. Stop! You are under arrest!'

So that's why the driver was sitting so motionless; they had ordered him not to move so that he couldn't warn me. And now I was dragged back into the vestry of Paul's Church.

Of course that made an incredible sensation. They commanded: 'You must leave this evening.'

I countered: 'I can't do that. I must preach here early tomorrow morning.'

'You are leaving!'

'We are in the German Reich. You just can't simply turn me out of Hessen. It's laughable,' I said.

'Then we'll put you on the train.'

'But I'll return on the next train; first I must preach here tomorrow morning early.'

'Then we must arrest you.'

Christic or Hitler?

'As you wish.' I didn't yet know what that meant. I really didn't know.

Then came the awful moment when they put me in an open car, an SS man in front and one next to him, then myself and the commissar. It was a big Mercedes, a little old fashioned. Round us were thousands of people; those inside had come out, and outside more people had come together. News spread quickly in those days.

I was afraid that the people might use force to set me free. That would be the worst that could happen, for then the Gestapo would take my family. I could only cry to God that the crowd would stay peaceful.

Then something happened which I'll never forget for the rest of my life. There was an excitement, a crackling tension among the people. The people cried: 'He didn't talk politics at all! "Jesus Christ the Lord!" Is no one allowed to talk about that any more?' Suddenly a young man stood up on the church stairs — I've never seen him again — and, over the heads of the excited crowd, called out the verse by Blumhardt:

> That Jesus conquers is for ever sure.
> The world and all in it shall yet be his.
> For this he says with full authority:
> The night of death is now for ever o'er;
> And God has put all things into his hand.

What that meant: the authority of Jesus Christ proclaimed so openly right next to the authority of Hitler!

> The conflict at the cross he has endured;
> And now he has ascended to the throne.
> This Jesus is for ever conqueror.

Before anyone could grab the young man he had disappeared in the crowd.

'Drive off!' yelled my escort to the driver, who had already been fumbling about a long time. The car just wouldn't start. It was as if someone was holding him back from behind. 'Go on! Drive!'

At that point the crowd sounded:

If God is for me, all may be against me;
But often as I cry and call and pray,
The enemies fall back before the Lord;
'Tis Jesus, and through him I'm loved by God.
What then can all the foes and haters do?

'Go on! Drive!'

Then at last we drove off. God had held the car there. They first had to experience this testimony! My heart was so full that I said to the commissar, 'You poor man!' He crumpled up and said, 'I was once in the Bible study group for senior pupils!'

'And today you're persecuting the Christians.'

'Oh,' he begged, 'please give in. Let yourself be directed out. Please don't make me have to arrest you.'

I said, 'You poor man, I can't preserve you from that.' Then he got really angry, and when the car arrived I was put in a cell.

Preaching via detours

Another time, when I went to preach in Kreuznach, the man who was to accompany me there was a young teacher. As the train reached

237

the stop before Kreuznach, he suddenly got on. All excited he said, 'Take your suitcase quickly, we're going into the last carriage.'

'Why? What for?'

'Look, the state police are patrolling the Kreuznach station and want to stop you from speaking. We don't know whether they're going to expel you straight away or arrest you, but they don't have the courage to forbid the meeting, because ever so many people have come from the whole of Hunsrück and from the Nahe Valley. They want to push you off quietly. We're going to do it this way: we'll get out of the last carriage and then get off the train under cover, not through the barrier, but straight back through the wood.'

So that was what we did. When the train stopped and everybody got off, we also left, under cover, over the rails and the wires. Then we disappeared into the wood. We made a great circuit round Kreuznach, then we thought about where to go. We couldn't go to the teacher's, nor to the pastor's home, in case the Gestapo were waiting there for me. We decided that the best place would be a large café. There would be lots of strangers, and I would be hard to spot in the crowd.

Imagination needed!

We arrived at the café and sat down in a corner. A few of the fellow activists had come there. Then we discussed what we should do. Messengers came, who said, 'The state police didn't find you at the station, so now they're stationed round the church. They obviously have a photograph of you to stop you at the church door and prevent you from going in to speak.' We knew this from past experience: once I stood in the pulpit they would do nothing to me; they were afraid to interfere then. But they could catch me at the door. I've often seen them standing at the door on the right and on the left and comparing a photograph with the faces of the people going in.

I never quite stooped to sticking on a false beard. But almost! It was decided: Pastor Busch would go in disguise. I put on a gown in a back room of the café. That was fixed with two safety pins which I just had to undo to make it fall down to my feet. Over that came a terrific camel hair coat, a hunter's cap, and a cigarette in the corner of my mouth.

I said, 'This is a bit overdone.'

'Yes,' said the fellow workers, 'but it can't be overdone enough. You now look like a spy.'

Then, just when a great swarm of people were going into the church, I forced my way in with them. The policeman gave me a funny look. I stood still on the stairs and threw the cigarette away in a big arc. Then the verger took off my coat and hat, two people tore out the safety pins, and I quickly ran up the stairs to the pulpit. At that point they gave up. Two of them took chairs and sat down at the right and left of the staircase that led up to the pulpit. They could no longer prevent my first talk.

It was good. This region was spiritually dead, not lively like Württemberg, yet it was glorious how this big church in Kreuznach was full. They were standing in the aisles, the wine-growers from the Mosel and the farmers from Hunsrück. Then I preached the gospel. I said that a heart is without peace until it has peace with God. For that peace we need the One who reconciled us to God, the Lord Jesus.

But while I was speaking, there was a question in my subconscious: How am I going to get out of here again? For I was due to speak again that evening. Then I had a thought: I would announce Luther's great hymn 'A mighty fortress is our God'. When this is sung, everyone immediately stands up. So at the end I said, 'Now we're singing in conclusion the hymn: "A mighty fortress is our God".' As expected everyone stood up, including the officers. During this 'holy activity' they couldn't very well arrest me. I hurried down the stairs and, while they were standing there, threw the coat over myself, took the hunting cap and was gone.

It was Saturday evening about 5.00pm on an autumn day. Now I couldn't go to any café or house anymore. Everywhere would be searched. Friends led me to the end of the resort park — Kreuznach is a health resort — and it began to rain. Then they all went away so that we wouldn't be a conspicuous gathering. There I was, sitting in the darkness and the rain, all alone and feeling rather cold. Later someone brought me my luggage and a bite to eat. I needed to be alone, for two men together were already conspicuous, and three was a gathering of people. True, a lot of people had come to listen to me, but which of those was ready to confess Jesus if it came to it? In that situation you can be tempted to lose courage: 'Man, it's all in vain anyway. You can't win against a whole state's power.' Then you learn what it is to pray.

In the evening I received another disguise. I went in and held my evening meeting, and then the Gestapo arrested me and insisted that I leave. I said, 'I was going to do that anyway.' The people who were speaking the next day were not yet regarded as suspicious.

The power of the lie

But let me stay for a moment with this ghastly loneliness that I experienced there in the resort park. That was the situation of Christians being faithful to the Bible in the Third Reich. We stood there so utterly alone, surrounded by walls of a demonic power. Let me describe these walls to you a little.

There was the power of the lie. It was an astonishing thing, how the Gestapo and all involved with the state had got so used to lying. We're so sensitive now when someone lies in parliament. But when the Gestapo arrested me — it only happened a few times — then two men came and said, 'We have to interrogate you, you must come with us.'

I said, 'You can interrogate me here.'

'No, you must come with us.' Then I knew already that meant arrest.

'You want to arrest me. Let me just take my toothbrush with me.'

'No, no, you come with us; you'll be here again in an hour. We're just going to Gelsenkirchen.'

That's where I had preached in the morning.

'Just tell me that you want to arrest me.'

'No, really not, only an interrogation, and because the witnesses are all in Gelsenkirchen we have to go there.'

When I arrived there, the red form was lying on the desk. I looked at it and saw the name — Busch. I said, 'But that's an arrest warrant!'

'Yes, you are under arrest.'

I asked them once: 'Why did you lie like that? Why didn't you tell me that you were going to arrest me?'

'Oh, you know, then the wives make such a scene and the children howl, we want to avoid that.'

I said, 'But you know very well that my wife doesn't make a scene, nor do my children. You know that perfectly well. Why do you lie then?'

Then the realization came to me: one can lie so much that it becomes an addiction. The Lord Jesus said that the devil is 'a liar, and the father of the lie' (John 8:44). With every lie you run into his camp. You grip the devil's hand. And after a while you find you have to lie even when it's not necessary. Perhaps you have experienced this yourself, this dreadful compulsion that people have to lie! That went on even into the concentration camps. When they drove the Jews into the gas chambers, they said, 'You're having a bath.' They had to lie. 'He who practises sin', says Jesus, 'is the slave of sin' (John 8:44).

The whole of public life was poisoned with lying. I was once brought out of my prison cell for interrogation. They took a statement, which I was to sign. The official rummaged about as he sat on my right at the typewriter and said, 'I'm going to make five copies; for the state police, for the state lawyer, for whatever. You can sign the whole lot in one go.' He passed me the whole packet.

But I said, 'Just a moment, can I just read through the statement?'

'You needn't bother to do that. I suppose you don't trust me!'

'You cannot expect me to give you unreserved trust. My mother taught me as a child, if I signed my name, then I must know what it is that I'm signing. Allow me.'

At that moment he tore away the papers and I saw that the sheets under the top copy were completely different. So they would have had me sign something I knew nothing about in the carbon copies. I didn't sign. What was it all for?

The compulsion to lie seems to me so scary, because it still exists in our day. There is still a devil and a compulsion to lie. And this having to lie went so far that they even enlisted the dear true prison chaplain to do it. I had been locked up and was to betray a name. I didn't give the name. Then the chaplain came in and said, 'I am to tell you, that your situation is hopeless. You will be transferred to the concentration camp the day after tomorrow.'

I said, 'Dear brother, don't frighten me. Have you got a sermon with you?'

'Yes.'

We squatted down in our cell, and he read out the sermon to me. Later he said, 'They worked on me beforehand so I would paint a bleak future to scare you into doing what they wanted.'

I was not due to go to the concentration camp at all. Do you see, even the poor chaplain was enlisted to intimidate me by lying? That was a wall against which we stood so alone, the wall of the lie in great and small.

The other wall was lawlessness, the dissolving of justice. It's bad when a politician drives the wrong way up a one-way street and then wants to get rid of the policeman who is trying to deal with him, or that a leading politician gets himself a hunter's licence in a crooked way. I am just giving examples. You know what I mean. You say that these are small things. But they make me nervous, because the dissolving of justice is the end of every community. I remember how the honoured Professor Heim once gave a sermon on the text from the Psalms: 'In the empire of this king they love justice.' He simply expounded that without any digs at anyone. That caused a huge storm. The published version was confiscated. It was forbidden. The dissolving of justice!

Despair, fear and loneliness

Right at the beginning, in my first encounter with the Gestapo, I had a shattering experience. There was an SS man I knew, who had been in the church service now and again — at the beginning that was still possible. He had got into trouble, had been ordering suits for his troupe and earning a bit on every suit. Naturally that wasn't allowed. So he had been arrested, and now he wanted Pastor Busch.

The Gestapo allowed that. I went into the headquarters and there were the officers of the state police and the SS leaders, and they said, 'Pastor, the man wants to speak to you.'

I said, 'That's nice that you allow me to go to him.'

'Look, we can't carry out the usual procedure in this case. Then he'll get three months. But that is impossible. For him, there's only one way: he must shoot himself. We've put a revolver for him in his cell. Can we ask you to do your ministry to him in such a way that the man shoots himself?'

'You can't ask that of me.'

'We require you to help the man to take this step.'

I said, 'Look, what I do in caring for a soul, you must leave to me.'

I came into the cell. It was a dreadful hole, and right at the top was a light. This was no way to treat an animal. I had no clue then that later I myself would be spending weeks sitting in this same cell.

But now this desperate man was sitting there. On the small table lay the revolver.

'Pastor, shall I?'

'No, don't do it! God does not want the death of the sinner; rather he wants him to live. Dear friend, that means that first you repent before God and then receive the one who is life, the Lord Jesus.'

It was a heart-rending conversation. The man didn't shoot himself. This was, I suppose, the first reason why the state police were angry with me — that I did not do them the favour of driving a man to suicide.

But at that time it came to me in a shocking way: justice has become powerless. In the prophet Habakkuk it says about the end time, 'No matter of right can win any more.' Justice has become unconscious. It is dreadful when that happens.

And then a Christian was unspeakably lonely. I believe that all real Christians experienced this terrible loneliness in those days, particularly because the 'Christian citizen' withdrew himself from us. 'We're Christians as well, but Pastor Busch doesn't need to hit people over the head.'

There was a saying in those days: 'When Daniel came into the den of lions, he didn't go around treading on their tails.'

I said, 'On the contrary, he went around and said: "Away with your tails, I'm coming in the name of the Lord!"' I am convinced of that.

Christ or Hitler?

As a youth pastor I used to hold an assembly in a senior school on Monday mornings. When I had my first spell in prison behind me and came to the school again, the headmaster stood trembling in front of me and said, 'I have forbidden the pupils to come to your assembly.'

From then on, he didn't greet me any more, although we knew each other well. He was a Christian man, an elder in a congregation. That all fitted in with the 'field, wood and meadow Christianity.'

Hand in hand with this sense of loneliness there was sometimes a deep despair. What an abyss of despair I went through in those first days after my arrest! I don't know whether you've ever heard of Jochen Klepper. He was a Christian whose wife was Jewish. It was now too late for her to emigrate. He said, 'I can't do anything about the fact that my wife is going to be gassed.' He was going to be forced to divorce her. So then he took his own life. Who can judge here? I can just dimly imagine what darkness and despair this man must have gone through.

We got to know a Jewish lady whose husband was a doctor. They were happily married. He got a divorce and drove away his wife, with whom he had lived in harmony for thirty years. One day the woman stood in front of me. What darkness and despair! She was taken away and then killed in the gas chamber.

In the corner of a cell where I was once sitting I saw scratched with fingernails: 'Oh, you place of my dark despair!' There, clear before my eyes, was what someone had gone through in the way of despair, in the way of darkness, in this Gestapo prison cell.

Along with despair came fear as well. I was afraid. There was a story told about me that at my seventy-fifth interrogation I had taken a bunch of flowers, put on a dinner jacket and said, 'This is a jubilee.' Whoever believes that has no idea of the deathly fears we went through. We had fallen into the Gestapo's hands, and that was terrifying. What we preachers had to go through in a special way, every disciple of Jesus basically experienced in the Third Reich.

How much fear my wife went through when they were looking for leaflets in our house. While I was talking to the officials downstairs my wife saw these leaflets on the first floor and thought: 'Where can I hide them?' She pushed them under our little thirteen-year-old daughter, who was lying ill under the blanket, and then the state police searched through the house. They came into the room in which the sick child lay, but they found nothing. The children also shared in the fear.

Now the question arises: What about God? Did he just keep silent? When everything went wrong, the bombs crashed and the towns burned, then the people cried: 'Where is God then? Why is he silent?'

I want to say to you clearly: God, the living, holy God can be silent and have nothing more to say to a whole people; though he speaks to his children. And I want to tell you this: do not fear anything so much as coming into the place of God's total silence.

God is in the game

I want to tell you just one more story. It illustrates the point I most want to make. The moment I put myself on God's side, God is secretly taking part in the conflict.

My brother Johannes had been arrested in Bochum. I heard that he would be released the next day. I went there and collected him. The two hours we had together I will never forget. He had experienced the same as me: two days in an abyss of despair and fear and then finally an ear that could listen to God. When God speaks in judgement, you recognize Jesus as Saviour in a completely new way. He said, 'For me one of the most staggering experiences was the following' — and he told me:

> Outside the police headquarters there was a stairway of three steps, which were rather smooth. The police had arrested me in the evening. That caused a lot of excitement, such a well-known pastor being imprisoned. It would immediately be reported in the foreign papers, in Switzerland, Denmark and Holland. So, of course, there was a heated discussion among the officials: is this right or is it not right?
>
> One of them kept shouting: 'This is right! The clerics must have their mouths stopped!'
>
> This loud-mouth left the headquarters that evening. Someone had thrown a banana skin onto a step. The man slipped on the step so awkwardly that he hit the back of his head and died.

Can you imagine the situation? Half an hour after he had shouted out: 'The clerics must have their mouths stopped!' he was lying dead on the stairs. You may say that's a coincidence, and I can't prove that it's not.

But this I know, that the Gestapo officials didn't believe in coincidence any more. My brother said, 'That's when they began seeking spiritual help. One after another came to me totally deflated and said, 'Tell me, is there a God who can kill?'

'Yes. — But that is still child's play, to slip on the stairs and die. But what comes after that...'

My brother said, 'Those few days were an opportunity for evangelism such as I have never experienced in my life.'

10.

Prison

Peace with God

Now I must tell you how God set me free from the fear of the state police, through my coming to know a greater fear.

The first time I went to prison for preaching the gospel I sat in the cell, overwhelmed by loneliness, despair and fear, until I suddenly noticed that God wanted to speak to me. Then God began to talk to me about my life. I experienced the same after every arrest. When it became quiet, God began to speak, and went through my life with me: all the arrogance, all the impurity, the lies and the lack of love.

Suddenly I realized that God was angry. 'The wrath of God', says the Bible, 'burns against all the sinful ways of men' (Romans 1:18). God's wrath was blazing in my cell. When the thought comes to you that God wants to speak to you, then perhaps you go to the cinema or get on with some business. Here in prison I couldn't run away. That was the scary thing. And yet there was blessing in the fact that God said, 'This is why I'm talking to you! You are a sinner.'

Christ or Hitler?

I know today what it's going to be like on the Day of Judgement, when God throws your life in front of your feet, and your sins are lying totally open there. Don't be deceived, God is not mocked! At that time I learned what hell is. Hell is staying for ever under the wrath of God. I don't know what hell looks like, but this I know, one is thrown away, put out by HIM. I learned the fear of God, so I lost the fear of these ridiculous SS men.

Have you ever had the fear of God? If not, you haven't yet begun to see reality. This holy God sees us, he surrounds us, and we can't just tread his commands under our feet and get away with it! Perhaps he needs to lead you for a while into the stillness where you can't run away from him any more.

Then, just when I was thinking 'Man, I am lost!' came Jesus and showed me his hands with the nail marks. Suddenly I grasped what in my mind I'd always known: he bore my sins away. The punishment was laid on him, so that I should have peace. He makes me righteous before God. He is our peace.

I've had many years working in pastoral care. I meet so many Christians who have no joy and no assurance of salvation. That's because they've not yet understood the cross of Jesus. He redeemed me. I belong to him. He paid for me. I may be a bad piece of property, but I am his!

My cell became bright; it was almost like when King Solomon consecrated the temple. Then it was so full of the glory of the Lord that the priests couldn't stand in it any more, they had to go out. But I couldn't go out! It was so strong, that I almost couldn't bear it for joy, that I have a Saviour who

From the crib to the grave,
From the grave to the throne,

Where his are the praises for aye,
Is the one who is mine,
The one I can claim,
Though but a poor sinner I am.

He gives peace with God, peace in the heart, which tells me I am a child of God, so I can laugh in the devil's face, and all the more at those who serve him.

Officials: the men behind the masks

What sort of men were they, these Gestapo officers? After all, they were not just officials. Behind the façade they were people. When I sat in the cell or was being interrogated, then I sometimes asked myself whether there was any possibility of breaking through this layer of hate, enmity and officialdom, through to their hearts and consciences?

I had some remarkable encounters. Once, when I was youth pastor with fifty young fellow workers, who did house visits every Sunday, there was a raid on the Youth Centre. Everything possible was confiscated and driven away in a lorry. Then the fifty leaders were investigated; each one's house was searched. The parents came rushing to me, because the officials were just throwing whole cupboards down, the flats looked like battlefields. It was already wartime, so they didn't have to show any consideration, they could just do what they liked. Fifty homes were devastated.

Then the boys were questioned, and finally they summoned me, after they had interrogated the fifty young men, whom I could not prime beforehand. Then I saw how a hard crust like theirs could break. They said to me, 'Pastor Busch, we have interrogated fifty young people of yours, and not one has lied to us. They have openly said that they secretly held camps. They spoke to their own harm, but they didn't lie — what kind of a world is that?'

I said, 'That is the world that you hate.'

He was staggered by the fact that there is a world in which people don't lie.

Once, when I sat in the cell and said to an official, 'I would not like to change places with you,' he went really wild and said, 'But that's madness.'

'No, I wouldn't want to change places with you. To belong to Jesus, with all my sins and follies, to be a child of God — I don't want to change places with you.'

At that he roared, and I could tell that this was something he just couldn't grasp. There I sat in the cell, shamed and humiliated, next to the proud man in uniform — and I didn't want to change places with him. Those were moments when I could sense: now the crust is breaking and he's homesick. I am convinced that every man is homesick.

When it all fell to pieces at the end, they gave up and committed suicide in droves. The chief of our state police, who had been speaking to me only a few days before, hanged himself in the cell. There was nothing left.

Poor in spirit

Breakfast was finished. In a mad hurry I had rinsed my mug, rushed back to the cramped cell and was standing to attention by the door. I had to smile to myself: Why did everything have to be done in such ludicrous haste in prison, when, after all, there was unlimited time?

The warder looked in: 'Everything all right?'

'Yes, officer.'

The door banged shut, the iron bolts crunched. I was alone!

Now I would have peace till midday. I moved my stool under the narrow window high up in the wall and opened my Bible.

Oh, this wonderful quiet! All alone and undisturbed with God's Word! I opened the letter to the Ephesians. I had read that many times before, but now it spoke to me in such a new way! That was surely because Paul himself was in prison when he wrote this letter. There are paintings which you can only see properly when you stand where the light is just right. It's like that with this letter. The place where you can understand it best is — prison.

I read, and everything that was oppressing me became small and insignificant. What did the threats facing the church and my own life in this Nazi regime matter compared with the message even in the first few words: 'God has chosen us before the foundation of the world'? (Eph. 1:4).

There was quiet around me, and quiet in my own heart. But suddenly there was a murmur in my heart, when I came to the place where Paul writes: 'I am a messenger of the gospel in chains' (Eph. 6:20).

These words touched my deepest needs. Out there was my great and fruitful youth work. What would become of that if I was to be detained for weeks on end? Being a 'messenger of the gospel' had defined my life. And now I was excluded from this work. That was hard.

Could I be a messenger of the gospel even in a prison cell? The thought came to me that I was responsible to make the gospel known even to the prison officers. But how was I to say it to them? They would surely not get into any conversation with me. How was I to be 'a messenger of the gospel in chains' here?

I thought about it and reached the conclusion that if I was really patient, quiet and cheerful, then the warders must notice that I have a different spirit from the other prisoners. Then perhaps they will ask me what it is that makes the difference…

So I decided to be a model prisoner, one who honours the Lord Jesus 'in word and work and all his being.'

Into my cogitations came noisy steps outside. My door flew open. A Gestapo officer stood there and said, 'Your wife has come. She has received permission to give you fruit. You are not allowed to have your wife's basket. Bring your wash basin with you!'

Excitedly I jumped up and went over to the wash basin. In my haste I grabbed it clumsily; it slipped out of my hand and fell to the ground, so that some enamel pieces came off.

'Man!' bellowed the officer, 'What are you doing with government property?'

Anger rose in me: 'Just let me go home, then I don't need to demolish your stupid pots!'

Now the man was wild: 'What? You want to be cheeky? Now you won't get the fruit at all!'

Prison

The door flew shut, the bolt crunched. I was alone…

'…messenger of the gospel in chains…' My heart was heavy when I thought of how my dear wife was now going home sad. But much, much worse was the fact that I had so thoroughly failed. The man had definitely noticed nothing of the fact that I belonged to the Lord Jesus. He had seen nothing of a different spirit…

It was lunch time. 'Come out and get your food!' bellowed the warders and unlocked the doors. When I stepped outside one of them said mockingly, 'Faster, faster — but don't throw the state-owned food bowl on the floor!'

I kept quiet. But the very young officer gave me no rest. With more and more remarks he mocked me in front of the grinning fellow prisoners.

Then anger gripped me. I must not say anything. But — now I deliberately did everything very slowly, till he too was white hot with rage. It was a teasing game — careful and mean…

And then I was back in my cell, a 'messenger of the gospel in chains'. I could have cried. Was I really not going to succeed in being friendly, quiet and patient? No! It went on worse than ever before. It was as if the devil had broken loose. Every meeting with the officers brought a clash. Even friendly officers became noticeably cooler…

Despairingly I sat for long hours in my cell. And what I had long known theoretically I then learned practically in my abysmal need: *The Heidelberg Catechism* is right; yes, it is right when it says, 'We are so corrupt that we are completely incapable of any good, and inclined to all evil.' And the dreadful answer to Question 5 sounded in my ears: 'I am inclined by nature to hate God and my neighbour.'

Christ or Hitler?

But then the liberation came! Never in my life will I forget that Sunday morning. I had wept as I listened from my wretched cell to the bells of a nearby church ringing. I was finished, my nerves had had enough. Hunger and misery had worn me down. But more than that, I was at the end of all self-confidence and self-righteousness. When I collected breakfast the warder had spoken a few friendly words, but I had maintained a numb silence. What were men to me now? God had abandoned his servant...

Just then the door opened again. The prison officer came in and brought a thick book: 'Your wife has brought this. Permission has been given for you to have the book in your cell. This old tome is not going to be a danger to the state!'

Oh my dear wife! I recognized the volume immediately. It was the sermons of the Württemberg pastor Hofacker. My wife knew what these sermons meant to me.

I sat down on my stool and began to read — anywhere, just where the book opened. And then — then I realized that it was not my wife, but my heavenly Father, that had sent the book. It said there:

> The Saviour begins the sermon on the mount with the words: 'Blessed are the poor in spirit, for theirs is the kingdom of heaven.' But what does he mean by such spiritually poor people? A poor man is one who does not possess what he needs for his upkeep. And poor in spirit is the one who with humility and lowliness feels that he lacks what he needs for a spiritual and godly life, but that he may and must beg this for himself from the great God...

I had to jump up. My heart beat wildly. However could Hofacker, who lived in the beginning of the last century, so exactly have known my situation? Oh no! Not Hofacker — the Lord Jesus knew my heart. So I read further:

> Such spiritually poor people the Saviour places at the top of his beatitudes, and thereby makes spiritual poverty the gate through which one can enter the kingdom of heaven…

When I had read the sermon I sang cheerfully in my cell:

> Mercy's been shown to me,
> Grace which I never deserved…

till the warder came and roared: 'Quiet! Singing is forbidden!'

But no one could forbid the singing in my heart.

The hanging pulpit

One day I talked to the architect about my pulpit. Our church hall was to be altered, and so the architect was asking where we wanted the pulpit.

How one's thoughts wander: on the way home I recalled the many pulpits from which I was permitted to proclaim the glorious gospel.

One of those was my remarkable hanging pulpit.

I was then — probably in the winter of 1940 — again a prisoner of the Gestapo because I had preached a celebration sermon in a big industrial city. So now I sat gloomily in my ice cold cell.

It was dreadful down there. The slimy walls! The gloomy darkness! And most of all — the atmosphere! All you heard was the occasional banging of iron doors, the scolding of officers or the cursing from neighbouring cells.

But then a beautiful thing happened, already on the first evening. We had our meal, and the officers checked all the cells again. Then we heard them walk in their hobnailed boots away down the long corridor. We heard the great iron door to the cellar being locked — then all was still. Now before us was a long, sleepless night on the cold, hard wooden plank bed.

There, what was that? Was someone speaking? I rose up. But I was alone! What was that? Again I heard a man's voice. It spoke in whispers, but it was so clear, it could have been a man in my cell.

'New one! Hey, you new one!' called the voice. Apparently he meant me; for I was a 'new one' here.

'Yes!' I answered spontaneously.

But the stranger obviously didn't hear me; for he kept calling, 'Hey, new one!' and finally: 'Climb up to the window and whisper out of the window. Then we can talk!'

I pushed the little table under the window, climbed on the stool, then on the table. Now if I raised my hands I could reach the window grill high up on the wall.

I pulled myself up… Yes, that is simple to describe. But I am not a great athlete, so it was quite an effort. But it worked. Thus I came to know the amusing secret of this dreary prison: the windows were at ground level, and very close to them was a high wall. If one spoke towards this wall, one could be heard clearly in all the cells. Some prisoner had once discovered this strange acoustic effect, and now the secret was passed from one inmate to another.

Prison

So there I hung with my legs dangling in the air and got to know my companions in suffering. What a motley company! Black marketeers, gypsies and Jews, political suspects and even a prostitute, guilty ones and innocent ones, old and young. I was shaken by this glimpse behind the façade of life. Soon it became apparent that there was something we all had in common: great fear and despair. We had all fallen 'into the hands of men'. And even the Bible says that is the worst thing that can happen.

Of course our conversations were not exactly free flowing. You couldn't hold yourself in mid-air for long. You had to keep letting go and gather new strength.

So there I stood once again on my little table, breathless and panting. An old man was just telling us with a moaning voice that he had been sitting in this cellar for two years, while a cheeky woman was interjecting malicious remarks.

Then the light dawned on me: these here are the labouring and heavy laden, the tax collectors and sinners of whom the Lord Jesus spoke! You have been brought here to tell these wretched ones about the gospel!

But what would happen if I began to do that? Would it not raise mocking laughter from hell? And there was no way I could give long explanations. After hardly a minute I had to let go of the grill, because my hands were burning like fire.

Suddenly it was as if all the demons here present in what seemed like the vestibule of hell were urging against it. But — God was calling. So I pulled myself up again and said during a pause in the conversation: 'Now I am going to tell you a glorious word from God. Listen!' And then I whispered against the wall: 'God so loved the world — *this world!* — that he gave...'

Hardly had I said, 'God', when the impudent woman swept in with a malicious curse.

But immediately the others shut her up: 'You be quiet, Frieda!' And then the word was 'Just carry on!'

So I spoke the gospel: 'God so loved the world that he gave his only begotten Son, so that whoever believes in him should not perish but have eternal life.' I added just a few words about the burning compassion of the Lord Jesus — then I let myself fall.

A great silence followed. No one spoke any more. They sat in their dark cells. Jesus had come to them — in their despair, in their guilt, in their ungodliness, in their night...

Now I had my 'hanging pulpit.' Every evening, when the general conversation was finishing, I held my 'shorter-than-short' sermon. There I hung — myself an outcast — ridiculous like a climbing monkey at the grill. But my heart was glad.

I saw none of my hearers. I just dimly saw the dreadful wall. But I could really sense the rapt listening. Even Frieda said not a word any more.

Do you know what moved me most in this strange preaching of the gospel? The more deeply it reaches down into the abyss of human need, the more brightly shines the message of God's mercy through Christ Jesus to the lost.

Evangelizing the Gestapo

One day when I was in the Darmstadt prison the door opened. A guard came in, an SS man. He pulled the door shut behind him and I thought he was going to do something to me. I put the stool in front of me and thought, 'I'll defend myself.' That was the old Wilhelm Busch appearing again, in spite of all my resolutions to suffer.

Then the guard said, 'Just a moment, I'm not going to do anything to you.' He pulled from his pocket a cutting from the Sunday paper and said, 'My father-in-law is a Christian man and reads the Sunday paper. There was a story in it: "Jesus in the Sarasani Circus" by Wilhelm Busch. I liked it so much that I cut it out and always carry it with me. Is that from you?'

'Yes,' I said. 'I once told that story.'

I had had to take a funeral in the Sarasani Circus, to bury an Indian woman. All kinds of people were there, Mauritanians, Americans and so on. Of course they didn't all speak German. Then it occurred to me: there is a word that everyone will understand: the name Jesus. So I gave a talk in which the word Jesus kept appearing. And suddenly everyone became quiet.

The story has gone through all the earth. It even appeared in Arabic writing. And so the SS man asked: 'Is that from you?'

'Yes,' I said, 'it is from me. But now it's not a question of Jesus in the Sarasani Circus; it's Jesus in the state police prison in Darmstadt.'

'I would have to be off my rocker to accept that from you.'

I said, 'On the contrary, you are off your rocker if you don't accept that from me. But if we want to talk about this — I'm suffocating in this cell. Let's talk in the corridor. At least that has a window to get some air.'

'Yes, come out with me.'

Ten minutes later I had the whole work force around me. Evangelization of Gestapo officers. Amazing!

I said, 'Before we talk, we must know what we want to talk about. Men, there are only two world views, in the whole world only two! One is all the world views together that there are, and the other is the revealed gospel. Give me some paper and a pencil.'

They gave me that, and I drew a line right down the middle of the paper and said, 'Here I'm going to write "all world views" and here "revealed gospel". These two differ decisively in four points: in what they say about God; in what they say about man; in what they say about salvation; and in what they say about hope.'

I explained: 'First: all world views and religions call something within the world "God". For example they say, "My nation is God." That's something within this world. The bourgeois says, "Nature is my God." Others say, "The depth of our being is God." But what God really is, is absolutely clear. I can say that "he doesn't exist," but I can't call something within this world God. That is a fraud, after all. So, for instance, Goethe says that "God is a feeling." The Bible says against that: "God stands outside the world as its Creator and Lord."

'Secondly: the world views and the gospel differ in what they say about man. All world views believe that man is somehow good. Idealism says, "Man is good at heart." Some say, "The Aryan man is good." The communist asserts: "The classless man is good." A grandmother comes to me and says, "Pastor, my grandson, he steals and beats up his sisters — but he has a good heart." So, all world views say that man is good. The revealed truth of the Bible says on the other hand, "Man is wicked before God and therefore most urgently needs salvation." In the *Reformed Catechism* it says, "I am inclined by nature to hate God and my neighbour."'

So there I stood before these SS men and made clear to them how bad we humans are, and that we're going to hell.

'Thirdly: they differ in what they say about salvation. Somehow all world views contain an element of self-salvation. "Whoever constantly strives and tries," says my dear compatriot Goethe, or, "If we breed pure Aryans, then we are saved." The Bible says, "God has provided salvation. Now receive it."' At this point I drew a cross on the piece of paper.

'Fourthly: they differ in their hope. The world views say, "Somehow, some time the great German kingdom will come." Or: "Some time the classless society will come." Some time… But the Bible says, "Some time Jesus is coming again." At the end there's a catastrophe awaiting the world, because the Lord of the world will step onto the stage, visible and glorious!'

While I was giving this lecture to the SS men, a friend and colleague of mine was sitting behind the cell door opposite me. I knew nothing about that. But later he told me: 'I was sitting there so desperate and suddenly I heard somebody talking. "Hey, man," I thought, "that's Wilhelm Busch; what's he crying out like that for? Man, he's evangelizing here in the Gestapo prison!" Then I fell on my knees and begged the whole time: "Lord, give him authority. Open hearts!"'

When I heard this I thought: 'This is the church of the future.' The church in prison: one is giving testimony and the other, behind a bolted door, kneeling and crying to God. This is the true church which experiences defeat with Jesus and yet conquers.

11.

The Second World War

Encouragement in a mountain chapel

Slowly we wandered back with our friends through the Fex Valley.

I wanted to tear myself away from the dismal conversations we were having. Oh, how glorious the world really is! I took deep breaths of air, the wonderfully pure air up there in the Engadin at 2000 metres, where the eye can hardly take in all the beauty: the wide green meadows, the white glaciers, and the deep blue sky.

My friend began to sing one of the lovely Swiss songs, but he stopped halfway through. There was an oppressive spirit surrounding all of us. It was July 1939. The shadow of the looming war lay dark over us. In a few days we would have to travel back to the Ruhr region. What a heap of rubble that would become if the war went ahead!

And that was not all. We were already undergoing tormenting persecution. What would happen to the evangelical youth work, to my family and to me, if at the outbreak of war Hitler stopped considering reactions abroad and aimed even stronger blows against Christians?

So we had come with heavy thoughts to the edge of the valley, where the path descends to the blue-green lakes of the Engadin.

A small, snow-white chapel stands at the edge. As we were approaching it we heard the tones of a violin coming from inside. We stood still. My Swiss friend went to the door; it was open. Quietly we entered. The sunshine lit up the plain room in which the mountain farmers would gather for the Sunday service.

At the front a woman was sitting at a harmonium. The violinist, a young girl, stood next to her. For a moment she took down her violin and looked at us. But when we quietly sat down in the benches at the back the two played on. We presumed they were guests at the nearby sanatorium.

The peaceful sounds did our hearts good. Now they played a simple chorale. My friend tried to see whether it would disturb them if he sang along with them. But the violinist just gave him a friendly smile. So he sang along cheerfully. And the rest of us joined in one after another.

The door opened, and a few health resort guests came in and sat down in the pew in front of us. They found hymn books lying in the pews. My friend helped them to turn to the hymn, and soon they joined in the singing.

Again the door opened. A few farmers came in with their wives. Quickly they turned to the hymn and their powerful voices strengthened our choir. More and more people came in, until we really were a little congregation. One hymn after another was turned up and sung, till the violinist let her instrument sink down.

'One more!' someone begged. And then we sang — I don't know who suggested it, for it came to us as from God himself — the mighty verse:

> Your glorious work you will complete,
> You Saviour of the world.
> Man's tide of misery you'll turn,
> Though dark is now your way.
> Faith's supplications never cease,
> Above our prayers and thoughts you'll work.

And with this song it happened; bit by bit the load fell from our hearts.

Happily we stepped out into the radiant summer world...

In dark, horrifying nights of bombing, in the gloomy prison, in raging fires and the destruction of a world, in all these the brightness of that day revived me. It was not the shining glory of the mountains and meadows, but it was the song that stayed with me:

> Your glorious work you will complete ...!

In scenes of darkness and horror we sang:

> Above our prayers and thoughts you'll work.

'Paula thought of it!'

Laughing, chattering hordes of children thronged the wide doors of the Cross Church. They brought all the noise of the city street with them into the vestibule. But when they stepped into the large room with its subdued light from a stained glass window they turned quiet.

Quickly the milling crowd sorted itself out. The organ began to play with a mighty sound. Then the children sang aloud:

> Now let us go and tread
> With singing and with prayer
> To God, who to our life
> Has given strength thus far.
> We travel and we wander
> From one year to another...

Did the children notice that on this first Sunday in 1943 every verse in the New Year's song by Paul Gerhardt had a new light? The older ones surely felt it! Their fathers were out in the war, in Africa, Russia, France, Norway, or somewhere else far away. And the mothers had faces full of care, because the food supplies were getting so scarce. The first bombs had fallen on Essen.

> Through many fears and plagues,
> Through trembling and dismay,
> Through dreadful war and shocks
> That cover the whole world...

sang the children. How relevant to today was this song from the seventeenth century!

The organ fell silent; the singing ceased. I read the 23rd psalm: 'The Lord is my shepherd ... though I walk through the dark valley, I fear no evil; for you are with me...'

I felt constrained to say a few words before the group discussions began.

'Children! What exactly is a dark valley? What does David mean when he speaks of the "dark valley"?'

One of the big boys knew: 'When you have to die!' he called.

'That's right! Death is a very dark valley. It's good then to be able to say, "You are with me!" What other kinds of dark valleys are there?'

The children thought about it. Then a little girl answered. She was wearing a bright dress and had a big blue bow in her hair. 'A dark valley is when the planes are dropping bombs and the sirens are howling and you feel so terribly afraid.' While saying this she nodded her head earnestly.

I felt my heart constrict. I didn't know yet how many terrible things awaited us: that this church would stand there bare and burnt out; that the busy streets round about us would soon be desolate heaps of rubble. But a premonition of what was to come lay over all of us.

'Yes, my child!' I turned to the little girl. 'That is a dreadfully dark valley. And now we want to agree on something: when it comes, we'll say: "You are with me, dear Saviour!" And then we won't be afraid anymore. Do you want to think of that?'

'Yes!' called the children. They all wanted to think of that word: 'Though I walk in the dark valley, I fear no evil; for you are with me!' It seemed so good to them to have an antidote to fear.

Just before midnight on that Sunday the sirens began to howl. Wildly their noise tore through the silence of the night.

I was still sitting in my study. Suddenly I heard steps running in the bedrooms upstairs. Quickly I stood up to see to my children.

Christ or Hitler?

Then the youngest stormed down the stairs in her nightdress, pale with shock, her little face distorted with fear. I caught her up in my arms. 'Daddy, I'm so scared!' she stammered.

'But Renate!' I said. 'What did we learn only this morning? Though I walk in the dark valley, I fear no evil; for you, Lord, are with me!'

'Oh Daddy,' she sighed, as her face became calmer, 'I forgot all about that.'

'Of course!' I answered, somewhat bitterly. 'The grown ups do that as well. The most important thing gets forgotten.'

Then we went into the cellar; and soon the bombs were falling…

Next morning the sun was shining. Our house had been spared. All was peaceful.

I was working in my study. Suddenly — crash, bang! — the door flew open. My youngest one came storming in. She had a little girl in tow who didn't really want to come with her.

'Daddy!' shrieked my little daughter in excitement. 'Paula thought of it!'

I turned round, somewhat annoyed, a bit absent-minded, also curious — just like any father who has been torn away from his thoughts about his work.

'What's the matter with Paula?'

Of course, I knew Paula. She was my daughter's dearest friend. Not a meal could we have without some event in Paula's life being recounted. She was Catholic; but the little girl's friendship was so

272

heartfelt that Paula had just been dragged along into our service the previous day.

My daughter got annoyed because her father was so slow on the uptake. 'Paula really thought of it! You know, don't you? — about the dark valley — they had fire — fire bombs — that's when she thought of it!'

Light dawned on me. 'Tell me, Paula. How was it?'

And then followed a moving story of how the incendiary bombs fell into the house, how the men excitedly rushed out of the cellar to extinguish the blaze, how the mother wept and was full of fear. Then little Paula had stood up in front of her mother and recited to all the people in the cellar: 'Though I walk in the dark valley, I fear no evil; for you, Lord, are with me!' Then the mother had become quite calm.

I was sitting still at my desk again. I could hear the voices of the little girls happily playing outside. But I was in quite a solemn mood. And then I had to sigh a little. How lovely our life could be, if we always had a great word from God ready for when it really matters!

'I can't!'

'Right — listen everybody!' bellowed the mate. 'Early tomorrow morning we're taking the minesweeper out. And you well know we've got a slim chance of returning. Oh yes! War is dangerous...'

The young men looked at each other in dismay. But the mate didn't leave much time for dismal thoughts: 'So this evening we're going to have a real celebration! We're going ashore together! There'll be enough *Schnapps* and women for us all to have a great time!'

Joyful roars answered him as they all imagined the coming pleasures.

All except Fritz, who had become very quiet. One of the others observed that and asked: 'Fritz, you are coming with us, aren't you?'

Fritz shook his head.

The others began to notice. 'What's wrong over there?' 'Of course we're all joining in!' 'No one's going to keep out of it!' came the word from all sides.

Now the mate had heard something too: 'What?' he roared. 'Who's not joining in? That one?' And now he became official: 'Right, now listen! We're comrades here! Understood? Sworn comrades! Is that clear?'

'Yes, sir!' cried the rough crew.

'So...' the mate continued, 'we do everything together! One for all and all for one! Understood?'

'Yes sir!'

'Well then, that's settled!' the mate said, ending the discussion.

There in the middle of this mob stood young Fritz. He sensed that the hour of trial had come. And though his heart trembled a bit, yet the path was clear before him. He must not give way...

He had come to know the Lord Jesus first in his parents' home, and later in our evangelical youth work. On a wall in the Youth Centre he had read every Sunday the words: 'My son, give me your heart, and let your eyes delight in my ways!' (Prov. 23:26).

Fritz had heard this call, he had clearly decided for Christ and had followed him.

But he had not had much time to grow. It was wartime, and soon he was called up to join the marines. At his departure I gave my young friend a pocket Bible and urged him: 'Fritz, confess your Lord bravely!' At that he squeezed my hand hard…

And now the hour of confession had come! Noisily the comrades left the ship. 'Once more — are you coming with us?'

'No! I can't take part in your boozing and unclean revels.'

Again a wild tumult arose; biting mockeries ended with the threat: 'Just wait till we come back! But then…!'

Fritz turned pale. They had rough ways on these ships. And who was there to defend him? So the young lad stayed back feeling alone and forsaken. Finally he lay down in his hammock, took his Bible and prayed to the Lord Jesus to help him remain steadfast.

It was towards morning when the comrades came on board, loud and drunken. One had a bottle of *Schnapps* in his hand. He brought it to the hammock. Fritz was immediately wide awake. 'Right, comrade,' the sailor began. 'We want to be patient with you, because you're such a mother's boy. But, one thing you must do now: you must drink *Schnapps* with us! Then we'll leave it at that!' The others were lurking in the background.

For a moment Fritz thought it over. Then he remembered the early Christian martyrs. They were only required to do a small thing: 'A little incense to the divine Caesar!' was the word then — and all would have been well. But those Christians had said a difficult 'No' and had gone to their death.

Christ or Hitler?

It was clear to Fritz: the one mouthful of *Schnapps* — that was at this moment the 'incense' to the 'God of this world'. So he shook his head.

At that the band was furious. 'What, you don't want to drink with us?' they roared. 'Then we'll teach you!'

Now they fell upon him. Two grabbed his legs, others his arms. One held the bottle to his mouth: 'Drink!'

Fritz pressed his lips together. Furiously they tried to push the bottle between his teeth; they pulled open his mouth forcibly: 'Come on: drink!'

And while the *Schnapps* flowed over his face, Fritz pressed out between his teeth: 'Look, I can't!'

'What?' roared the mate. 'You can't? Nonsense! You don't want to!'

'No!' cried Fritz. 'I can't!'

The mate stopped. Then he beckoned to his rough companions: 'Leave him alone a minute!' And to Fritz: 'Why can't you?'

I don't know exactly what Fritz answered. But it was probably something like what Luther said at the Diet before the Emperor and the whole realm: 'My conscience is captive to God's Word … I can do no other! So help me God!'

The mate then mumbled: 'Leave him alone!' and no one dared do anything to him.

A few days later the roughest of the whole crew came to the boy and poured out his heart to him. And he was not the only one. People who follow their conscience are a great help to the world.

The synagogue that preached

God sometimes has strange and wonderful preachers. Luke the doctor tells us in his Gospel that a criminal on the verge of death gave a deeply impressive sermon from the cross on which he was hanging. And the Old Testament tells us that even a real four-legged donkey once preached.

Some people don't believe these stories. I believe them, for I know that God often chooses wondrous preachers of his truth.

Among these I am particularly impressed by a great, dead, burnt-out building. Every time I pass this house it begins to preach to me. And I know that it once preached for a whole night to many hundreds of people.

This strange preaching building stands in the middle of a noisy city in the Ruhr district.

There must have been a rich Jewish congregation once, to have built such a magnificent synagogue. It is a huge domed structure made of grey natural stone. Years ago I went into it once, and the glory inside matched the wonderful exterior. You could see that a great artist had designed and built this house.

Then came that dreadful day which is a dark blot on the history of our land: the day in which the German people completely forgot that they had had Luther, Kant, Bach and Goethe, when with a huge leap they went back from the twentieth century to the Middle Ages.

Christ or Hitler?

The mob raged; the Jewish shops were plundered, the Jews' apartments were demolished. Innocent people were kicked, beaten and shot.

A wild mass penetrated the glorious synagogue and set it on fire. Everything that could burn was devoured by the flames. But at the end the huge bare domed structure still stood. The great stone blocks had defied the flames.

Then this building began to be an embarrassment. It was not speaking yet, but with its dead silence it began to worry people. The loudspeakers droned out about 'the German cultural will' — and there stood this house! Above the entrance the passer-by could still read: 'My house shall be a house of prayer for all peoples.' There it stood with its smoke-blackened walls and gaping windows while the loudspeakers announced that German armies had moved into Russia to carry forward German culture. People kept saying that this house ought to be pulled down. But — they never got round to it. It was as if they had lost the courage to lay hands again on that huge, mute building.

And the synagogue was silent — silent — as if waiting for the day when it would speak.

And that day came!

It began like any other day in the city. The shopkeepers opened their shops, the housewives did their washing or queued in front of the shops, whose wares were already becoming scarce; the miners went down into the depths, and others came up to the surface. It was just like any other day. Evening came, the streets lay dark. All the houses were darkened; all lights off. It was war, after all, and some bombs had already fallen on the city.

The Second World War

At 9.00pm the sirens sounded. The people ran into the cellars.

And then came the shock!

It was the first great carpet bombing attack, in which whole districts were set ablaze. The people in the cellars felt the terrible heat. They rushed out. No! Many never made it to the outside. They found the entrances caved in, and were burnt alive.

But those who came out were horrified. All round the synagogue were narrow, densely populated streets. And now everything was in flames. Wherever you might turn — Fire! Fire! The terrible blaze generated its own storm, which carried the roaring fire still further.

People covered themselves in wet cloths and ran to see if they could find protection somewhere. But they found the exits from the streets blocked with rubble. The smoke robbed them of breath. Many keeled over and were struck down by falling walls, suffocated by the smoke or devoured by the fire.

Those who got through searched, their eyes mad with fear, for a place that offered protection from the fire. They found only one: the huge, bare, burnt-out synagogue. Hundreds found rescue there in that terrible night.

There they sat, packed together and shivering on the cold floor, while everywhere else horrific death went about. There they sat and could not run away, when now the synagogue began to preach.

It was a terrible sermon, just one sentence: 'Be not deceived; God is not mocked; for whatever a man sows, that he will also reap' (Galatians 6:7).

Christ or Hitler?

Some of those there had taken part in setting this synagogue on fire. And others had watched with curiosity, laughing perhaps. Or at least they had kept silent and not objected. But — who had thought of God, the God who is not silent?!

Then the fire had devoured this one building. Now the city was engulfed in fire… And just this building was the refuge!

The synagogue preached. And even the most stubborn heard the sermon in that night of horror: 'Be not deceived; God is not mocked…'

But the story is not finished yet. The synagogue had a special sermon for one of the refugees.

He was a simple coal miner on a low wage, but he belonged to those who are 'rich in God' according to the Lord Jesus.

This man sat among those desperate people and was neither surprised nor worried. He was not surprised because he had long known that his nation was heading for dreadful judgements. And he was not worried because he had peace with God.

So now he sat in a corner, after he had helped many others. He was tired, but there was no way anyone could sleep.

And then the synagogue began to preach a special sermon to him. It asked: 'Do you know why you are safe here from the fire?'

And he answered, 'Yes, because the fire has raged here once already and has consumed everything that could burn.'

'Do you know also,' asked the synagogue, 'that there is another more terrible fire than the one from which you have sheltered here?'

'That I know well,' said the man, 'that is the dreadful fire of God's wrath and judgement that will one day flare up against all the unholiness of ungodly men.'

'Then you already know a lot!' said the synagogue. 'But do you think you will find a refuge then, when that fire is kindled? Will there be a place that can offer refuge because the fire has gone over it already?'

Now the man smiled among all those shocked and miserable people and said, 'I know what you're getting at. Yes, there is just one place where the fire of God's wrath has already gone, that can offer refuge: that is the cross of Jesus at Golgotha.'

'You are right!' said the synagogue. 'Just look at me! How safe you are in my bosom, because I previously suffered the fire. And thus you are safe at the cross of Jesus. How the fire burned then, when Jesus cried: "My God, my God, why have you forsaken me?" — Now you are safe there for ever from the judgement of God.'

At that the simple man rejoiced that he knew about this eternal refuge. Then he lay down as well as he could in that crowded place and went to sleep after all, resting peacefully, comforted like a child at his mother's heart.

'How sad!'

During the war many soldiers came to Essen for a while. Among them were Christians who had heard of me somehow and wanted to seek me out.

These visits led in time to the forming of a soldiers' group, which met in my home once a week. We looked at God's Word, shared our spiritual experiences and finished with an evening meal using the meagre rations allowed us.

Although the members of the group kept changing, yet a close fellowship existed between us, and all who took part in those evenings found them a pleasant oasis in the desolations of war time.

One day a middle-aged man found his way to us. His accent immediately gave away that he was a Bavarian. He had a quiet, refined manner. Only gradually did we discover that he was a very cultured man who had been through incredibly difficult times. Because of his frank confession of faith he had spent a long time in a concentration camp. At last he was released and then immediately called up for military service. The rough officers naturally regarded him as a suspicious concentration camp convict; so he got used to leading a quiet, unobtrusive life.

One evening however he opened up and told us something that made a deep impression on us all.

He was quartered in a room occupied by about ten soldiers. They were a noisy lot, especially a young man from Hamburg who had the most to say. He had obviously gone through all the cesspools of the city, and now he filled the room with his filthy talk. The curses and dirty jokes came like hail, and the others gave their delighted applause. The quiet man was just ignored.

One day the post came. The soldiers opened their packets and read their letters. The man from Hamburg also had his little parcel; presumably some girl had thought of him. And while he proudly displayed the contents — cigarettes and sweets — he boasted of his many treacherous love affairs.

Then came the point where the quiet man couldn't bear it any more. To the astonishment of all he stepped forward and said in his weighty, emphatic way, 'What a poor fellow you are! If what flows out of you is so dirty, what must it look like inside you? How sad that is!'

With that he went out of the room, and strangely it was suddenly dead quiet, while he pulled the door shut after him.

He had not gone far down the corridor when the other man ran up behind him. 'Comrade, stop!'

'What's up?'

'You said it's sad about me. No one has ever said anything like that to me. That — how shall I say — that looks as if I used to have some value. I don't understand that. Tell me, what do you mean by it?'

The quiet man stopped. And then he said, again in his remarkably emphatic way: 'God wanted to make something of you. You were created by him. And now — such filth! That's sad! Yes, comrade, when I know that God wanted to make something of you, then I can only say, that's sad about you!'

Straight after that they all had to report for roll-call. The quiet man went to his place. Suddenly, while the rows were forming, he felt someone gripping his hand from behind, and then a sweet was pressed into it. When he looked round he saw the rough Hamburg man standing behind him.

This was no time for a conversation. But when the roll-call was finished, the quiet man asked: 'Why are you being kind to me of all people? I've just given you my opinion very severely.'

Then it came out of him: 'You're the first person that has ever taken me seriously in my life! You do really think that my life could have value, do you?'

That was the account the quiet man gave in our soldiers' group. For a long time no one said a word. Everyone was thinking about the fact that most people — like that man from Hamburg — wear a mask, behind which the real person, with all his need and longing, is hiding. At last one of us asked: 'How did it go on?'

The quiet man smiled: 'We are friends now; yes, more: we are brothers. We read the Bible together. And my friend has found the Lord Jesus and knows that he is his Saviour. Sometimes the old, self-important man wants to break out. But then he gets a shock and looks at me. And I read in his look the question: Do you think that Jesus still has patience with me? But we both know that we live on his patience.'

The quiet man has gone from my circle of friends. I don't even know whether he is still alive. Perhaps he is buried somewhere in Russia. World history has taken no notice of him.

But I think that a story like that about the man from Hamburg is more important in the light of eternity than all the great battles of this dreadful war.

Deborah in the air raid shelter

To be honest, I was always a little afraid of 'Mother B' because she had a suspicion that pastors were lacking in true zeal for the kingdom of God. No doubt she had found this at times during her long life.

And because she was not a person who criticized people behind their backs, she visited me now and again and told me what she thought, or mentioned things that I ought to do. That was not always easy to bear, but often I had to admit she was right. And when at the end of the conversation she prayed, that made up for everything. Her prayers were mighty. You could sense a dread of God's majesty, as well as a burning love to the Lord Jesus and to lost men. I was shaken by her zeal for the kingdom and the glory of God.

That is how I imagine Deborah, the wife of Lapidoth, who as a judge in Israel defeated the Canaanites. You can read about her in the fourth chapter of the book of Judges. And I always felt that with Mother B I was like Barak, of whom the same chapter tells us that he did not fully match Deborah's mighty faith.

The terrible bombing raids came to Essen. There were many dreadful nights in which desperate people wandered through the streets not knowing where they could take refuge from the fire.

Hundreds of thousands fled to the countryside. When it was put to Mother B that she should also be evacuated, she disposed of that idea briefly: 'I have my work to do here.'

Indeed, so she did! How many in those days had new heart put in them through this woman so strong in faith!

One night she sat in the cellar again with the other residents from her block. Those were ungodly people who only smiled about the old woman.

Then came the air raid. Anyone who has experienced an hour of that knows what torture it is for the nerves: the whine of the high explosive bombs, the devilish hissing of the incendiaries, the rending crash of the explosions. A minute then becomes an eternity. And such a raid often lasted fifty minutes!

The people in the cellar screamed. They clung to each other. Any moment they could be buried in rubble or blown to pieces.

Suddenly a woman cried: 'Mother B, please pray!'

Mother B, who up till then had been sitting calmly and quietly, looked up. 'How can I pray for you to the God whom you have always despised?'

'Mother B, pray!' screamed the woman.

'I will do it,' said Mother B, 'if from now on you want to seek the Lord.'

'Yes, we do!' came the call from every corner of the cellar, in which dread had now completely taken over. The light had long since gone out. The cellar rocked like a ship in a storm. The bombs crashed, howled and hissed. Chalk dust filled the air. The people felt they were in the jaws of death.

'Yes, we want to seek God!' they called. 'We will go to church with you next Sunday!'

And then this poor old woman, who was strong in faith and had quietness and peace from God, prayed out loud. She placed this cellar with all its lost inhabitants into the hand of the Lord. She thanked him for his presence and called with a strong voice on him for help, strength and comfort.

This prayer of faith had a calming effect on all. The people experienced something of the 'peace that passes all understanding.'

286

The Second World War

At last the horrific raid was over. Quietly they went to their flats…

And now came Sunday morning. Mother B went from door to door and invited people to the service: 'You promised me that you would seek the Lord. Now come with me to hear his word!'

But in the end she had to go on her own. In one flat the door was slammed shut in her face, in another they stammered out apologies. In a third they chased her away with a curse, and in a fourth they just laughed at her…

A fortnight later another shocking night came to Essen. The people sat in the cellar again, with the light gone out as the bombs howled, crashed and hissed over a dying city.

The people in Mother B's cellar wanted to be strong this time. They were a bit ashamed of so 'losing their nerve.' But when half an hour had passed and the horror was only getting worse and worse, it was all over with being strong. And then no doubt they remembered how their hearts had been quietened by the old woman's strong prayer.

Mother B was among them again. Yes, calm and still she sat sunk down in a corner.

And then a heavy bomb landed right nearby. They heard the whine of its approach … a second of shock … then a deafening crash and bursting asunder … chalk dust… They thought now they would be choked to death…

Then a man cried out in horror: 'Mrs B! Please pray!' And they all joined in: 'Mother B, pray!'

For a short moment there was silence; only the din of the air raid could be heard. Then came the voice of Mother B through the darkness — and the hearers couldn't tell whether it sounded hard or sorrowful: 'With you I cannot pray any more, seeing you despise my God.'

And she left the people to their horror...

Deborah in the air raid shelter!

Later Mother B became very ill with cancer. For a long time she lay in hospital. Then they sent the old widow back home as a hopeless case.

Soon after that we met her on the street. She was, as so often, active in showing love. She could not stop helping those that had needs she could meet.

We were shocked: 'Mother B! But you are ill! How can you go around like that? How is the cancer doing?'

She waved her hand with a little annoyance and then said calmly, 'What has my cancer got to do with me?'

So she stayed strong and powerful, till the Lord called her home. Then we mourned the loss of a 'mother in Israel'.

When my house burned down

Until 1943 I lived in an enormous vicarage. I had a huge library and next to it a smaller study. And there was also another very small room with a high desk, in case I really wanted to be undisturbed. The great house had three guest apartments and enough rooms for every need.

For a housewife there were drawbacks to such a big house, and often we were miserably cold. We couldn't possibly keep all the stoves burning, and central heating was a rare luxury in those days.

Still, the house had many advantages. Meetings were often held in the big ground-floor rooms. And there was room for all my books… The building was marked as a vicarage by having a plaster head of Jesus mounted under a little gable facing the street. When my children were small they used to boast: 'In our house the Lord Jesus is looking out of the skylight!'

This house was destroyed on Sunday 5 March 1943 when Essen experienced its first heavy air raid.

I had just come with a young man from a meeting at the Youth Centre when the sirens began to howl. Quickly everyone ran into the cellar. My wife had always turned the previous alarms into a little feast; she made cocoa on a small cooker, and there were rusks to eat with it.

But on 5 March 1943 we lost the appetite for such little feasts. This raid was different! All hell was let loose above us. The house shook to its foundations. And when at last the crashing and destruction ended and we left the cellar, everything around was on fire. We could hardly breathe; the fire was consuming all the oxygen.

My wife gathered the five children and ran through fire and smoke to a place where they could still get a little air. And in all the tumult a young man kept on asking whether anyone had seen his hat. It was as if the world was coming to an end, and the man was looking for his hat! I have often thought what a picture that is of this world: it is heading for the judgement of God, the earth is already shaking under our feet, and yet people cling to trivialities.

Christ or Hitler?

At last I stood alone in the flames and tried to put them out. But — there was no water in the main! Helpless, I had to watch as my vicarage burned from the roof down to the ground.

Round about in all the streets, as far as the eye could see, were flames and rubble — and no man in sight! I stood there helpless in the horror. Enormous despair and rage rose in my heart. But in my confusion it was not clear against whom I should direct my anger: against Hitler, who had begun this stupid war? Against the fools who still talked about victory, though even a blind person could see that it was all going to end in catastrophe? Against the Americans who were smashing us to pieces so mercilessly?

Weigle House after its destruction in 1943

Suddenly, I remembered something that gave me a shock. In the morning we had worshipped together and had read the text for the day in the well-known booklet from the Brethren assembly. For 5 March 1943 the text was: 'Is there evil in the city, and the Lord has not done it?' (Amos 3:6).

So — God was responsible! God had burnt my house down! How could that be? But then a deep peace, even joy, came over me. *He* had the right to burn my house. *He* after all has thoughts of good towards us. *He* always leads his children in the right way.

I cannot express the peace that filled my heart. Now I began to put out fires here and there by beating firebrands together, pulling down walls and pushing beams away.

We carried on like this for another two days, and thus managed to preserve the ground floor of the house. My library was saved.

While we were still putting out fires a kind acquaintance came running and said, 'Would you like an apartment? My widowed daughter-in-law is finding things too hot round here. You can move into her flat.'

So I found a new home where I have stayed to this day. I sensed in all this the good leading of my heavenly Father.

I will never forget our delight as we moved into this flat. We came from streets full of rubble to a part of the town that was still fairly undamaged. In front of the house forsythias bloomed in brilliant gold. Behind it, in a little garden next to the park of the evangelical hospital, the birds awoke us with their song.

True, we still experienced plenty of air raid alarms here during the remaining war years, but our home was spared.

It was all on one floor. There was just a single room for me to work in and for my books. It's quite a spacious room, yet gone are the days when I could put out all my books.

Christ or Hitler?

The torch of love

For a moment I stood stunned. In the twilight I had stumbled over something, and as I looked closer I saw it was a corpse lying in the middle of the road, surrounded by dust and rubble.

I made a quick calculation; the last dreadful air raid had been at midday on Sunday. Now it was Wednesday evening. So there were still unburied corpses lying on the street!

A word from the Bible came to mind: 'Their corpses lie like dung in the street...'

'Like dung in the street...' I kept murmuring to myself.

Then I noticed a man watching me from a half-destroyed house. 'Do you think that's bad?' he asked. 'I'll show you something worse. Come with me!'

He went ahead through the rubble on the street, round a large wrecked building and into the yard at the back.

'Here!' he indicated. A cry of shock stuck in my throat. There lay perhaps eighty corpses. I had seen dreadful sights on the battlefields, but this was much worse. It was not soldiers that were lying here. Oh no! Here were old men, women worn out by work, and — children! Little girls with scrawny arms and thin little legs, showing the signs of the long war! Oh, children! What had they to do with this senseless war?

In my mind's eye I saw a picture by Hans Thoma: a meadow covered in blossoms, where happy children are jumping and dancing, with garlands of flowers in their hair.

Yes, that was how it should be! That meadow was where children should be! ....

The man had gone. The evening grew darker.

Somewhere in the ruined house a beam blown by the wind struck monotonously against the wall. Otherwise there was a deadly silence.

And as I stood like that between these corpses, so infinitely alone in the horror, in this dreadful stillness, a question sprang up to choke me — a terrible question: 'Where is God now? Why is he silent? Has he forsaken us? — Yes, we are God-forsaken!'

Forsaken by God! — That is hell! I felt horror. It was like a string tightening round my throat. I could have screamed with dread.

But then — I can only testify what I experienced — it was suddenly as if someone had spoken out loud a word from the Bible: 'God so loved the world that he gave his only-begotten Son, so that whoever believes in him should not perish, but have everlasting life' (John 3:16).

That word was suddenly there! The Holy Spirit himself must have called it to me in my desperation.

There stood the cross of Golgotha before me, on which the bleeding Son of God hung: 'God so loved the world that he gave his Son...' And suddenly I knew: 'Here is an everlasting sign of God's love: a shining torch of his endless love.'

I don't understand God. No! I will never understand his ways and his judgements. But one thing I know: he loves us! He loved us so much, that he gave his Son. The cross of Jesus calls the message loudly in a dark world: 'God does love us!'

Comforted, I left the dark courtyard.

12

The aftermath

'In ten years…!'

The bolts of my prison cell clanked. The door was torn open. 'Come out for interrogation!'

Yet again I was led down the long corridors to the Gestapo office.

I was unspeakably tired. What did they want from me now? Oh, I knew exactly what they wanted: to force me to make statements about the Confessing Church. And there was just no way I could betray my brothers.

By now this had gone on for weeks: nerve-racking waiting in the cramped cell, and even more nerve-racking interrogations.

Soon I was standing again before my tormentors. I knew well these three faces behind the broad table, these pale, soulless and cruel faces!

But — wonder of wonders — today they were showing friendly smiles. I got a fright: what did this mean? I was even offered a chair! That was new. Was the 'carrot' now going to be used because the 'stick' had failed? Inwardly I went into defence mode.

And then one of the three began: 'We have been observing you now for a while. And we have noticed that you are really not that bad. Only...'

He cleared his throat. And I knew: here it comes! He continued: 'Only — you are riding the wrong horse.'

'Yes, Sir?'

'Yes, it's time you began to realize that this occupation is completely redundant. In future we will not need youth pastors any more.'

I must have looked a bit astonished, so he tried to make himself clearer: 'Today we have a new world view. Christianity has had its day. In ten years no young person in Germany will know who your imaginary Jesus is! We will see to that!'

And then came a friendly offer: I should just take another job. They would be glad to help me. Yes, they even made various suggestions. It was touching to see how these hard men were concerned about my future.

Unfortunately, I was not in a position to accept such friendly offers. So in the end they got annoyed, and I wandered back down the long corridors — into the cell.

That was a difficult evening! 'In ten years no young person will know who Jesus is!' I kept hearing this hard sentence. Why should it not become true? After all, God can take away the gospel from a people! But what darkness would then cover my people!

The aftermath

It is an odd thing when people speak so definitely about the future. This was one of the marks of the Third Reich, that everyone, from the Führer down to the smallest official, could see into the future with an astonishing confidence. But above all this was the Word from the 2nd Psalm: 'He that dwells in the heavens shall laugh...'

In that dark evening hour in the prison cell I could not hear this comforting and heavenly laughter. My faith was so weak. I only heard the malicious laughter of hell: 'In ten years no young person will know who Jesus is!'

But God does more than our faith can grasp!

It was seven years later, on a Sunday in 1945.

Brilliant sunshine woke me early. Immediately the thought of our current situation descended on me and produced the most contradictory feelings. Gone was the honour of our people! Cities were destroyed, including Essen where I lived and worked. My dear old church lay in ruins; my house was burnt down; my son was buried somewhere in Russia. Everywhere the terrible hunger went through the land. Oh, how we hungered in those days after the war! But what was that compared with the unspeakable sorrow; the flower of young manhood was dead, sacrificed to the mad dreams of politicians!

And yet, the war was finished. No more terrible nights of bombing. No more senseless destruction. Finished also — I breathed a sigh of relief — the cruelties of the Gestapo and all the pointless prohibitions of our youth work...

Suddenly an unspeakably happy note broke into my thoughts. Somewhere outside a trombone choir drew near and played:

Christ or Hitler?

Go out, my heart, and seek your joy
in this most lovely summertime
from grace, the good gift of your God…

Now I couldn't stay in bed anymore. I jumped to the open window!
What an overpowering sight: in the morning sunlight lay the
wooded heights of the Siegerland.

O valleys wide, O verdant heights,
you lovely woods so green…!

My window was a vantage point, with a view that stretched far over
the land.

But my view was captivated by what was happening under my
window on the main road from Siegen to Dillenburg. A procession
was approaching with trombones in front. Jubilantly they sounded
out Paul Gerhardt's summer song:

I cannot rest, nor want to sleep;
the doings of our mighty God
my senses all awake…

After the trombones followed young men. There were not many
yet! Most of the young men were still prisoners of war. And how
many would never come back home! But this little troop of twenty
men did still make my heart glad.

Then came the boys, and then the girls; then a mingled crowd of
men, women and little children.

Over the whole procession there was a joy that cannot be described!
For years such Christian festivals had been forbidden. For the first
time we could meet again!

The aftermath

Just under my window the happy procession met another group of people coming round the bend from Siegen. The trombones stopped, the processions broke up. Joyfully the young people greeted each other.

I thought I was dreaming!

But now the joy with which I remember that great day has made me run ahead of myself in writing, and the poor reader has no real idea of where we are.

Between Siegen and Dillenburg the road goes over one of the highest points of this mountain region. It is called the Rödgen. There are only a few houses there, two farmsteads, a health resort, a vicarage and a great ancient church.

Here God gave mighty awakenings in the nineteenth century; to this day the 'pious Siegerland' is known for its lively spiritual life. This was also shown by the mission festivals on the Rödgen, to which many young people came in former years. That annoyed the rulers of the Third Reich, and so the festivals were forbidden.

Now the bonds were broken. A youth mission festival was to be celebrated once again on the Rödgen!

The news spread through the region like wildfire. 'Youth mission festival on the Rödgen!' The people came streaming together! And all the misery of that time, all the worries and needs were submerged in the indescribable joy of God's people when they come together.

That is what I saw from the upstairs window of the vicarage. On all the roads people were approaching. From all directions came the sound of trombones!

Christ or Hitler?

Quickly I dressed; and now downstairs!

When I saw the young pastor's wife I was cut to the quick. Here, too, the sorrow of that time had spread its dark wings: the pastor had gone missing in Russia. The young woman had already laid down her suffering before the throne of grace. And now she was rejoicing with those who were happy.

What a teeming throng under the old trees in front of the house, in the vicarage garden, at the edge of the wood, in the meadows!

A church elder came rushing toward me: 'The church is much too small for the festival service!'

We considered the matter. Yes, what was now to be done?

Behind the church a meadow sloped steeply up the mountain. 'If we open all the windows, then the people can sit in the meadow and follow the service.'

Yes, open the windows! That was not so simple. They were a few hundred years old. The glass and lead fell out of the first one with a clatter. 'Never mind!' said the elder smiling. I don't think he was usually so generous. But today was special!

I will never forget that service as long as I live. I could hardly find room to get to the communion table, from which the Scripture was to be read. All the gangways and even the pulpit steps were packed with young people waiting expectantly. And the meadow outside was like a brightly coloured carpet — radiant youth!

The trombones began. The glorious Tersteegen hymn sounded out powerfully:

The aftermath

> Lord of victory, King of honour,
> Majesty enthroned on high.

And then, exactly at that moment, the memory came back. I saw myself standing again in that disgusting office, and I saw the empty, cruel faces: 'In ten years no young person will know any more who your imaginary Jesus is!'

But here the young people were singing:

> At your feet shall I not fall
> while my heart exults with joy
> when the eye of faith beholds
> all the glory of your might?

With some astonishment the young people saw the festival preacher wipe away tears which just could not be held in. I was hardly able to finish the Scripture reading:

> …and it happened, while he blessed them he was parted from them and went up into heaven.

Then the choir began and sang the verse from the 126th psalm: 'When the Lord sets free the captives of Zion, we shall be like those who dream. Then will our mouth be full of laughter and our tongue full of praise…'

Now that had happened all around us. And this great crowd had an inkling of what it will be like in the future new world, when one day all, all bonds will fall,

> …when altogether free of woe
> His countenance I'll see.

Christ or Hitler?

Luke 15 in the camp

'Dear Pastor, that idea of yours is impossible. Right on the first night your tents will be taken down and sold on the black market.'

'Let that be my problem, director! Just send me four of the young people from your mine, and don't worry.'

'Well, you should know. You have been warned! Goodbye!'

'Goodbye!'

I put down the phone very thoughtfully. What the man had said was quite right. It really was risky to arrange a camp for young miners in the chaotic time between the end of the war and the reform of the currency. Would it be better to give up the whole thing?

But then I saw them in my mind's eye: All these young fellows, whom the war and the economic collapse had brought flooding into the Ruhr district. Homeless ones, orphans, young men without any roots! There were hundreds of them in the wretched barracks from which the Polish forced labourers and all the displaced persons had recently moved out. The works managers tore their hair at the thought of these strange 'miners.' Sixty per cent of them ran away as soon as they had received their first wages, and then sold their shoes, their tools and whatever else belonged to the mine on the black market.

Should I not bring the gospel to this 'lost generation'? Surely yes! I could take at most seventy boys in one camp, and our souls were burdened with thousands. But just at that time I heard the beautiful Chinese proverb: 'The greatest darkness cannot stop us from lighting at least one candle.' I just wanted to light my small candle.

The aftermath

Then suddenly everything seemed to happen of its own accord. The American military authority was interested in my attempt. They made tents and provisions available. The YMCA let us use their country house. And so out went the invitations: 'Every pit to send four young people!'

So far all was going well. But now the works managers got worried. They knew their men, and thought that a pastor would probably not be up to such a responsibility. No doubt they were right. But — did they know the power of Jesus?

I went to the American military authority. The colonel laughed: 'Just give it a try! The USA can stand the loss of a few tents!'

And then came the day when the young men arrived at the camp. I can't remember now whether I laughed or cried. In no time at all there was the most terrific tumult. One of them had brought cigarettes and opened up a black market. Another sat with an accordion on the grass and sang out loud, with his companions, coarse pop songs that made my face redden with shame. Not far off a few were already having a fight.

It was just as well that supper was ready. I even managed to say grace. Then I sat down next to the darkest looking lad, who was brooding as he stabbed fiercely at his plate. Grumpily he moved to one side.

'Where are you from?' I asked.

'Crailsheim.'

'Oh, you're a Württemberg man! Then we can chat in Swabian.' He looked up, astonished. 'D'you know the Swabian land then?'

'Of course, man. When I think of it I get homesick!' He nodded understandingly.

I asked: 'You homesick, too?'

He nodded again. Then he ponderously pulled out his wallet, and searched in it for a long time. At last he laid on the table before me a cigarette card with a picture. It was so battered there was no way I could make out what it was.

'Crailsheim?' I asked. Again a nod. And moist eyes. From that moment on he was my best helper and support…

But then came the first morning; and now I had to come out with what I really wanted to do. The whole company was gathered in the day room, rather curious to see what was coming.

I stood on a chair: 'Men! Brothers! A question: What can you take seriously?'

Laughter! Roars: 'Nothing!'

'Don't you take me seriously either?'

More laughter. 'No! Why should we?'

'Don't you take yourselves seriously?'

This time there was no laughter; just a bitter 'No!' as from one mouth.

'So that's how it is! Well, that's good! Now there's some room in your hearts for something that you can really enjoy taking seriously. That Is God's Word. Here is a heap of Bible portions. Please distribute them among yourselves. We are now going to read together in this New Testament for half an hour. If you find it boring, then we will never do it again. But — for my sake — let's give it a try today.'

With that I pulled out a packet of booklets containing Mark's Gospel, with a brightly coloured picture on the title page. I had got them from the British and Foreign Bible Society.

Astonished, the young men helped themselves. I almost lost courage. Some grinned, some made great big eyes, others were already thinking about lighting up cigarettes. A few were making really stubborn faces.

I cried inwardly to God and then called: 'In the first chapter there's a really great story — from verse 40 onwards. Please turn to it!'

Then they all began to search, and so found their way into the Bible study. And now this wonderful story became alive before our eyes. How there is a great crowd thronging around the Lord Jesus — how suddenly there is excitement: a leper dares to come near; how the crowd want to chase him away — how they scatter in all directions, shocked, for of course no one wants to be infected with this gruesome illness — how the miserable man, this disgusting, pus-oozing rotting little heap of misery lies before Jesus in the dust...

And then — now the young men hold their breath — then the Saviour takes a step towards him and lays his hand on his head. The Saviour's hand on that pus-covered, evil smelling head! He does not turn away from anyone that seeks him. He loves the one who is lying there like dirt in the dust.

And then the Saviour raises him up and heals him ... that's how it is with the Lord Jesus!

Christ or Hitler?

The half hour was over. 'Shall we do it again tomorrow?'

'Yes!' was the call from all sides. I didn't hear a single 'No.'

'So, everyone out! Now we're going swimming. Afterwards it's handball.'

The company charged out. Matches were lit. The black market cigarettes spread their biting smoke. I kept standing on my chair and looking. It seemed to me — or was I imagining it? — as if something had changed. And suddenly I realized with a great joy: I am not alone in wrestling for the hardened souls of these boys. He himself is among us, the only One who loves lepers.

Lunch hour. Most of them were lying in the grass or in the tent and having a 'kip.' That was how they put it. Their vocabulary was small and very rough.

I went through the rows of tents… There, wild laughter! A loud voice! The tent walls were so thin. I hurried over to ask those who were making a disturbance to respect the others' rest time. But then I had to stop: someone inside was telling a joke. But what? A joke? That wasn't witty, that was just revolting and indecent.

Indignant, I threw back the door sheet and entered the tent. What I saw took my breath away. There were the two youngest in the camp, boys of fifteen or sixteen.

I lay down with them on the straw: 'Boys, I'm afraid I heard what you are telling each other.'

'So?' said one of them calmly, and began to roll himself a cigarette.

'You must be very poor lads. Inside you must look like a bucket of filth; because what is coming out is stinking dirt.'

The aftermath

'Yes, that's how it is,' said the boy, who was really still a child. His fingers meanwhile rolled the cigarette nervously. 'The boys here in the camp are all saying the pastor is really putting himself to a lot of trouble with us. But…!'

Now he looked at me with eyes that were frightening to look at, because their light seemed to have gone out. Then he put the cigarette to his mouth, passed it over the tip of his tongue and carefully stuck it together. And while he looked for matches in his pocket he said, '…Just leave it! With us two all effort is in vain. No one can rescue us.'

He lit the cigarette and took a deep pull into his lungs: 'Look, this is how it was. Back home in Silesia they said that the Russians were coming! Then everybody hopped it, including my mother and me. There were five of us.'

'And your father?' I interrupted.

He shrugged his shoulders: 'Fallen somewhere or other. We were a little column, almost all women and children. On the way we met an anti-aircraft battery. They took us boys with them; they needed helpers. Well, then we came among men. What we saw and went through then! And afterwards in a POW camp in Italy.'

'Italy?'

'Well yes, that's where we landed in the end. There's no misery, no dirt, no filthy swamp that we haven't seen. We were poisoned with dirt. And therefore…' he took another deep pull, '…and therefore all this is no use. No one can rescue us.'

I felt something clutching at my heart. These were children after all! Who would have to answer for that, these children's souls, defiled and trodden into the dust?

And suddenly I saw a picture before me: The Saviour's hand on the head of the leper, the one who was lost without remedy. 'Oh my dear boys,' I said. 'Have you completely forgotten this morning's story?'

'Naa, that was good.'

'Lads! Don't you know that the Lord Jesus has a burning love for you? For him there are no hopeless cases. He detests no one. He brings people back from the brink of death...'

I couldn't stop speaking about Jesus. Four boyish eyes stared at me. The message was so incredible! Slowly the cigarette went out between the fingers. The boy throws the stub out past the tent door. A few others were standing there. 'Just come in!' I called. Soon the tent was full.

And once again was enacted the wonderful story, that has at all times agitated and baffled the Pharisees: 'This Jesus receives sinners and eats with them.'

That's what it says in Luke's Gospel, chapter 15. And this is still happening, even in our own day.

Echoes from the preached word

When I say 'Amen' in my pulpit on Sunday, then the sermon is not over and done with, because a few years ago a publisher began to print my sermons, and so every week about ten thousand copies flutter over the land.

I have often wondered how these printed sermons get on. Will they find open ears and hearts? Do they get read? Are they understood?

The aftermath

Sometimes I feel as if I've called out loudly, and I am waiting to see if an echo comes back.

One day such an echo came, a moving account from a man who regularly read these sermons. On Easter Sunday afternoon he was reading a sermon about the wonderful story of the seven disciples, who after a night of fishing and catching nothing are approaching the shore in their boat. There in the morning light they see a man standing on the shore. He calls to them. And suddenly young John cries out: 'It is the Lord!' Yes indeed! It was the risen Jesus himself who was seeking his timid disciples.

This sermon made a big impression on the man. He put the leaflet in his wallet and got up to visit a seriously ill friend in hospital.

He found his friend very troubled and downhearted. So he said, 'I'm going to read you a sermon.' He pulled the printed sermon out of his pocket and read it to his poor friend, who received the Easter message like a thirsty land drinking in the rain. And when the visitor said goodbye, the sick man asked: 'Can you please leave me the sermon here? I want to read it over again in peace and quiet.'

'Gladly!' said the man. So he laid the sermon on the bedside table. In big print the title on the first page proclaimed: '**It is the Lord!**'

A few hours passed. Quietly the door opened as the sick man's wife came to visit him. She had an eerie feeling as she saw her husband lying motionless. He did not answer her greeting. She hurried to the bed. She called him, but there was no response.

She took his hand. It was ice cold. The sick man had passed into the eternal world.

Christ or Hitler?

Desperate and shocked, the woman was about to scream. Then she saw the leaflet that was lying on the bed cover. The large type sentence struck her eye with forceful impact: **'It is the Lord!'**

The Lord! The living One! Shaken she realized: 'Here I am not alone with my dear deceased husband. A third one has come in. It is the Lord!'

She sank to her knees and prayed silently to the One who has overcome death, and who comforts the desperate. Her heart became still and full of consolation. Then she called the ward sister…

There is another strange echo I want to tell you about. The postman brought me a letter one day. I didn't recognize the sender's address. A bit half-heartedly I began to read. But then I started up. What that letter said — yes, that was just phenomenal!

The letter came from the typesetter at the firm where the sermons were being printed at that time. This was in the confused times after the war and before the so-called currency reform. It was very difficult then for the publisher to get the necessary paper. And when they had the paper, it was even more difficult to find a printer to take on the job. So the publisher had finally given the work to a small two-man business. One man set the type and the other ran the machine.

The typesetter had written to me. He had come back from the war as a totally distraught and unbelieving man. 'They made such fools of us!' he said. 'Now I don't want to believe anything any more, except that two pounds of beef make a good soup.'

It was no wonder that he was really annoyed when he had to set the type for a sermon every week. He of all people! He described very fully how week after week he had got angry about the 'stupid nonsense'. Yes, it really got under his skin that he had to help in the distribution of such 'rubbish'.

To work off his annoyance he deliberately made the most ridiculous misprints. He described this very fully in his letter.

It became so obvious that the misprints were deliberate, that he kept waiting every day for a big row. It was clear to him that the publishers couldn't possibly let this pass; the sermons were never fit to be printed, and the publisher had to keep on proof-reading them and send the corrections back to the printers.

The typesetter got cheekier and cheekier with his misprints. But nothing happened. The man who did the proof-reading showed such patience that our typesetter eventually began to feel ashamed.

And when he had become ashamed enough, he thought that perhaps there was something in the message after all. In the letter he described how from then on he began to read the sermons not with hate but with curiosity. And in that way the Holy Spirit of God touched his heart.

At the end of the letter came the words: 'Now I believe from my heart in the Lord Jesus, whom you proclaim. And I look forward every week to the new sermon. Yes, I am glad that I can help in the proclamation of this glorious message of the love of God, which has come to us in Jesus Christ.'

When I had read this wonderful letter, I went into my quiet study and thanked God that it is still true today what he said through the prophet Jeremiah: 'Is not my word like a hammer that breaks the rock in pieces?'

Christ or Hitler?

The uprooted ones

1. Salt of the earth

As I stood in the pulpit, I noticed a young man's face: pale, with dark rings round the eyes — a typical miner's face.

On further Sundays I saw him again, now accompanied by others. So one Sunday I spoke to him after the service. I discovered that he was from the east, that he was totally alone in the world and lived in a big hostel in which hundreds of young miners had found some sort of home.

'Why don't you pay me a visit?' he said. 'My friends would be glad to see you as well.'

So one day I stood in front of the huge, hideous, bare brick building in which six hundred young men lived. Behind the building the first mine tower reared up. Apart from that I could see well kept allotments and badly kept tenement blocks.

I went through the big gate. A rough voice called from a porter's hut, asking where I thought I was going. This was not somewhere that just anyone could enter.

A bit shocked, I was about to give the information when I felt a blow on my shoulder: 'Really! Why, this is Pastor Busch! My, that's great that you have come to see us!'

It turned out that the burly man was the house father. When I explained to him that I wanted to visit a young miner, he laughed in a slightly embarrassed way and said, 'There are rough fellows in this house. I think you could have all sorts of experiences.'

The aftermath

The man was right. I did have 'all sorts' of experiences.

My friend lived in room 23. When I opened the door, I remembered the time when I had lived as a young soldier in army barracks: that smell of spent air, of sweat, cheese, cigarettes and socks! In the middle was a huge table, round the walls iron lockers and camp beds.

My friend was a bit embarrassed to get such a 'middle class' visitor. The other young men looked up with curiosity and mistrust. At this moment it dawned on me that these young people were living in a totally different world from my own. They had no idea of what life can look like when one has a chance to make one's own choices. And most of all — they didn't know what it was to be alone! Surely, deep down they were all desperately lonely people — lonely, but never alone!

I had to break through the awkwardness. I managed that, and soon we were sitting round the big table having an informal conversation.

'Now just tell me how it was that you found your way into my church service,' I asked my young friend.

Without any inhibitions he answered: 'I used to be in a YMCA in Silesia. There I decided to belong to the Lord Jesus. When I came to Essen, I enquired where I could hear the Jesus message. And so I came to hear you preach.'

I was really astonished that nobody made a face at the mention of the Lord Jesus. Anyone who knows the atmosphere of such rooms knows that the name of Jesus always calls forth opposition, scorn and mockery. But here none of that happened. That was remarkable. So I asked the others: 'Well, and what do you say to that?'

For a moment there was silence. Then a tall chap raised himself up: 'OK then, we may as well tell him! At first it really annoyed us to hear that our comrade was going to church. After all, he had to get up so early that we were always disturbed.'

'Yes, yes,' another nodded, 'we made life hard for him. Now we can talk about it. I always threw my boots after him. But nothing would stop him.'

'On the contrary,' another chimed in, 'he kept inviting us to come with him. Of course, there was no question of that happening. But, at Christmas, early in the morning, he said he was going to the Christmas service. And — well, you know, Christmas is something special after all. In short, we all went with him.'

I was astonished. 'And since then have they left you alone?' I asked my young friend.

At that his face lit up: 'Why, now they come with me!' he said happily. And all the rough fellows looked embarrassed, as if they had been found out in some evil crime.

But I looked at my friend; and through my mind went the words of Jesus: 'You are the salt of the earth! You are the light of the world! A city that is built on a mountain cannot stay hidden' (Matthew 5:13-14).

2. A worrying question

I didn't get away as soon as I had thought. 'You must pay our comrades next door a visit!'

They led me to the next room, and there they left me alone. I had to smile. Those lads knew their buddies. And they were probably all agog to see how they would react to a visit from a pastor. But they had managed it so that he had to fight it out on his own.

There I stood in a big room that was home to sixteen young men. One was eating his soup at the table. Another was just getting ready to go out ('I'm off to the cinema for a bit!'). A third lay on his bed and told dirty jokes... In short, they were all occupied, so much so that they hardly looked up when I stepped into the room. And then everyone carried on as if I were not there at all.

An uncomfortable situation! I had to do something to change it.

'Hello men!' I called out with all the hearty openness that I could possibly muster. But my well-intentioned greeting had not the slightest effect. The young man who was eating soup from a tin bowl looked up without the slightest interest and carried on eating. The one at the window who was rolling himself a cigarette had obviously heard nothing at all. I felt — how shall I put it? — as if I was a wine salesman, who has, by mistake, offered champagne to a total abstinence society.

Now it was getting beyond a joke. I made a quick decision and sat down opposite the soup eater. 'So where are you from?'

'Upper Silesia.'

'And your relatives?'

'All dead!' End of conversation.

I turned to a second one: 'And where is your home?'

'East Prussia.'

'Do you have any relatives left?'

'My mother lives in the East Zone.'

I asked a third: 'Where are you from?'

'I'm from Bavaria. My parents are divorced. My, are they glad to be rid of me!' Everyone laughed.

'How old are you then?' I asked.

'Eighteen.'

From the background someone called: 'That's our youngest, our sweet little one!'

I turned to the man in the background: 'Whereabouts is your home?'

'Me? I scarpered with my old man from the East Zone. Now he is slowly starving to death in Hagen.'

It was nerve-racking how the most shattering life stories were being told with such utter indifference.

Then the young man lying on the bed raised himself up: 'Hey, I suppose you like interrogating people?' Scorn and threatening sounded in his voice. Now I must make a forward move.

'Yes,' I replied. 'Quite right! I interrogate people. Have you ever heard of the Gallup Institute?'

They knew about that: 'That's a sort of polling company in America!'

'That's right!' I continued. 'I'm something like that. But actually I have only one question. What I have asked so far was not the real one.'

'Well then, fire away!' said the soup eater comfortably and put his bowl to one side. He had finished and was lighting himself a cigarette.

I looked directly at him: 'My question is: Are you how you should be?'

He was astonished. He became embarrassed. Finally he said in annoyance: 'I am the way I am!'

I laughed: 'Look, you haven't the guts to answer my question.'

He flared up: 'What do you mean? Of course I've got the guts!'

'Well, then just answer me: Are you how you should be?'

He looked around desperately. Then he burst out: 'No one is!'

I kept at it: 'You are evading the question again! I didn't ask about all men. I asked, are you how you should be?'

A moment of silence, then he said honestly, 'No.'

I looked at a second man: 'Are you how you should be?'

He made no excuses: 'No.'

Suddenly there was a tremendous tension in the air as I now asked one after another: 'And you?'

Monotonously and honestly the answer each time was 'No! I am not how I should be.'

There was a tension in the air when I finished. 'Gentlemen,' I said, 'then you must allow me a second question: Why do you not change?'

This question suddenly galvanised all into life. The one on the bed jumped up and cried: 'Heavens! Yes! Why don't we change? I've never thought of that! I've always known that we needed to.'

One got very assertive and came right up to me: 'Well, you try living in such conditions! And then you say we should change! It's only because of the conditions!'

I waved him aside: 'That's nonsense! I know lots of people who live in first rate economic and social conditions, and still don't change, though they badly need it. No, that's not the reason!'

He saw the point of that. Everyone went quiet again. The one on the bed — he had thrown himself onto it again — just murmured: 'Why don't we change?'

'I'll tell you,' I answered him, 'because you can't! No one can change his nature and escape his own skin!'

It got lively again. All were talking at the same time: 'So there you are! Why do you first have to drive us mad?' … 'Sure, that's how it is.'

Once again I had to call for quiet: 'I haven't finished yet! Now I want to give you a hint. Have you ever heard of Jesus?'

Embarrassed and astonished, they muttered: 'Well, of course!'

'Has it ever occurred to you that Jesus might be relevant to a miners' hostel?'

Laughter and shaking of heads.

But they got a real shock when I actually shouted out: 'Then you are seriously mistaken! Jesus is relevant to you! This same Jesus is the one who said, "See, I am making all things new." He died for you on the cross, so that you could be different, totally new. So, start looking in his direction! And now I must go.'

As I pulled the door shut behind me a great conversation broke out in the room.

3. How do you know?

The next room was small, and only three men were in it. One was sitting at the table and reading. A second, who turned out to be from Berlin, was shaving. The third was frying a chop.

'Good afternoon!' I began bravely. 'I am the Protestant youth pastor. As I have just been visiting your mates I wanted to greet you as well.'

The man from Berlin grinned. While he scraped at his beard he declared mockingly: 'I always listen to pastors! Not wanted!!'

'What a big mouth,' I thought, and replied: 'Not wanted? What is not wanted?'

He just looked me straight in the face and said laughing, 'God is not wanted! We're not interested in him! So now you know!'

Livid anger rose in me: 'Man!' I thundered at him: 'That's not the issue, whether you are interested in God. Much more important is whether the holy, living God has any interest in such a windbag as you…!'

At this moment the wonder of the gospel gripped me, so that I added: '…and just imagine it: he does! It's wonderful but true: God is interested in you!'

This must have struck home, for he lowered his razor and said full of surprise: 'What makes you think that? So far no one has ever been interested in me!'

Now I just had to tell him the great word from the Bible: 'God so loved the world that he gave his only-begotten Son so that whoever believes in him should not perish, but have everlasting life' (John 3:16).

Then I knew that I had said all that was needed here. I gave him my hand: 'That's what I wanted to tell you. Goodbye!' I went.

In the next room I had hardly said 'Good afternoon' when the three stormed in, the man from Berlin at the head: 'Man! We must hear more about that!' And before the occupants of the room had a chance to know what was going on, we were sitting at the table and I was bearing witness to Jesus as the Saviour and the Son of God.

The green may-bug

Some years ago I was due to hold a week of Gospel Lectures in a South German town. In the middle of the week I was sitting together with a crowd of people from the town. One of them said, 'On Saturday night our streets are swarming with revellers. We have a lot of night-spots, and people come into our town on

Saturdays to have a good time. How about inviting them to a meeting at midnight?'

They were all for it, and decided to print special invitation leaflets. The young people would give them out at night in the streets.

'Yes, but what subject shall we take?' was asked. The discussion went back and forth. Meanwhile I was in the background talking to a young man. At last the chairman, somewhat annoyed, called across to me: 'Brother Busch, why don't you suggest a subject?'

I had not been following the debate and was far too deep in conversation with the young man to give a proper answer. So I laughed and said, 'You must decide the subject! I'm quite happy with whatever you choose, even if it's "The green may-bug"!'

I meant that as a joke, and was rather shocked when the next day I found that the dear people had taken my suggestion seriously! The printed leaflets showed a green may-bug, with an invitation to a midnight meeting. Now there was nothing else for it; I had to talk on the subject 'The green may-bug'.

Shortly before midnight I came into the meeting room. A strange room! It was a big tent, like a circus tent. Inside was a motley company, male and female, laughing, chattering, smoking cigarettes, some dissipated old people and some young blood.

I stepped onto the stage. 'Ladies and gentlemen, I am now going to entertain you for twenty minutes with the "green may-bug". What do you think? Are there green may-bugs?'

'No!' yelled most of them. I retorted: 'Do you know that absolutely for sure?' Then they were a bit uncertain. There was a general discussion. A few called out that you couldn't be certain that such wonderful creatures might not exist in the jungles of South America.

Now I spoke again: 'So we don't know for certain. Well, that's not so serious. It won't give us sleepless nights. But there is another question, which you treat in the same way: "You can't know for sure." But this is a question that must be settled before we can sleep peacefully. I'm talking about the question, "Is there a living God?"'

That started a commotion! 'There is no God!' shouted a fat chap laughing, with his hat tilted on one side. I turned to him: 'Are you sure about that?' Then he got embarrassed and was silent. The whole company became very still. And I continued: 'I know for sure that God lives.' A heckler called: 'How do you know that?' I waved my hand, and he was quiet again. I said, 'I know that because he sent his Son. It is really bad that you live as if you could know nothing for certain about God. He lives! He has declared his will in his commandments. And — one day you will be judged before his throne. You should live your lives in the light of that.'

I was interrupted. A drunkard stumbled out grumbling. At the same time a new group of merrymakers entered the tent. So I broke off, waited until all had found seats and then began again: 'We're talking here about the green may-bug!'

'There's no such thing!' called one of the newcomers.

'Well, we have just decided that we don't know that for sure.'

'Have you ever seen one?'

'No, but if I were to meet such a green may-bug I would say to it, "Friend, there's something wrong with you. A proper may-bug is brown."'

The aftermath

I waited a few seconds: all were listening with rapt attention. And then I continued: 'I fear that you are all green may-bugs. There is something wrong with you as well. We have just been speaking about the living God. What do you think? If God looks at your life, does he approve of it? I suspect that there are many things not right in your life. Or are you as you should be?'

A young man right in the front shook his head honestly. I went on: 'With one something is wrong in his marriage. With another it's to do with money. The third is having strife in his house. And you are all living without having peace with God.'

Every face was turned towards me. And believe you me, I suddenly discovered that all these faces looked tense and unhappy. It was as if the laughing mask had dropped off. My heart burned: 'Why don't you get your lives sorted out? It's not impossibly difficult!'

The faces suddenly looked full of doubt, as if they wanted to say, 'That is terribly difficult.'

'No, it is not so difficult at all. Because you can have a strong helper, the Lord Jesus, the Son of God. He has come to save sinners!'

While we were still talking about this, yet more people came into the tent and were very astonished to find such an attentive gathering. So I had to start again from the beginning. 'Dear people,' I called, 'we wanted to talk for twenty minutes about the green may-bug; and now three quarters of an hour has passed. Shall we go on?'

'Go on!' was the call from all sides.

'Good. Now listen. We don't know whether green may-bugs exist. But if they do, they have something in common with the brown ones. Do you know what? When they fall on their back, then they can't get up again on their own, and exactly the same is true of us. We have fallen, not onto our back, but into sin and guilt. None of us can come out of that on his own. But there is a wonderful hand that is stretched out towards us and wants to set us on our feet, and that is the hand of our Saviour Jesus Christ.'

We continued speaking about that for a long time. Late at night the people went quietly out of the tent. And to me it was as if I saw the Lord Jesus, how he goes seeking after these poor people, just the way he sought after us.

A strange visit

My heart was beating fast as I stood in front of the simple wooden house in Oslo. It was just like any of the brightly painted wooden houses that are to be found all over Norway.

But this house had a special significance for me: Bishop Berggrav lived here. How often I had heard his name! When Germany occupied Norway this man was a fearless witness for the truth, who finally landed in prison. It is a wonder that he escaped execution.

And when the war was over he showed himself to be a real brother to the Christians in Germany. Not just among our people, but all over the world he is known as one of the leading men in Christianity.

So you can understand why my heart was beating and why I hesitated a moment before I rang the bell.

A young student received my companion and myself and took us to the study. You could see it straight away: a stormy and wide-ranging spirit is at work here. Mountains of papers, books and manuscripts covering every possible surface! A massive office armchair was surrounded by these witnesses of a phenomenal mental diligence.

Then my gaze fell on the enormous relief that hung above the armchair. I recognized straight away the distinctive head that it showed; for a photo of this head had long been hanging in my study in Essen. The relief showed Hans Nielsen Hauge, the lay preacher through whom God gave the Norwegian people such a deep and powerful awakening.

The picture of the lay preacher, the revivalist, above the desk of the Lutheran bishop! That expresses perfectly a programme for the church in Norway.

Such thoughts filled up the time while we waited. He must be coming now. I expected a majestic bishop-like appearance. Then in swept — yes, I can only express it like that — in swept a small man in a yellowish suit. In one hand he balanced a tray with coffee, in the other he carried a tobacco pipe the like of which I had never seen before. It looked as if a lumberjack had made it with an axe.

I presumed that this was a servant, but then this man came towards me, silently extended his hand to me, silently motioned me into an armchair, poured out some coffee and passed me the cup.

So this was Bishop Berggrav! Silently he looked at me. I began to feel hot. What was I to say now? Then I just told him simply: 'I just wanted to have one look at you, Bishop. I am so curious.'

At that he laughed and said, 'That is a good curiosity!'

'I know,' I declared, 'that my standing before you is not good. I am German. And you and your people have suffered much wrong through the invasion of the Germans and through the occupation.'

Christ or Hitler?

'We can distinguish between Germans and Nazis,' he growled.

'No!' I said. 'I share the guilt of that wrong. If I had properly resisted the wrong, I would not be alive now. I cannot distance myself from the guilt. My people's guilt is my guilt.'

'It's good that you say that,' he observed seriously. 'I was in a German hotel recently. When the waiter noticed that I was Norwegian, he began to say, full of enthusiasm: "I was in Norway during the war. What a beautiful country that is!" — At that I got up and went to another table. I felt as if a burglar was saying to me: "Oh, I know your house. I broke in there once. It's a really nice place!" I believe that the Germans do not know to this day what they perpetrated in the war...'

He paused. I sensed that he wanted to say something and was not quite sure whether he should say it. Clearly there was a conflict in his heart between ruthless honesty and the tender love that did not want to hurt. Then he pulled himself together.

'I want to tell you why I brought the coffee myself. My long serving, faithful housekeeper told me brusquely: "If you have a German visiting you, then just bring in the coffee yourself. I cannot do it."'

I looked up, shocked. And he continued: 'I regret that this girl's Christianity is not stronger. But — one can understand it. When I was arrested, they didn't just take action against my employees, but against their relatives as well. My housekeeper comes from a little farm in the north near the border with Finland. One day the SS appeared there, burnt down the farmhouse, slaughtered all the cattle and drove the people into the woods.'

He was silent. Tears came to my eyes as I imagined the terrible tragedy in those lonely forests. I understood how it was that the girl could not bring the coffee to a German. And I was shocked at how quickly my people have shaken off and forgotten these fearful things.

Then the Bishop laid his hand with an infinitely tender gesture on my arm: 'I will tell my household staff about you.'

Now I do not give up hope that my sorrow can help a poor Norwegian girl — to forgive.

Closing days
(by Ulrich Parzany, Wilhelm Busch's son-in-law and successor as youth pastor in Essen)

The limitations resulting from a heart attack caused Busch serious thought. In May 1966 he was recuperating at Wildbad in the Black Forest. During these days he wrestled to know the will of God for his further service. Should he continue with tiring evangelistic work? A great field of work awaited him in believers' conferences, and more generally in ministry to Christians. Bible exposition for believers — that was not a wearing effort for him, it was what he greatly enjoyed.

During this time of wrestling he was informed that the permission he had sought to enter the GDR (Communist East Germany) had been granted. This permission was hard to get, and there was no way of predicting the outcome of an application. When it came, it was for Busch the 'Yes' from God to further evangelistic activity. He decided to take the opportunity thus offered.

He spoke at the believers' conference in Bad Liebenzell, and ten days later led the Tersteegen's Rest conference in Essen. Then he travelled to Sassnitz in Rügen (in the GDR) for an evangelistic outreach. It was on the return journey from this outreach that he died in Lübeck.

Only a dash
(Wilhelm Busch again)

Silver light shone over Lake Constance. I have seen many glorious lakes on my journeys, but I have only found this wonderful silver light on Lake Constance.

Wasserburg is a peninsula, which swings in gentle curves into the lake. It has a bustling jetty for ships. It swarms with health resort visitors, with radios blaring out from the pubs.

But there is also a small, old church building right by the lake. Surrounding the church is a cemetery.

Here there is stillness. Red, blue and yellow flowers decorate the graves. Silently we went through the rows of sleepers to the low, mossy, battlemented wall, which closes off the cemetery from the lake.

The stones were hot from the sun. It was good to rest my arms on the wall and look out to the glistening silver. All was still; only the waves pattering quietly on the stones. Next to me stood my companion, a deaconess, who had led me to this wonderful place. She knew it from her youth, for her parents' house was not far from here.

Suddenly she pointed to the water just before us and said, 'Here is where the decision of my life was made!'

The aftermath

I looked into the clear water, and saw something strange: there were old gravestones lying there. Presumably in former days, when space was needed for new graves, they just threw the old stones into the lake. There they now lie between the stones on the water's edge. When the water is clear you can still read the inscriptions.

The deaconess continued: 'Here I once stood as a young girl. My glance fell on one of the gravestones. The name was weathered away; but the year numbers were still clearly to be seen: 1789 – 1821. And the thought went right through me: the dash between these two numbers; that was a whole human life. Only a dash! Our life is no more than that! And then I realized what a responsibility we have, the enormous responsibility to make something of this pathetic dash … yes, then I gave up my life to the Saviour, and decided to put this poor little life at his service. So I became a deaconess.'

A quarter of an hour later we were walking over the jetty, where there was a merry throng of health resort visitors. I was tormented by the thought: 'Do they really know what their life is? A dash between two numbers. What will they make of this dash?'

And I myself? I grasped the fact that it is a really great thing if God makes something out of this poor little dash 'to the praise of his glory'.

Acknowledgment of sources

All books used are by Wilhelm Busch himself (apart from a short section near the end about his death, see below). They are nearly all now under the imprint of Neukirchener Verlagsgesellschaft in Neukirchen-Vluyn (though the copies I used appeared under other publishers' names). The one exception is *Pastor Dr Wilhelm Busch, ein fröhlicher Christ*, which is now issued by Brunnen Verlag in Giessen.

Other books used:

Freiheit aus dem Evangelium — Meine Erlebnisse mit der Geheimen Staatspolizei, 4. Auflage, Aussaat Verlag, 2000.
Pastor Wilhelm Busch erzählt — 2. Aufl. Gütersloh, Quell, 2001.
Plaudereien in meinem Studierzimmer, Schriftenmissions-Verlag, Gladbeck, 1965.

Also, five volumes of *Kleine Erzählungen*, all from Christliche Literatur-Verbreitung (CLV), Bielefeld, 1. Auflage, 2005. They are:

1. *Kleine Erzählungen*
2. *Man muss doch darüber sprechen*
3. *Variationen über ein Thema*
4. *Leben ohne Alltag*
5. *Unter Menschen*

The section 'Closing days' in chapter 12 is from Ulrich Parzany's *Im Einsatz für Jesus. Programm und Praxis des Pfarrers Wilhelm Busch*.